The Boston Tea Party

The Boston Tea Party

The Foundations of Revolution

James M. Volo

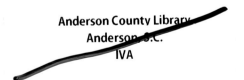
 PRAEGER

AN IMPRINT OF ABC-CLIO, LLC
Santa Barbara, California • Denver, Colorado • Oxford, England

Library of Congress Cataloging-in-Publication Data

Volo, James M., 1947–
   The Boston Tea Party : the foundations of revolution / James M. Volo.
      p. cm.
   Includes bibliographical references and index.
   ISBN 978-0-313-39874-2 (hbk. : alk. paper) — ISBN 978-0-313-39875-9 (ebook)
  1. Boston Tea Party, 1773. 2. United States—History—Revolution, 1775–1783. I. Title.
   E215.7.V65   2012
   973.3'115—dc23   2012010987

ISBN: 978-0-313-39874-2
EISBN: 978-0-313-39875-9

16 15 14 13 12   1 2 3 4 5

This book is also available on the World Wide Web as an eBook.
Visit www.abc-clio.com for details.

Praeger
An Imprint of ABC-CLIO, LLC

ABC-CLIO, LLC
130 Cremona Drive, P.O. Box 1911
Santa Barbara, California 93116-1911

This book is printed on acid-free paper ∞

Manufactured in the United States of America

Contents

Introduction

Who knows how well tea will mingle with salt water?
—*John Rowe, merchant of Boston, 1773*

Our old North-Enders in their spray
Still taste a Hyson flavor.
And Freedom's tea-cup still o' flows,
With ever-fresh libations.[1]

—*Oliver Wendell Holmes*

THE INCIDENT AT GRIFFIN'S WHARF

On the night of December 16, 1773, several thousand people massed on the chilly streets of Boston to listen to a speech given by political radical and longtime colonial rabble-rouser Samuel "Sam" Adams. With white plumes of frosted breath rising from the audience that strained to hear his words through the open windows of the Old South Meeting House, Sam Adams targeted the shipment of tea belonging to the East India Company (EIC) sitting on three ships tied up at Griffin's Wharf. His speech was filled with bold utterances of colonial consensus and dire warnings of an impending loss of liberty. These filtered through the open windows of the packed hall and were repeated in bits and snatches from neighbor to neighbor throughout the immense crowd. This made it difficult to follow the gist of the speech, but the handbills announcing the meeting beforehand had given its main thrust. "Whoever supports the unloading, the vending, or the receiving of the tea [is] an enemy to his country."[2]

That night, almost half the population of Boston listened, and cheered, and booed at appropriate moments during Adams' harangue. Although described at times as fractious and unrestrained, no other man in Boston seemed to have a greater influence over or a better understanding of the popular mind of the city. People liked tea, but the tax imposed on it by Parliament had given offense to all but the staunchest friends of the Crown. Their indignation was manifest not only in terms of ideological concepts like taxation without representation and government by the consent of the people but also with regard to the practical consequences in America of granting the powerful EIC an even stronger monopoly over a heavily restricted colonial trade. "Friends! Brethren! Countrymen! That worst of plagues, the detested tea . . . is now arrived in this harbor."[3]

Mr. Samuel Savage of Weston (president of the Massachusetts Colonial Board of War) was the appointed moderator of the meeting, but Adams was clearly in charge. As Adams spoke, a mock Indian war whoop split the night air, and a few in the crowd made to answer it. But rather than spur on his listeners to give further voice to their discontent, Adams commanded complete silence. A peaceable, almost religious deportment overcame the crowd as first one, then another, and another in the assembly suggested quiet to his neighbor. This was pure political theater. No Mark Antony speaking his part over the blood-soaked corpse of Caesar in a Shakespearean tragedy could have employed better stagecraft than Sam Adams. He fully apprehended the gravity of the moment, but he was less certain that his own seething passion to be free of British rule would overcome the natural inertia of his audience to accept the tea at its greatly reduced price and submit to the tax. Although among the first to articulate the call for independence from Britain, it is doubtful that Adams knew on this specific occasion that he was helping to give birth to the newest great nation on the earth.

"This meeting can do nothing more to save the country," he finally pronounced with all the gravity he could summon.[4] With this statement, a group of men, loosely disguised as Mohawk Indians beforehand, and joined by their confederates from the Sons of Liberty and the Patriot Party, made their way through the crowd to Griffin's Wharf bearing torches, followed by a nearly silent throng of eager onlookers. The disguised "Indians"—using no more words than necessary—boarded the three ships in the harbor and smashed 342 chests of tea worth approximately £18,000 (pounds sterling) and tossed them into the water. This was equivalent to £1.4 million sterling or $2.2 million (USD) in today's money.[5] Each chest represented the value of a full year's income for an average working-class family. Its loss would seriously sting the proprietors of the Company and its investors among the members of Parliament in faraway London. The incident at Griffin's Wharf has come to be known as the Boston Tea Party—one of the most iconic events in the history of the United States.

To consider the Boston Tea Party as an isolated incident, however, is equivalent to watching only a small scene in a long three-act play. No matter how dramatically staged or well written, much is missed. The Tea Party was a brief incident among the many scenes composing an economic and political crisis that ultimately produced a revolution. That which went before is necessary to the meaning and understanding of what took place, and that which follows provides the observer with context and closure.

Moreover, the silence necessarily preserved by the actors in this daring exploit has rendered the task of writing its history one of no little difficulty. Their secrets were remarkably well kept; and but for the family traditions and scraps of documents which survive, we should know very little of the people who comprised the cast of the famous Boston Tea Party. Henry Bass, a cousin of Sam Adams and one among the many that planned the Tea Party, wrote to his father-in-law describing his part in the plot and sending him some incriminating letters and documents. Bass, at least, seemed acutely aware of the historic nature of what was taking place: "I must desire you'd keep this a profound Secret and not to Let any Person see these Papers, and should be glad when you come to town you'd bring them with you, as we have no other Copies, and choose to keep them as Archives. We do every thing in order to keep this . . . Affair Private."[6]

It is the purpose of this book, through insights like this, to give the reader a front-row seat before the entire drama—all three acts, from the prelude to the climax to the final curtain call. The cast of characters is immense and appropriate to the significance of the drama: firebrand radicals and a subjugated but hardworking populace; a youthful king, devious advisers, corrupt officials, and greedy businessmen; self-interested conspirators, dedicated ideologues, an army of occupation, and an arrogant navy; animated mobs and passive extras; and more than one buffoon to provide comic relief. The reader will find that, in a period that valued formality and ceremony in society, commonsense restraint and essential decorum were conspicuously absent from many

political processes. To be fair, the identities of the protagonists and antagonists, of the good guys and the villains if you will, must be left to
an understanding assessment of the facts and the educated impartiality of
the reader.

TO RIDE UPON THE WINDS OF HISTORY

Historian Colin G. Galloway has aptly described the fundamental
nature of historiography and importance of studying history: "Battles
over history—dry, old history—and whose history gets to be told can
become heated and emotional because the ways we behaved *then* say so
much about the kind of people, society, or nation we have become."[7]
Many modern readers labor in ignorance under an incapacity with history—that is not their fault—that comes from an incomplete knowledge of the *then*, to which they must be exposed in order to form a
better understanding of the *now*. They should be more than curious in
the passing of these inquiries, for it is by the means of a wider knowledge that centuries-old connections between fundamental principles
are made. There are important connections between the Magna Carta
of 1215 and the Declaration of Independence of 1776, between the
battle for political freedom in Scotland at Stirling Bridge in 1297 and
the battle for independence in Massachusetts at Concord Bridge in
1775, and between the evangelical revolution of John Knox in 1560
and the political revolution of Samuel Adams in 1773—and among all
of these and our present day.

On the surface, the causes of the American Revolution have disappeared along with its lappets, bonnets, and periwigs. We no longer wear fichus, embroidered pockets, and hip-enhancing panniers,
or hunting shirts, knee breeches, and neck stocks; but the causes of
dissatisfaction with government were deep rooted and sprout new
growth periodically. In almost every case, a widespread and unremitting contempt for established authority coupled with a libertarian
leave-me-alone attitude seems best to characterize many of the cross-
generational attitudes toward government passed down throughout
these histories. There is perhaps no better example of this fundamental character in American history than the importance and meaning
of the Boston Tea Party *then* to the rise of the T.E.A. Party political
movement *now*.[8]

Historian Jill Lepore has written, "The importance of the American
Revolution to the twenty-first-century T.E.A. Party movement might

seem to have been slight, as if the name were a mere happenstance, the knee breeches knickknacks, the rhetoric of revolution unthinking, but that was not entirely the case."[9] Political opponents and media pundits have derided the three-cornered hats, the red, white, and blue ribbons, and the yellow "Don't Tread on Me" flags; and they have berated the T.E.A. Party demonstrators as clinging to their Bibles and guns in ignorance of more socially progressive ideals.

However, activists from a variety of political viewpoints have invoked the Boston Tea Party as a symbol of protest. For instance, when the university-trained lawyer Mohandas K. Gandhi in frock-coat, striped tie, and vest led a mass protest against institutionalized racism by burning the registration cards issued to those from India living in British South Africa in 1908, a British newspaper compared the event to the Boston Tea Party. Some years later in 1930, the same man was the now revered *Mahatma* (Great Soul) with his head shaven, dressed in the traditional *dhoti* and shawl of India, woven by his wife, Kasturba, with yarn he had spun by his own hand. Gandhi met with the British viceroy after his walk to the sea during the India salt tax protests. During the meeting, he took some duty-free sea salt from inside his shawl and reminded the official again of the Boston Tea Party. Would the modern media pundits have disparaged him for his choice of traditional dress the way they do T.E.A. Party demonstrators for their colonial dress, or is their own partisanship coloring their analysis?

The Boston Tea Party has often been indirectly referenced in protests from both extremes of the American political spectrum. In 1973, on the 200th anniversary of the original Tea Party, a mass meeting of liberal protestors and environmental activists at Faneuil Hall—calling for the impeachment of President Richard Nixon—retired to a replica tea ship in Boston Harbor to hang Nixon in effigy and throw empty oil drums into the harbor in the cause of environmentalism. In 1998, two conservative U.S. congressmen put the federal tax code into a chest marked "TEA" and dumped it also into Boston Harbor to protest added taxation under the Clinton administration. In 2006, the modern T.E.A. Party was founded, and one year later, on the 234th anniversary of the Boston Tea Party, Libertarian candidate Ron Paul, evoking many fundamental American ideals concerning smaller government, broke the existing one-day political fund-raising record by raising $6 million (USD) in just 24 hours.

It must be remembered, moreover, that the American Revolution began first as a crisis of trust, over-taxation, debt, and out of control spending, coupled with an arrogance of big government, partisanship, and demagoguery. This may sound familiar to the modern reader. The British government, in the person of its monarch, had a long history of extending its sovereignty over unwilling peoples. These included the Welsh, the Scots, and the Irish; the Native Americans of trans-Appalachia and Canada; and the populations of India, Australia, and parts of Africa and Indonesia. British policies in the 18th century were designed to defend the empire from foreign threats. American colonials did not consider themselves either threatening or foreign.

Modern America is exhibiting many of the characteristics and governmental challenges of its colonial period, but they are only symptoms of a deeper crisis—a culture war for the soul of America. Big government has entered beyond the thresholds of American homes dictating by law the size of toilet tanks, the efficiency of refrigerators, the mechanism of light bulbs, the flow of showerheads, and a myriad of other regulations on everyday devices. For the protestors *then* (and *now*), government had come to stand for extensive disruptions of their chosen lifestyle, intrusions into the social fabric of their communities, and a loss of control over their local policies and their most heartfelt issues. It was shared issues of personal, economic, political, and religious liberty that brought on demonstrations and calls for change in the 1770s.

Moreover, it must be recognized—and often is not addressed in standard treatments of the subject—that 18th-century Americans were acutely aware of the business climate and political activities taking place across the British Empire and not only those of local importance. While the speed of modern communications would be incomprehensible to colonials, Anglo-Americans did not live in a box sealed off from the rest of the 18th-century world. As will be seen, there is ample evidence that Anglo-Americans affected and were affected by occurrences that took place right across the globe. They were expansionists, not isolationists. Theirs was the first *emerging economy* of the New World in an era during which Europe attempted to colonize and overrule the globe. An emerging economy is one that experiences rapid growth under conditions of limited or partial industrialization, a definition that certainly reflects 18th-century Anglo-America. Moreover, colonial Americans were seamen, merchants, and traders; students, visitors and expatriates, who—living and acting under the British flag—fully participated in an empire of goods governed from London but coming from sources in every corner of the world. Even the everyday English word for money, *cash*, was derived from the Tamil dialect of Southeast India (*kaasu*). The term *cash* was used with great specificity in the 18th century to describe legal tender and various instruments of value transfer and payment other than gold and silver coins. The availability of coins and the severe demands made on the stock of precious metal coinage in America, Britain, and around the world will be a repeated theme of this work.

Unreasonable demands on the imperial economy were especially evident in the case of the business affairs of the EIC, the greatest corporate monopoly in recorded history up to that time. If corrected for inflation and fluctuations in the value of money, the EIC would be rated among the greatest non-manufacturing corporations of all time. Yet there is evidence that more gold and silver was transferred through the EIC to China and India in the 18th century to satisfy the desires of European fashion than the Spanish Conquistadors stripped from all the mines and native temples of America in two centuries of rapine and greed. This circumstance left the British Empire rich in goods but with a net loss in real wealth.[10]

When the EIC and its corrupt allies in Parliament and the government ministry precipitated a world credit crisis in the 1770s, Americans were made to suffer and were asked to pay for it. The despised Tea Act that caused protests in America over the demand for increased taxes in silver coin was passed almost simultaneously with the East India Company Act (Regulating Act) that transferred £1.4 million of scarce imperial revenues from the colonies to the EIC to prevent its bankruptcy. This is the approximate equivalent in modern money of £1.3 billion sterling or $2.1 billion (USD).[11]

Here is the nexus, the unheralded financial connection between British policy and American protest. Asian trade sucked up Britain's wealth as a sponge absorbs water. The Company's failed attempt at landing a few hundred chests of China tea in Boston had been initiated by economic, political, and military concerns in far away London, Calcutta, and Canton. A historian of the Company has observed of the EIC, "What was supposed to have been a trading company with an eastern monopoly vested by Parliament had become a rogue state." To those it enriched, the EIC was the familiar John Company; to those it impoverished, it was the Devil's Company.[12]

The British Crown was, and had been for almost two centuries, the legitimate government of the Anglo-American colonies before the revolution. Anglo-Americans were a conscious part of the empire and lawfully subject to its legitimate ruler, who from 1760 to his death in 1820 was King George III. Americans today bristle at the concept that they are subjects in any way. They believe that government should be subject to its citizens, not the other way around. Yet no serious American in 1773, even among the radicals, ever questioned the king's legitimate right to govern the empire, only the necessity that he expand his absolute rule in America.

Moreover, poorly defined political groups, such as Whigs and Tories or Patriots and Loyalists, continue to populate the history texts in American classrooms as if opposing one another on a weekly football schedule with the Battle of Yorktown (1781) looming as the Super Bowl of the revolution. Yet, even after two centuries, the political, economic, and social opinions that each group held remain somewhat unclear. Ironically, the least loyal to their legitimate and rightful king are commonly called "Patriot," yet the members of the so-called Patriot Party were no more patriotic (in the traditional sense of the word) than those colonials who ultimately became members of the Loyalist Party—just the reverse was true. The very name of Patriot was borrowed from a decades-old opposition political faction in Parliament known in Britain as the Patriot Whigs, who promulgated many of the same small government, free market, and strict constitutional principles aspired to by proponents of the American Revolution and by T.E.A. Party activists today.

Among the so-called Patriots were the Sons of Liberty—agitators, reactionaries, and, frankly, thugs—who habitually denied to the Tory opposition many of the fundamental freedoms Americans would ultimately demand for themselves in the Bill of Rights. This is not to disparage their devotion to the cause of independence. Sometimes a little benevolent thuggery is necessary in a crisis. Those loyal to the Crown had formed no parallel street organizations, relying instead on the instruments of government to maintain the status quo until it was too late to avoid the crisis.

Among the objectives of this book is an attempt to make the reader aware of the parallelism and relevance to modern times of the history surrounding the Boston Tea Party and its role in the genesis of the modern T.E.A. Party movement. In this regard, those who attended the Boston Tea Party of the late 18th century and those who demonstrated in the streets of the 21st century seem to be driven by similar circumstances. Among these were intrusive regulations and an unresponsive government; a credit-starved global economy increasingly dependent on foreign resources; and an arrogant cadre of public employees dictating debilitating lifestyle changes to average Americans while attempting to maintain their own position of advantage. Among these

Americans was a vocal minority who seemingly found such intrusions into their daily routine unacceptable and un-American.

The recent electoral successes of 2010 for T.E.A. Party-backed candidates strongly suggest that, under circumstances similar to those of the late 18th century, modern Americans remain equally as cynical as their revolutionary predecessors toward government and its officials and as unsympathetic and distrustful of government's underlying goals and regulatory policies. In both cases there seems to have taken place a substantial deterioration in the underpinning of trust that is necessary between the governed and the government.

A central theme of all recorded history has been the use or abuse of power—how it lurks in the shadows behind the professed idealism of politicians and reformers and the compelling reasons they expound when they encourage their followers to expand their influence and thereby secure for themselves the privileges enjoyed by their class or their associates, even unto war. Compelling and persuasive words are often used to cloak from closer scrutiny those who would wield political power indiscriminately and redistribute it unfairly among themselves or their supporters. In a crisis, whether real or imagined, both sides seem swayed more by the demagogue than the compromiser, and the best dissembler is often thought to be in ascendance. Thucydides, the ancient Greek historian of the Peloponnesian Wars, urged historians to embrace a healthy skepticism in their analysis of grand events and impressive speeches and to look to personal self-interest rather than publicized grievances and high-sounding intentions when writing their analyses. To paraphrase Charles Dickens, historians and chroniclers are privileged to enter their task where they choose, to come and go as through keyholes, to ride upon the winds of events, to overcome with their pen all the obstacles of distance, time, and place.[13]

Because the American Revolution gave birth to a nation, it has received the attention of countless historians, yet few have produced serious studies of the role of tea in America or of the integration and implications of business, society, politics, and religion in an import-based, mercantile economic model like that in the colonies. The Boston Tea Party itself is often reported as an amusing anecdote in the struggle between Britain and America, populated by fake Mohawks wielding tomahawks and urged on by a wild-eyed and slightly disheveled fanatic, Sam Adams, who railed against taxation without representation. Teachers are fond of this last concept, but few know that Cotton Mather raised the question of representation from the pulpit in a different war almost eight decades earlier (1689). It was resurrected in the political ranting of James Otis and finally made popular in Sam Adams' cutting series of articles in the *Boston Gazette* (1764–1772).

Shaking from palsy, weakened with age, disheveled, and poorly dressed in the crisis of the revolution that he had supported for almost two decades, Sam Adams is somehow portrayed as less important to the achievement of independence than his more reserved and erudite cousin, the future president, John Adams. Had Sam left a treasure trove of touching and whimsical letters to his wife, fathered a future president (or even a lowly congressman), and been portrayed as the main protagonist in a hit Broadway play and film *1776*, he would

The American radical and founder Samuel Adams in his prime. (Library of Congress)

perhaps have been better served by history. Yet in recent years, a like-minded segment of the voting public has rediscovered Sam Adams, the small government radical and firebrand revolutionary.

Many historians and academics writing during the 19th century took liberties with the facts surrounding the first Tea Party. The term *Boston Tea Party* did not appear in print in an American published history before 1834. Previous histories, many printed in Britain, began their chronologies with the aftermath of the Tea Party or skipped over it completely. "It became fashionable for American historians to make the 18th-century British look less oppressive and more sympathetic than they actually were by depicting Samuel Adams as a hate-filled and cunning conniver."[14] These 19th-century Federalist Era historians portrayed their revolutionary forbears as political geniuses and religious paragons. Sam Adams exhibited too many human foibles to fit the mold of genius, and James Otis became too clearly insane to stand long as a paragon. These Federalist writers also generally failed to note that the so-called Founders of the American republic were also inflexible ideologues and materialistic profit seekers caught up in the economic undercurrents surrounding the death of a mercantilist age and the birth of a capitalist one—a capitalism that gave these Federalist Era commentators the financial wherewithal to spend time writing history books in the first place.

Among the objectives of this book is an effort to relieve the reader of the many myths surrounding the Boston Tea Party. Although the incident warms the pens of historians and arouses the popular imagination with regard to calls for liberty and independence and protests against unfair taxation and tyrannical government, it was neither the only nor the most effective outpouring of Anglo-American ire toward the Crown during the 18th century. Moreover, although none called for their taxes to be raised, not all Americans agreed with the ongoing protestations. In fact, even a tenuous consensus for protest was not to be had outside New England.

In 1774, as the revolutionary crisis approached, John Adams wrote to a friend saying that about one-third of Anglo-Americans were loyal to the British Crown, one-third in favor of the cause of independence, and one-third undecided or too timid to take a stance either way. The characterization of timidity made by Adams was patently unfair. Most Anglo-Americans were deeply conscious of their British roots. Some, like Sam Adams, James Otis, and the radicals who hotly pursued independence, were anxious to remove the "Anglo" from their Anglo-American identity. Many more colonials simply could not countenance the traumatic loss of any part of their British being and were willing to take up arms as Loyalists.

For others—among them men of cooler political temper—submission to a traditional monarchial authority restrained by law, custom, and Constitution seemed preferable to submission to a new and untested American authority openly supported by mob violence and underwritten by foreign agents and recent former enemies. A successful Franco-American farmer living in New York and married to an Anglo-American woman, Hector St. John de Crévecoeur, a British subject by choice rather than by birth, anguished over the dilemma presented to him by loyalty to the traditions of monarchical rule or the innovations of an untried democracy. "How easily do men pass from loving, to hating and cursing one another!" he wrote. "I am a lover of peace."[15] Ultimately, these last undecided citizens were overwhelmed by the breaking storm.[16]

Much of what had happened at Griffin's Wharf was the end product of careful, long, and tireless planning, as well as many years of active protests and previous demonstrations targeting government policy. The signs of unrest appearing in the newssheets and diaries of the 18th century provide evidence of this underlying turmoil and are eerily similar to those troubling reports populating the tweets, blogs, and Facebook pages of an online America in the 21st century—unresponsive and arrogant government officials, insecure borders, non-Anglo immigrants, ethnic, racial, and religious hatreds, unfunded mandates, increasing taxation, ill-advised legislation, uninhibited corruption and cronyism, big business bailouts, bloated government spending, excessive executive compensation, partisan bickering, an angry and outspoken populace, and an economy seemingly on the verge of collapse under the weight of senseless regulations, a deficiency of currency, monetary devaluation, lack of credit, a debt crisis, and questionable leadership.

Some of the factors that spawned the Boston Tea Party were more than a decade in the making, with the Proclamation of 1763 and the Stamp Act of 1764 generally being assigned as points of departure between colonial acquiescence and active resistance to royal governance. The enervating Sugar Act and the Currency Act of 1764, the restrictive Townshend Acts of 1767 and 1769, and the despised East India Company Act and the Tea Act of 1773 followed.

As the reader will discover, 1764 was not a good year in American colonial history. Nothing that happened was immediately overwhelming, but nearly everything that happened had awe-inspiring consequences. It was in fact a pivotal year in the relations between the colonies and the empire. Until 1764, the Crown had seemingly chosen to govern its colonies with what amounted to benign neglect; thereafter, their governance can rightly be termed as bordering on the despotic, a word used by many Americans, including Thomas Jefferson. Some among the supporters of the Crown, however, suggested that the country had fallen into rebellion from an earlier point. Violence had become a virtual ritual of Boston culture. On November 5 each year, mobs from the South End and North End of the city held a mock street fight in celebration of the Gunpowder Plot of 1605 in which Catholic terrorists had attempted to blow up both houses of Parliament and King James I. The South End gang, a force of 2,000 men led by a shoemaker and Sons of Liberty leader Ebenezer Mackintosh, took the victory in 1764. The North End, led this day by Henry Swift, also a member of the Sons of Liberty, was declared the loser because they suffered more bumps, bruises, and broken heads.[17]

There is also evidence of a virulent antigovernment spirit taking hold in the frontier settlements from the Carolinas to Maine dating back to the circumstances of the French and Indian War (1754–1763). Land speculators with friends in government had taken possession of this land and sold it to hardworking American farmers. Forest clearings that had formerly harbored subsistence farmsteads had become substantial agricultural holdings, and these in turn had become commercial enterprises characterized by a growing interest in economic and political policy. Political demonstrations on the frontier had been met with armed confrontations, arrests, and executions. This circumstance will be discussed at some length in a later chapter.

This history is more than an account of how a simple pantry staple like tea became a symbol of government tyranny. It is also the story of how a largely grassroots movement, poised to protect its pocketbooks, its possessions, and its balance sheets from a tax-and-spend government, gave birth instead to a great democratic republic. The author of this history has tried to separate the facts from the propaganda and the politics from the policies. The words of persons from the prerevolutionary and revolutionary periods have been incorporated wherever appropriate in this study, and a meaningful analysis of the implications of what they did or wrote or said has been attempted. With respect to these sources, the rather free-wheeling spelling, grammar, punctuation, and sentence structure of the period have been modified to make what was recorded in the 18th century more reader friendly for a 21st-century audience. In order to prevent confusion between discussions involving

Native Americans and those regarding the subcontinent of India, certain items have been termed *India* goods rather than *Indian* ones, a device often used in period documents. Also the term *Indian* is used in context for Native Americans where appropriate (as in Indian fighter, Indian attack, or French and Indian War).

A further minor warning to the modern reader is necessary. The author's way is to avoid running straight at a thing as others have done in the past, pointing out instead the curiosities and unknown aspects among the characters and events that spring forward from the historical melodrama along the way. A favorite among books characteristic of the 18th century is Lawrence Sterne's marvelously humorous novel *The Life and Opinions of Tristram Shandy, Gentleman* published in England in 1770. Herein, the title character, Tristram Shandy, speaks out from the pages warning the reader that if he seems to *digress* somewhat in his historical musings, he does so to *progress* toward a fuller understanding of the topic. Writing, when properly managed, is after all nothing more than a one-sided conversation, and it behooves the author to anticipate both the questions and the speaking parts of the reader lest that conversation becomes a lecture, or worse still a sermon. In this book, American Revolutionary history and global economic history, Western Hemisphere and Eastern Hemisphere, are intertwined in a way seldom before attempted. Yet "like wit and judgment, seemingly incompatible movements on their surfaces by the end will be explained and reconciled."[18] Along with Shandy, the present author hopes that nothing that is touched upon in this history "will be thought trifling in its nature, or tedious in its telling."[19]

Finally, a further word concerning historians is warranted before proceeding, and this too comes by way of 18th-century anecdote. In the early days of the revolutionary crisis, Thomas Jefferson—when couched in Williamsburg as governor of revolutionary Virginia and before the outcome of the fighting was certain—was asked to identify the person then living who could write the real history of the American Revolution. Jefferson replied that *no one* could do it, but that *everyone* would try. The task was too important not to warrant the attempt![20]

CHAPTER **1**

The Morning After, the Night Before

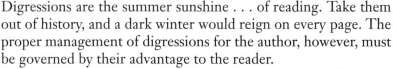

Digressions are the summer sunshine . . . of reading. Take them out of history, and a dark winter would reign on every page. The proper management of digressions for the author, however, must be governed by their advantage to the reader.

—*Lawrence Sterne, 1770*

O' conspiracy . . . Then honesty to honesty engaged,
That this shall be, or we will fall for it?

—*Brutus, act 2, scene 1*, Julius Caesar

A SALT WATER BREW

For almost three weeks before any EIC tea had arrived in Boston in December 1773, mass protests had been held at the Old South Meeting House. At one of these meetings, the portrait painter, John Singleton Copley, son-in-law to one of the tea consignees, had tried to negotiate a compromise agreement to allow the tea to be landed. At another, Sheriff Stephen Greenleaf interrupted the meeting with a stinging proclamation from Lieutenant Governor Thomas Hutchinson demanding that the assembly disperse and cease its unlawful proceedings. Failure to do so was to be at the peril of the attendees. The meetings resoundingly refused to comply with either the pleas or the implied threats. Meanwhile, the tea ships arrived: one on the 4th of the month, one on the 7th, and the last of the three on the 16th. On the morning of the Tea Party, December 16, Abigail Adams of Braintree wrote a letter to her friend Mercy Otis Warren of Barnstable: "The tea, that baneful weed, is arrived [in Boston]. Great and effectual opposition has been made to the landing of it . . . our citizens have been united, spirited and firm. The flame is kindled and like lightening it catches from soul to soul."[1]

On December 17, the morning after the Tea Party, friends of the demonstration greeted one another on the streets of Boston with childlike giggles, secretive glances, and smiling countenances. Others— friends of the Crown—averted their eyes in discomfiture, warned of the extent of the sure-to-follow retributions or spoke in critical whispers behind their hands or through perfumed handkerchiefs. A Tory handbill mysteriously appeared in the streets suggesting that the previous night's work was a "Tradesman's Protest," a combination of apprentices and indentured servants against their masters; but it was clear that the body of the people, regardless of their class or occupation, had approved of the Tea Party.[2]

Many people went to the wharfside to see the long soggy windrows of spoiled tea that floated with the tidal flotsam among the mudflats of Massachusetts Bay. But anyone who attempted to rescue the noxious weed was warned off by volunteers in rowboats or patrols organized along the shore. Broken boards from the distinctive black and red China motif crates, their bland canvas covers imprinted with the EIC logo, and any tea leaves recovered from the water were collected and committed to a smoky fire on Boston Common. The local Crown officials were outraged and issued a request for informers to supply the names of those who had destroyed the tea. Despite arresting a barber named Francis Eckley, who had openly bragged about his participation, the Boston authorities were unable to find anyone who could identify the protestors. Yet, no soldier, constable, or sheriff made an appearance as the protestors openly tended the fire or patrolled the shore; Boston had less than 10 constables, in any case.[3]

The previous evening (that of the Tea Party) had started quietly for Betsy Hunt Palmer. Considered a great beauty in her girlhood village of Watertown, the young woman had been married only a little longer than a year, and on the night of the protest, she had remained at home alone in Boston with her newborn baby. Her husband, Joseph Pearce Palmer, had gone out with a few friends, among them Foster Condy and Stephen Bruce, to listen to Sam Adams and, she suspected, to lift a few tankards of ale. Late in the night, she heard the gate squeak on its hinges, the frost crunch under foot on the walkway, and the front door open and close. She supposed it was her husband returning from the meeting or more likely from the tavern. She would have to chide him for staying out so late on a cold night leaving her alone to care for the baby. Turning into the parlor, she screamed at the sight of three stout Indians standing there. Betsy would have fallen to the floor in a faint except that her own husband was one of them. "Don't be frightened, Betsy," Joseph said wiping his blackened face with a cloth. "We have only been making some salt water brew."[4]

Betsy's husband Joseph was the son of Mr. Joseph Palmer, gentle-man of Roxbury, a local leader of the Sons of Liberty, and a grandson through his mother's side of Judge Richard Cranch of Braintree, who had introduced John Adams to Abigail Smith (Adams). Young Joseph had formerly traded in India goods and ironware—possibly as a re-ceiver of smuggled items or as a producer of illegal manufactures. He was an ironmonger (roughly speaking, a seller of hardware) and had attempted to expand his own small business with an iron furnace and foundry of his own. There were strict laws (the Iron Acts of 1710 and 1750) regulating and restricting the establishment of such an enter-prise in the colonies. A member of a local artisan's guild and a friend of Paul Revere, Joseph was quickly identified as one of the crowd of Mohawks and was warned the next day by a friend, Thomas Flucker, secretary of the Governor's Council, that he faced imminent arrest. The young family wisely fled to friendlier quarters with Betsy's father in Watertown.

IN THE GARRET ROOM

The evening's protest in Boston in 1773 and the destruction of the tea at Griffin's Wharf had been carefully devised in secret by a small group of men in a garret room over Edes & Gills printing office on the corner of Court Street, among them self-interested businessmen, partisan colonial magistrates, and antigovernment conspirators. The so-called Mohawks had dressed and painted themselves in the Green Dragon Tavern on the corner of Hanover Street. John Andrews, an eyewitness to the destruction of the tea, described the Mohawks, "The actors were Indians . . . being clothed in blankets, with their heads muffled, and copper-colored countenances, being each armed with a hatchet or axe, or pair of pistols."[5] Every person present on the night of December 17, 1773, had sworn on the Bible that they would keep their meeting secret. The identity of all the members is only partly known with certainty, and their working protocol was probably too close to treason to be committed to paper. Therefore, the absolute list of the participants can only be surmised from anecdote and tradition.

Dr. Joseph Warren and William Molineaux were members of the North End Caucus, a political club that also met there regularly. There were three caucuses in the city, but the North End was the most outspoken and active. There were also two Masonic lodges in Boston, St. Andrew's and St. John's, whose wealthy members included significant family names: Otis, Gridley, Rowe, and Quincy. Wealthy merchant John Rowe was the new Masonic grandmaster for all America, and the Quincy family was said to have realized a vast fortune in gold and silver bullion through privateering in the last French war. The two lodges often met together and were among the most active of 30 lodges in Massachusetts.

The three Whig political caucuses in Boston—North, Middle, and South—were well represented among the protestors. The Tories in the city had no such well-developed political associations and were curiously complaisant concerning local politics, possibly because they

Taverns like the Green Dragon pictured here were a favorite meeting place of the Tea Party planners and the Sons of Liberty. (Library of Congress)

felt that the establishment represented them. Molineaux, a middle-aged ironmonger and a reportedly angry and confrontational man made nearly bankrupt by the recent economic depression, was chairman of the North End group and spokesman for all three. The North Enders were not above doing the necessary dirty work of the protests. The Middle Caucus was often overwhelmed by the activities of the other two groups, but the workings of the three caucuses often interlocked. They could carry the vote in many public meetings even over the wishes of the majority.[6]

A dozen men—among them Sam Adams, James Otis, Paul Revere, Thomas Young, and John Hancock—were members of the Long Room Club (formed in 1762), a so-called social organization that met in the garret room over the printers shop with some regularity. Three of the conspirators were respected medical doctors (Warren, Young, and Benjamin Church); others were considered well off, if not conspicuously wealthy, like Rowe and Hancock. If gentlemen like these were going to draw up the proposals and policies for the group, however, it was thought best to have a mechanic as its moderator and the public face of its leadership, in this case Benjamin Edes, the printer.[7]

Joseph and Betsy Palmer had celebrated their marriage in the upstairs room of the Green Dragon (one of the largest spaces in the town) with many of the same persons now conspiring against the tea. Most taverns then had a large room that could be hired for special occasions. This was often upstairs on the second floor above the bar room and public rooms, where it could span the entire length of the building with no intervening walls from fireplace to fireplace to allow space for dancing or large groups. Consequently, Sam Adams and several others among the designers of the Tea Party—being Freemasons, caucus, guild, or club members, or simply public-minded citizens—were in the habit of holding gatherings at the tavern. They had all gathered many times in the room upstairs and cemented the bonds of their friendship in the usual manner, with a mug of hot flip or a glass of Brandy Port or Canary or Madeira wine, and talked of business or scandals or politics, or quietly conspiring toward independence before the warming fireplace.

O' CONSPIRACY

In his Pulitzer Prize–winning book, *The Radicalism of the American Revolution* (1993), Gordon S. Wood wrote, "The institution that best embodied these ideals of sociability and cosmopolitanism was Freemasonry. It would be difficult to exaggerate the importance of Masonry for the American Revolution."[8] Yet, too much can sometimes be made of the interconnections among Freemasons in the revolution. Many references to Freemasonry will be noted in any history of the period, including in this one, but a Masonic-inspired conspiracy to overthrow the British government in America is highly unlikely. This supposed connection between revolution and the saga of Freemasonry must be immediately exposed for the myth that it is.

Certainly, one of the personal objectives of Masons, consistent with their class status as gentlemen, was to position themselves or their fraternity brothers at the top of any organizational hierarchy, and it seems that they did so in the case of the Tea Party also. However, stronger statistical associations among possible conspirators can be made among beer drinkers frequenting the same tavern, churchgoers who followed the same sect, or men who rode astride rather than in carriages.

There were two Masonic lodges in Boston—St. Andrew's and the more elegant St. John's—but there were not many Freemasons in the city. When Jeremiah Gridley, the grandmaster of all America died in 1767, the Boston brethren exerted themselves to turn out 160 mourners in a grand procession that drew members and non-members from among all the surrounding colonies. By way of comparison, there were more than 300 active members of the Sons of Liberty just in Boston alone. Nonetheless, efforts to promote the notion of a Masonic conspiracy have successfully created a mythology that has seeped into many mainstream historical texts.[9]

It should be noted that there were as many Masons among Loyalists as there were among Patriots, and that the Order was a powerful cultural influence that promoted the ideas of the brotherhood of man, not a political agenda. The Masons, however, met in ritual secrecy (as would perforce the Tea Party conspirators) and surrounded themselves with symbols and regalia the meaning of which was only vaguely understood by those outside the order. The very silence of the order concerning politics led some in the government, Lieutenant Governor Hutchinson, in particular, to believe that the opposition to themselves and the government emanated from the Masons. The Hutchinsons and their kin the Olivers were very conscious of their wealth, breeding, and influence and were consequently not well liked. They were not democrats in the small "d" sense, but somewhat snobbish elites appearing in public with lacquered coaches and matched teams with liveried servants and not interacting with anyone whose own power and influence was not considered important. The position they chose to hold in the social hierarchy inevitably led their dealings with local tradesmen and artisans to be businesslike and aloof rather than sociable and friendly. Yet the Masons allowed for interaction among many levels of men—artisans, mechanics, doctors, soldiers, and farmers—as long as they were considered gentlemen.

Among those whose efforts affected the myth of a Masonic conspiracy was 20th-century historian of Freemasonry, Sidney Morse, who seemingly saw Freemasons everywhere he looked in American history. Based only on little more than hearsay, conjecture, and half-truths, Morse published *Freemasonry in the American Revolution* (1924) and *Freemasonry and the Drums of "Seventy-Five"* (1927). According to Morse, the Masonic brotherhood not only orchestrated the Boston Tea Party but also sank the revenue cutter *Gaspée* and dominated—throughout all the colonies—the committees of correspondence, committees of safety, provincial conventions, and both Continental Congresses. Demonstrably false claims were made that *almost all* the signers of the Declaration of Independence were associated with Freemasonry, some simply because they did not openly condemn it.[10]

A decade later, historian Bernard Fay identified to his own satisfaction profound Masonic influences in both the French and American revolutions of the 18th century. In *Revolution and Freemasonry, 1600–1800* (1935), he made emphatic claims for Freemasonry's importance to these revolutionary movements. Fay saw the fraternity as the wellspring and main conservator of intellectual and political thought of the age.

Of particular concern was the work in 1884 of Harvard professor Eliot Norton, who may first have introduced the persistent myth misrepresenting the so-called all-seeing eye on the Great Seal of the United States as a Masonic emblem. This piece of popular claptrap was made with regard to and for the benefit of the third-party anti-Masonic candidacy for president of the United States of Jonathan Blanchard of Wheaton College in 1884. The anti-Masonic Movement, beginning about 1820, was particularly active throughout the 19th century. Yet, the single eye was clearly a well-established artistic convention for an omniscient and universal deity dating from the Renaissance, and it can be traced back less convincingly to ancient Egypt.[11]

Certainly Sam Adams, John Hancock, Ben Franklin, Paul Revere, George Washington, and other figures prominent in textbooks numbered themselves among both the ranks of Freemasons and Patriots, but a far greater number of significant players in the revolution were not associated with Freemasonry in any direct way. Moreover, many persons, who were nominal members of established churches, used the opportunity to join a fraternal order, any popular fraternal order, in order to abandon formal religious services without cutting themselves off from regular contact and sociability within the wider community. Detailed studies of 18th-century Freemasonry provide evidence only of a casual link between the organization and the revolution with Masons representing approximately 25 percent of the major figures among the founding fathers—a proportion among that class of persons not inconsistent with their membership in other colonial organizations that researchers might choose to study.[12]

FREEDOM'S TEA CUP

The Boston Tea Party was not an isolated event, and it can be shown that the protests against the tea were more widely founded than a Freemason conspiracy in Boston would suggest. The Tea Party was no spontaneous event isolated to a small geographic area. The overall resistance to the tea—and the meticulous planning that forged it—helps to illustrate two insightful notions concerning mass protests, whether they are held in the 18th or the 21st century: silence sometimes speaks volumes, and restraint often reveals underlying strength. Initial plans for the tea protests had included discussions of methods for preserving the property of the EIC and plans to return it safe and untouched to its owners.[13] This was an attempt to keep faith with a core Patriot concept of the sanctity of private property—even if that property belonged to a large corrupt corporation like the EIC. Sam Adams later attempted to rescue his conservative principles by shifting the blame for the destruction of the tea to the Hutchinson's, the tea consignees, or the customs officials for insisting that it be unloaded and not allowed to return to England in safety.

The subsequent decision to destroy the tea was the start of a long history of bad relations between the EIC and America (and New England, in particular), which would shadow the young nation's maritime trade into the next century. The company greatly feared American competition and with good reason. Even before the ink had dried on the Peace of Paris (1783), American vessels were taking on cargoes in formerly forbidden places and intruding on EIC profits. So ubiquitous was the appearance of these Yankee traders that in some regions of the trading world the natives called all those who spoke English "New England men." By 1825, more American vessels traded with India and China than did the ships of any nation save Britain, and the two merchant fleets conducted an economic trade war at sea until the American focus was distracted by its own Civil War.[14]

At Griffin's Wharf in 1773, however, not one article of EIC or other person's property other than the tea was disturbed, and the vessels had been left "ship shape in Bristol fashion" after the protest, a common allusion to well-ordered seafaring.[15] When the destruction of the tea had ended, the murmuring crowd dispersed in twos and threes. The city had remained quiet. No riots or burnings followed. Sam's cousin, John Adams wrote, "There [was] a dignity, a majesty, a solemnity in this last effort of the Patriots that I greatly admire."[16] The *Boston Evening Post* of December 20, 1773, published a letter from an observer of the incident visiting from Rhode Island: "I cannot but express my admiration of the conduct of the people. I shall go home doubly fortified."[17]

Nonetheless, not all had been done with polite decorum. An elderly man in a wig and a large cocked hat made an attempt to save a little tea by filling his pockets, but he was detected. The tea was seized, and the hat and wig committed to the water in its place. George Hewes, a Patriot shoemaker, noted, "In consideration of his advanced age, [the elderly man] was permitted to escape, with now and then a slight kick."[18] The only two samples of the tea known to have survived the protest were taken from inside the shoes of Thomas Melville, one of the Sons of Liberty, where it had inadvertently fallen the previous night, and a tiny sample taken up on the Dorchester shore in the morning by Dr. Thaddeus Harris, a witness to its destruction and an avid antiquarian who gave it a valued place on a museum shelf. Many Americans knew that these were momentous times worthy of documentation.

A single empty China tea chest survived ravishment and was purchased as a curiosity by Historic Tours of America in 2005. Known as the Robinson Tea Chest, it was found half submerged in sand some days after the Tea Party by a teenager, John Robinson, who took it home as a souvenir. The box is actually a half chest that held a smaller quantity of tea than the standard chest. It is displayed in the Boston Museum.[19]

The rigorous attitude, dogged continuity, and attention to details that the individual Patriots exhibited during their protests were also important. A fourth tea ship, *William*, approaching Boston, for example, had wrecked itself on Cape Cod a week before the Boston Tea

Party, a fairly common occurrence in the days of sailing vessels. The Patriots in this case attributed the wreck to the intervention of Divine Providence. Some of the 58 tea chests were seized from the vessel and burned by the Patriots of Provincetown on the far tip of the Cape. Two dozen tea chests—of uncertain origin, but thought to have survived the wreck—were brought to Boston a short time after the Tea Party. These were also seized and burned by a small party of protestors in disguise. Like the stamps associated with the Stamp Act almost a decade earlier (of which more will be said later), none of the detested tea was to be permitted.

In October 1773, seven ships had left England, bound for America with significant cargoes of tea from the EIC. Four of them, named respectively the *Dartmouth*, the *Eleanor*, the *Beaver*, and the *William*, carried more than £18,000 of tea consigned to merchants in Boston; the ship *Nancy*, with £36,000 of tea, was cleared for New York; the ship *Polly*, also with a cargo of £36,000 of tea, was destined for Philadelphia; and the ship *London*, with just £12,000 of tea, was routed to Charleston, South Carolina. The total value of tea in the seven ships was roughly £100,000, but whether valued in sterling or colonial paper is uncertain. The EIC had hired these private vessels specifically to carry the company's tea to EIC consignees. They should not be confused with the East Indiamen of the company's own navy or the private vessels of other merchants carrying promiscuous cargoes of tea that happened to be caught up in the tea protests.[20]

Various authorities seem to disagree as to the amount of tea in the EIC shipments. The weight shipped in *pounds*—which may be confused in some texts with the value in *pounds sterling*—does not compute with the number of hundredweight chests known to be among the cargoes or with the wholesale or retail values per pound of tea that are often quoted. There is documentary evidence that there may have been some packing and repacking of teas in London for the convenience of the shipment with the division of whole chests into half chests and quarter chests by quality for the accommodation of the smaller shopkeepers. Chests of both Bohea and Singlo teas, together with smaller assortments of Hyson, Souchong, and Congou teas, were jointly consigned to a number of merchants. This repackaging represented a recent change in the trade regulations, which had formerly required the shipments remain in bulk as they had come from India. An additional problem faced with regard to the value of the tea (discussed later) was the intrinsic difference among the values of the various currencies and types of teas that were being reported in the primary sources. The directors of the EIC noted the difficulty of comparing and tracking prices:

> Public notice should be given in the [news]papers of each Province at least one month preceding the sale, and the following valuation prices affixed for the buyers to bid upon . . . Boston, at 2s, lawful money, per lb. [Massachusetts had no legal paper currency]; New York, 2s 9d, currency; Philadelphia, 2s 3d, currency; Charles Town, South Carolina, 10s per lb., currency. These prices are for Boheas . . . as each of the species going under the same general denomination of Hyson, Souchong, Congou, and Singlo vary almost 100 per cent in the price they sell for, according to quality, & not 10 per cent in the purchase [price].[21]

The movement for liberty and personal rights was no short-lived matter of a single night's mass protest in Boston over tea.[22] Similar, if sometimes less dramatic, protests against the tea were held in other colonial cities as word of the Boston Tea Party passed by mounted couriers down the length of the Atlantic seaboard. New York, Philadelphia, and Charleston hosted the most significant demonstrations, but generally all merchant ships carrying tea were simply refused a landing or were warned away by pilot boats at the approaches to the ports.

Only a quirk of weather or of fate kept an EIC tea ship to New York from arriving before those to Boston. A meeting called with the New York consignees, Pigou and Booth, to decide how to proceed when the expected tea should appear failed when the radical Sons of Liberty absolutely refused to allow the tea to be landed and stored, and the moderates among the attendees left in disgust. The EIC tea ship *Nancy*, Captain Benjamin Lockyer (a.k.a. Lockier) did not arrive in New York until February 1774, having been caught in the same winter storm that had wrecked the tea ship *William* on Cape Cod and having been redirected to Antigua for repairs to its masts and rigging. Four months passed before the shipment of 680 chests of tea was quietly and safely returned to England.

A private merchant vessel owned and under the command of Captain James Chambers was the first to arrive in New York with 18 chests of tea hidden away in her cargo. Chambers had been among the first to publicly refuse to transport the company's tea, but the vigilant and attentive Sons of Liberty, suspecting smuggling, searched the vessel and on finding the tea cast the whole of it into the waters of the harbor.

"The people all dispersed in good order, but in great wrath against the captain; and it was not without some risk of his life that he escaped." The captain was advised to leave New York as quickly as possible.[23]

The affair at Philadelphia, on the other hand, was particularly well managed. The consignees, among them Thomas Wharton, Gilbert Barkley, and the firms of James and Drinker and Willing and Morris, resigned their agencies early (although Barkley was a passenger aboard the tea ship *Polly*). More important, the local customs officials stayed out of the matter. Pilot boats had alarmed the tea ship at the Delaware Capes, and the ship's captain, Samuel Ayres, had anchored in the river off Chester and had bravely come ashore. He formally asked if the consignees would accept the cargo of 598 full chests and 130 half chests, and when it was refused he begged only the reprovisioning of his vessel and returned to England. "Be assured," wrote Wharton, one of the consignees, "this was as respectable a body of inhabitants as has been together on any occasion, many of the first rank. Their proceedings were conducted with the greatest decency and firmness, and without one dissentient voice."[24]

In Charleston, the consignees, Richard Smith and the firm of Leger and Greenwood, were also quickly convinced to resign their commissions, and the customs officials seized the shipment of 257 chests of tea aboard *London* when the 20-day grace period for the payment of the duties had passed. The cargo of chests was stored in the basement of the Exchange largely forgotten and moldering until supposedly sold by the Patriots after the opening of the war.

In Maryland, the decorum of the Boston tea protests dissolved into mob rule and flagrant injustice. Anthony Stewart, the private owner of the Maryland brig *Peggy Stewart*, arrived at Annapolis and paid the import duties on his cargo. The vessel contained a ton of tea (20 chests, 2,000 pounds by weight) privately consigned (not EIC tea) to a local Tory merchant named Thomas Charles Williams. Also aboard were 56 seasick indentured servants who had experienced a storm-tossed crossing. Going ashore, Stewart became terrified as a mob confronted him concerning the tea and demanded that he burn his vessel! The angry crowd had given Stewart no choice: burn the ship and its non-human contents or be hanged at his front door. Here was an escalation of dignified protest to levels of unwarranted vitriol that certainly constituted a violation of the very property rights that formed the core of America's political philosophy. Nonetheless, Mathias Hammond, a political rival of Williams and a spirited leader among the local Patriots, had roused the city beforehand with handbills making a case of disaffection to the cause against both Stewart and Williams. Claiming unconvincingly that he had paid the tea duty only to affect the landing of the sick passengers, Stewart appealed to one of the protest leaders, Charles Carroll, who would later sign the Declaration of Independence. Carroll convinced the man to submit to the demands of the protestors, and the vessel with all but its human cargo was set aflame. Stewart attempted thereafter to reconstruct his business, but plagued by death threats, he removed to England where he petitioned the Crown for compensation for his losses.[25]

ALTERNATIVE LIBATIONS

Most of the EIC tea sent to America—save the fewer than 350 chests that flavored Boston harbor—went untouched by the tea protestors. Two private cargoes had been destroyed. Other surviving cargos were ultimately redirected to friendlier ports as word of the Tea Party protests spread. Nonetheless, hundreds gathered in small groups elsewhere to destroy their own tiny stock of tea regardless of its source. Pound by pound and ounce by ounce tea went up in flames on village commons or was ceremoniously committed to the sea throughout the colonies. Devoted tea resistors condemned even their smuggled Dutch tea so that no question of its possible British origin might be raised. Many more shillings worth of tea went up in flames than could have been bought with any savings in tea duties, dramatic evidence that the tea protests were about process and principle, not money paid in taxes.

Meanwhile, the matrons of each town made a great spectacle of brewing alternative beverages from native leafs, stems, seeds, and flowers. The creativity of the ladies knew few bounds in producing alternative libations, although some of their concoctions were barely palatable. Labrador tea (made from the leaf of Red Root), Hyperion Tea and Yeopann Tea (from the Carolinas), and Oswego Tea (a Native American brew made from Bee Balm) had been used for decades as money savers "among the lower sort."[26] Teas made from Loosestrife (a four-leaf plant and stem) became widely known as Liberty Tea, although the term was applied to many other tea substitutes. These included rose hips, mint, sassafras, chamomile, sweet gum, lemon balm, and many berry flavors. Some of these were acceptable, and the modern reader may note some popular herbal flavors. Others were horrid. The reader should not be surprised to learn that the people did not totally abandon their beverages. The estimated consumption of smuggled Dutch coffee and cocoa, subsequently, rose more than 700 percent.

YOUR TEA IS DESTROYED

Ironically, very little English tea had been imported into the American colonies in the decade before the passage of the Tea Act. The determination to send 5,000 chests of EIC tea to America in 1773 had been based on a solid business calculation of the previous 10 years' average. The populous colony of Pennsylvania imported an average of only 2,000 chests of tea annually (200,000 pounds by weight), and New York used about the same. The southern colonies used tea in proportion to their smaller populations, and populous New England imported hardly any at all—only about 500 chests. This was partially due to the strength of the non-importation agreements and partially because Dutch smugglers swarmed in and out of most New England ports with their own East Indian tea, thereby filling much of the demand. Only in Boston had the customs officials attempted to effectively suppress the illicit trade in tea.[27]

Tea prices demanded by London ranged from 2s. 0d. (24d.) per pound for Bohea to 5s. 0d. (60d.) for quality Hyson. The company made a great deal more profit on quality teas. Hyson, Souchong, Congou, and Singlo sold for up to twice the price of Bohea, but they cost less than 10 percent more for the company to purchase and not a penny more to ship or handle.[28] In 1770, quality tea in New York was

Table 1.1
An Account of the Amount of Tea Imported at Boston

Year Imported	No. Chests	No. Merchants
1768	942	82
1769	340	33
1770	167	22
1771	890	103
1772	375	70
1773	378	61
Average	515	62

Source: A Letter from Mr. Clarke to Mr. Draper (Drake, 3358).

purchased wholesale at 4s. 6d. per pound and sold at retail at 5s. 6d., and in Maryland its retail price rose to an astounding 10s. (120 d.) per pound.[29] Dutch traders could have paid the British duty on tea and still undercut the London tea prices, but they were prohibited from entering the closed market in any case. A letter from Boston to the EIC directors written in 1771 noted of the sale of tea, "Were it not for the Holland tea, the [sale] of English would have answered . . . but the profit is immense upon Holland tea, which some say cost but 18d, and the 3d duty here is saved. . . . So much tea has been imported from Holland, that the importers from England have been obliged to sell for little or no profit."[30]

Although the government rescinded all the other import (Townshend) duties by 1773, it left in place most of the offensive and intrusive trade and currency restrictions. It had also hoped to reaffirm the right of Parliament to tax the colonies as Americans submitted to the payment of the duty on the tea for the sake of their pocket books. The tea duty from the year 1764 had averaged approximately £7 per ton.[31] Parliament passed the Tea Act in 1773 authorizing the immediate shipment of 5,000 chests of tea (250 tons) to the colonies and demanding that the tax (£1,750 sterling) be paid in coin by the importers when the cargo landed. The ostensible purpose of all this change was to grant the EIC an ironclad monopoly on the sale of tea that would drive the smugglers (free traders) out of business, but its hidden concurrent purpose was to maintain the effective tax of 3 silver pennies (3d.) on every pound of tea that had been in effect for almost six years under the Townshend duties and quietly direct the silver into the coffers of the EIC as a draw back.[32] Ironically, the plan would have made legal tea in the colonies less expensive and more competitive than the smuggled product, but seeing "the hook through the bait," Benjamin Franklin noted, "The British Ministry . . . believe that three pence in a pound [by weight] of tea, of which one does perhaps drink ten pounds in a year is sufficient to overcome all the patriotism of an American."[33]

In May 1773, months before the crisis came to a head, William Palmer had written to the directors of the EIC:

> The act allowing a drawback of the whole of the customs paid on tea, if exported to America, is now passed, in which there is a clause empowering the Lords of the Treasury to grant licenses to the [East] India Company, to export tea, duty free, to foreign states, or America, having at the time of granting such licenses upwards of ten millions of pounds in their warehouses, and as the

present stock of tea is not only near seventeen million, but the quantity expected to arrive this season does also considerably exceed the ordinary demand of months. It should be the opinion [that] an immediate consignment [to America] should take place . . . conducive to the interest of the Company.[34]

Writing under a pseudonym, *Anglo Americanus* noted the effect of the tea protests in a letter to a contact (George Dudley, Esq.) at East India House, the sumptuous edifice in London that served as the world corporate headquarters of the EIC. Included with the letter was a recent copy of a Boston newspaper describing the Tea Party: "Your tea is destroyed . . . finally the people were obliged to destroy it. . . . There is [in America] the utmost detestation of tea . . . as so much chains and slavery. . . . I am sorry the Company are led into such a scrape by the Ministry, to try the American's bravery, at the expense of their [EIC's] property. . . . Get the Tea Act repealed, and you'll sell all your tea."[35]

LET MY PEOPLE GO

The use of florid language was not unusual in 18th-century rhetoric, yet the extremes of *death* or *slavery* when applied to the sale and use of tea seem demagogic. Sam Adams—certainly no stranger to extravagant language—was a man driven more by biblical allusions than by Enlightenment philosophies. As such, he can be seen as a conservator of the Puritan ethic, fond of comparing the American revolutionaries to the Israelites who had escaped the slavery of Egypt, "to die freemen, rather than to live slaves." Adams' biographer, Ira Stoll, noted, "Samuel Adams was the archetype of the religiously passionate American founder, the founder as biblical prophet, an apostle of liberty." John Jay also proclaimed the essence of the biblical Exodus the "true cause" of the revolution—the deliverance of America from the "threatened bondage of Britain" through "the interposition of Heaven." The idea that Americans were like the enslaved biblical Israelites and that God was intervening directly on their side is essential for understanding the American Revolution.[36]

The archaic language of the 17th century was not only the language of Locke, Hobbes, and other political theorists whom Americans read but also the language they encountered when they opened their Bibles and worshiped in their churches. It conjured up visions of the sacred while signaling Americans to shift from their colloquial mode of everyday speech and thinking to one of liturgical interpretation and revered importance. It was also the language that Americans after 1763 used in scores of partisan newspapers, pamphlets, and books. This unique and often overlooked American tradition of writing "in the style of antiquity" opens a window onto a lost American world of biblical imagery. American authors, thereafter, reverted to this pseudo-biblical language and more clearly to its accompanying structures, forms, and cadences when discussing their difficulties and represent their grievances, past and present.[37]

For many of even the most conservative thinkers, God was a democrat (small "d"), and this God of Democracy allowed his followers an unfettered freedom of religious expression that led wherever its adherents chose. For some, this was considered a great cultural weakness and a danger to social order. Democracy was seen as a threat to the power of the elite—a capitulation to the mindless mob or to the tyranny of the majority. In the Declaration of Independence, however, American revolutionaries had relied on the Laws of Nature and of Nature's God to justify and underwrite their separation from Britain. Americans understood the words of the French philosopher Blaise Pascal who wrote that the king was a king because his subjects believed he was. Without that belief, the king had no power and no identity as a king. Many Americans highlighted the idea that religious beliefs as well as political structures were the products of social protocols and authoritarian pressures, and not the reverse.

Reverand Gad Hitchcock of Pembroke, Massachusetts, preaching a sermon at the Old Brick Meeting House in 1774 referred to God as "the great patron of liberty," and, quoting Psalms 118:9, he said, "It is better to trust in the Lord than to put confidence in princes." Hitchcock then made the connection between the Bible and the situation in America:

> They [the people] are sensible of their own happiness in having men of uprightness, honor and humanity to rule over them— Men, who make a proper use of their authority; who seek the peace and welfare of the whole community, and govern according to law and equity, or the original rules of their constitution. But when the wicked bear the rule, the people mourn; they are dissatisfied and grieved when contrary to reasonable expectation . . . it turns out . . . that their rulers possess opposite qualities; are inhuman, tyrannical and wicked; and instead of guarding, violate their rights and liberties. . . . Although government is not explicitly

instituted by God, it is, nevertheless, from Him. . . . He has signified it to be his will, that, as a security of property and liberty, and as necessary to greater improvements in virtue and happiness than could be attained in a state of nature, there should be government among them [the people]. . . . The people in this province, and in the other colonies, love and revere civil government. They love peace and order but they are not willing to part with any of those rights and privileges, for which they have, in many respects, paid very dear.[38]

Sam Adams, who was in attendance, later wrote confirming his dedication to the religion and government of his Puritan forefathers: "By the blessing of Heaven, we shall shortly be confirmed in that freedom for which our ancestors entered the wilds of America."[39]

As an additional example, a little-known Baptist minister named John Allen preached a sermon regarding the *Gaspée* incident in 1772 using biblical language and references to warn his listeners about greedy monarchs, corrupt judges, and conspiracies at the highest levels in London. Allen first appears in 1764 as a Baptist pastor in London, and around 1767 he moved to America. He then published *The Spirit of Liberty* (1770), pleading the case of John Wilkes, urging that the Member of Parliament be restored to his seat in the House of Commons or that the body be dissolved for abridging English liberties.[40]

His thanksgiving sermon delivered on December 3, 1772, *An Oration, Upon the Beauties of Liberty, or The Essential Rights of Americans*, was printed seven different times in two years in four colonial cities in string pamphlet form, becoming one of the most popular Patriot pamphlets in America. The pamphlet, in the form of an open letter to the colonial secretary, along with the incendiary rhetoric of numerous colonial newspaper editors, awoke colonial Patriots from a yearlong lull of inactivity prior to the Boston Tea Party: "When the king, judges, and senates, unite to destroy the rights of the people by a despotic power, as the [biblical] text expresses it . . . then the prosperity of the nation totters; the crown shakes; and the destruction of the people's rights is near at hand."[41]

Historian Bernard Bailyn included Allen with James Otis and Thomas Paine as the only three colonial pamphleteers who were able to demonstrate the "concentrated fury" to be found in tracts and treatises by Europe's more imaginative and capable writers. Until the publication of Paine's *Common Sense* in 1776, the Patriot protests—other than those of Allen and Otis—were notable for their careful avoidance of directly blaming George III for the troubles in America.[42]

The adoption of biblical language for non-religious purposes eventually became a distinct American form of intellectual expression. The first identifiable American piece in biblical style, *Regeneration and Conversion*, was produced in 1763 by Samuel Hopkins of Rhode Island (whose family helped staff the Continental Navy), and a pro-American tract, *The Book of America* (1766), also exhibited the biblical style. Many early Federalist writers, wishing to strengthen American attachment to the parent England after independence, applied the language of the King James Bible to describe American history and politics. The pinnacle of the tradition of writing in biblical style in America was reached with the publication of Richard Snowden's *The American Revolution; Written in the Style of Ancient History* (1796).[43]

THE PRINCIPLE OF SELF-INTEREST

It is safe to conclude from the available evidence that the tea leaves of Boston had become a symbol for deeper grievances than a mere dispute over taxing beverages. Traditional histories tend to focus on the legislative acts passed by misguided ministers in Parliament and the sometimes illogical willfulness of the colonial assemblies in resisting them. These are significant factors in any history of the revolution. Yet, in these analyses the seeming animosity of the ministry toward America and the will of the people to involve themselves in resisting their government is often taken for granted. This was not always the case. While there was a sizable number among Anglo-Americans who were anxious to separate themselves from Britain, many more were glad to be subjects of the British Crown that had just recently beaten down the almost century-old Bourbon alliance of Catholic France and Spain. The almost hysterical response of Anglo-Americans to the toleration of Catholicism represented in the Quebec Act of 1774 evidences this attitude. Other Anglo-Americans were simply unsure of their place in an untried republic independent of the so-called Mother Country. Until the success of the American Revolution, words like *democracy* and *republic* were tinged with negative connotations.

For many Americans, the political questions surrounding taxation, which seemed so clear to the leaders of the protests (and historical analysts today), had become muddled among a number of practical considerations that affected their daily lives and interests. These included the future availability of money and credit, of manufactured goods and inexpensive cloth, of precision tools and printer's type, of brass buttons and silver shoe buckles, and even of housekeeping items of many kinds.

Benjamin Franklin believed that "the British Ministry have no idea that any people can act from any other principle but that of [self]interest."[44] But he was not precisely correct. Although most Patriots were concerned for their rights as Englishmen, many others had only their own best interests at heart whether they were associated with finances, business, political power, or simply what was available from the local peddler. Many other Americans supported the Crown and ignored, mocked, or resisted the tea protestors. Others, who initially supported the non-importation of British goods and the non-consumption of tea, ultimately failed to support the revolution. A consumer's *boycott* had never before been attempted, and even the generic term would not be coined for a century.[45]

An anonymous opponent of continuing the tea protests, identified only as "Z," noted his own state of confusion regarding the conceptual foundations of America's tea crisis:

> The objectors say the tea duty will be a means of supporting the Parliament of Great Britain in raising money from us. How it can affect this matter I am utterly at a loss to comprehend. . . . How in the name of common sense does it differ . . . for a New England merchant to have his tea shipped from Great Britain, on his own account, or receive it on commission from the grocers there, and on its arrival, paying the customary duty, than if it had been shipped by the East India Company, who were the original importers? [And] be it considered that by this step the East India Company have taken of sending their tea to market themselves at their own cost, and the saving that is thereby made to the merchants here [in America] of commissions, freight and charges of importing it, which will be equal to the whole annual tax.[46]

There were a number of factors that militated against the tea protests of 1773–1774. The demonstrations engendered by the Stamp Act crisis of 1764 had been more effective than the question of tea in uniting the resistive spirit of the Anglo-American population. The Boston Massacre of 1770 had brought equally large and much angrier crowds into the streets of Boston, and the burning of the revenue cutter *Gaspée* in 1772 had engendered a greater reaction in political circles with the appointment of a Royal Commission of Inquiry.

Moreover, the year immediately prior to the Tea Party had been one of increasing disunity among the Patriots, and absent the tea crisis of 1773, political agitation in the colonies had largely subsided. When Richard Snowden published his history of the American Revolution, he started with the Boston Tea Party and made no mention of the *Gaspée*, the Boston Massacre, or, for that matter, any event prior to 1773. Mercy Otis Warren gave note to the Stamp Act crisis but skipped the entire period from 1770 to 1773 in her massive two-volume history of the American Revolution (1805).

The collapse of the non-importation agreements among New York merchants with the repeal of the Stamp Act in 1766, and the speedy acquittal won by the legal firm of John Adams and Josiah Quincy for the British commander, Captain Thomas Preston and the six soldiers involved in the Boston Massacre case in late 1770 also had seemed to portend a cooling of colonial ardor. The Royal inquiry into the burning of *Gaspée* brought forth no informants but also engendered no additional protests or demonstrations. Consequently, Lieutenant Governor Thomas Hutchinson of Massachusetts—no friend of the radicals or their tactics—called the Boston Tea Party "the boldest stroke that had been struck in America" because it reignited the quarrel between the people of the colonies and the king's ministry in London on many levels.[47]

The renewed imposition of the non-consumption agreements in 1774, in particular, allowed many of those who held no previous claim to a formal franchise (vote) to partake actively in politics for the first time even if they could only stand in protest. Sam Adams noted that the royal charters issued to many of the colonies and sanctioned at the end of the previous century by William III and Mary in 1689 secured to the people "all the English liberties" and "some additional privileges which the common people [in England] had not." The provisions contained in these documents were more than mere abstractions for the Patriots.[48]

SOME DIFFERENCES IN RANK

We accept the ideas of democracy and universal equality today, although we do not fully experience them in practice. Before the 18th century, it was nearly impossible to imagine a society that did not have a permanent hierarchy of some kind with the bishops, or the land-owners, or the employers, or the monarch at the top, and the ordinary people below taking their cues from above. Arthur Browne, an Anglican minister from New England, regretted the general lack of a more sharply defined hierarchical presence in the colonies, saying that "some differences of rank, some inequality must and ought to grow up in every society."[49] Yet, these distinctions were not equivalent to the concepts of fixed classes (lower, middle, upper) promulgated in the 19th century by social reformers, utopian ideologues, social Darwinians, and progressive academicians.

Unlike France, where nobility was extended to all the offspring of the aristocracy, in Britain only the eldest male line retained its hereditary rights. Those scions of noble British houses who fell by the side of the road due to the misfortune of their birth order or gender added to a numerous and growing mass of lesser *gentry*—a middle ground between the nobility and the common people. The title of *gentleman* was used to distinguish between these well bred but less-than-fortunate souls and just ordinary people of unimpressive bloodlines.

By the middle of the 18th century, genteel status no longer required a landed estate or a coat of arms. It was more a matter of opinion. A gentleman recognized another gentleman when he saw one. A gentleman due to his family means (wealth), but not an ordinary person, could enter freely into the "cosmopolitan world of scientists, philosophers, statesmen and men of business from all over Europe who were united by their curiosity."[50] The law, the pulpit, the royal court, or the military camp could make a gentleman, but a person could also establish himself as a gentleman "by a good garb, genteel air, or good education, wealth or learning." This was no easy matter for those rising to the level of the gentry from the merchant classes, but growing wealth and increasing political influence assured that no small number of so-called ordinary people might enter the ranks of gentlemen in the English-speaking world. Nonetheless, there was a taint to *new* money that was most perceptible among those who had *old* money.[51]

Most persons chose their day-to-day associates from among their own social class, and they frowned on anything other than necessary business dealings or unavoidable discourse with any others. Young men of a certain level of social birth were, therefore, under immense pressure to acquire the correct manner and air of a gentleman if they wished for advancement. Consulting physicians or university professors could be gentlemen, but barber-surgeons and tutors were not considered so gentlemanly. Military officers, naval commanders, barristers, and clergymen displayed their gentility with colorful uniforms, powdered periwigs, formal gowns, and ritual vestments. Private persons displayed their gentility in their dress, speech, and manner. Absent these outward symbols of gentility, titles, salutations, and suffixes, such as Reverend, Esquire, KC (Kings Counsel), MP (Member of Parliament), or Doctor of whatsoever (Letters, Philosophy, Theology, etc.) became socially important as descriptors of a gentleman of accomplishment.

In 1762, Oxford University awarded Ben Franklin an honorary degree for his studies in electricity, and he used Doctor Franklin to refer to himself thereafter in almost all circumstances. In the London of the famous Dr. Samuel Johnson, the prefix *Doctor* had great power, and no one ever referred to the noted essayist and author without his title. The great actor David Garrick, the author Oliver Goldsmith, and Dr. Johnson's own biographer James Boswell might have been insulted if "Gentleman" were to be omitted after their names in print.[52]

Walter Jones, a young Virginian studying medicine at Edinburgh in Scotland in 1766, reported that the medical students at the university were divided into three ranks, or orders of gentlemen. Jones described the characteristics of these gentlemen, as he considered them, in a letter to his brother: "First. The fine gentlemen, or those who give no application to studies, but spend the revenues of gentlemen of independent fortunes. Second. The gentlemen, or students of medicine. Strictly speaking these live genteelly and at the same time apply themselves to study. Third. The vulgar, or those who, if they are not indolent, are entirely devoid of every thing polite and agreeable. . . . The last is chiefly [composed] of Scotsmen."[53]

Although Englishmen, Americans, and Scots were educated together, Jones distinguished Scotsmen by their separation. The Scots, even those who were well educated or financially successful, were very conscious of being Scots, and they were not allowed to forget their supposedly inferior ethnicity. In England, the Scots and the Irish were treated with open hostility and sometimes with physical abuse—even among gentlemen. Moreover, Englishmen and Americans sounded essentially the same when they spoke—especially if they were studied to do so—while the lilting speech of a Scotsman or an Irishman generally betrayed their origins. "Although the Yankee twang had emerged by the 18th century, there is no evidence that Londoners could recognize it or any other colloquial colonial speech as American. After all, there were enough dialects spoken in the British Isles alone to confound the average London shopkeeper."[54]

Nonetheless, the moralist Dr. Johnson looked on most Americans as inferior to Englishmen: "They are a race of convicts [probably referring to criminals sent to the colonies as indentures], and ought to be thankful for anything we allow them short of hanging."[55] Most Londoners did not actually know much about America, although they thought they did. To many of them, America was a land of tropical plantations and slave compounds.[56] Indeed, most distinguished American visitors to London were from the slaveholding South or the West Indies, and many brought slaves with them as servants and attendants. The fact that the fabulously rich sugar planters of the West Indian islands were classed as Americans added to the confusion. All of New England, New York, Philadelphia, and Virginia were thought by some to be in the West Indies. James Otis, one of the leaders of the Sons of Liberty, complained that the people of London thought American colonials were "a compound mongrel mixture of English, Indian, and Negro."[57]

Whatever other assumptions Englishmen made about America, they were well aware of there being a large number of African Americans there. "Americans were a colonial people, English, Scottish, Irish, European and African, direct spin-offs of Britain's Atlantic trading empire."[58] A British officer told Josiah Quincy (law partner to John Adams) that a majority of Londoners thought Americans were all black, or at least that they secreted so-called Negro blood. This infuriated Otis, who heard of the comment. "You are wretchedly mistaken," he wrote, "there is as good blood flowing in [America's] veins, save the royal blood, as any in the three kingdoms."[59]

YANKEE DOODLE, GENTLEMAN

The number of the gentry in America—as a proportion of the larger population—was not unlike that to be found in England. Moreover, there was clearly an attempt among the better sort to create an informal American aristocracy. A cultured man from the colonies who enjoyed refined living, wrote poetry or erudite treatises, and filled his home with expensive art might use his gentility and his wealth to acquire a knighthood or baronetcy and overawe his neighbors as Sir So-and-So, Baronet. Of course, he might have to purchase his elevation, and after the opening of the revolution his new rank might serve to mark him as "a rascally friend of the King."[60]

There were a few legitimate members of the aristocracy present in America in the form of royal governors, well-bred military officers, or visiting landlords to overawe the public, but the appearances of new-made knights and baronets among the ranks of base-born colonials, like Sir William Pepperell, Sir Peter Warren, or Sir William Johnson, were considered events of consequence because the men themselves were of consequence. They had undertaken two of the signal victories of colonial forces in the wars with the French—Pepperell and Warren the capture of Fortress Louisbourg (a.k.a. Louisburg) in 1745 and Johnson the defeat of the French at Lake George in 1755. A self-made man, gentleman, and so-called Mohawk Baronet, Johnson was one of the most highly respected colonial personalities of his day. His early death in 1775 was widely mourned everywhere.[61]

During the French and Indian War (and later the War for Independence), the martial spirit that pervaded the New England colonies was personified in a rather ill-defined character known as Yankee Doodle. During the French and Indian War, American provincials made up a substantial portion of Britain's military force and their snobbish British cousins in the regulars initially assigned the sobriquet to colonial militiamen from Connecticut. These men had been among the admittedly rag-tag militia of Colonel Thomas Fitch of Norwalk, who had fought alongside Johnson at Lake George. Although Fitch was the son of the sitting colonial governor (also named Thomas Fitch), he commanded only a local company of citizen soldiers. His young sister had placed chicken feathers in the hatbands of the Connecticut men to simulate some uniformity among their nondescript militia clothing. A poem naming the men Yankee Doodles had been circulated among the regulars by Colonel Richard Schucksberg, a British army surgeon, in derision of the unkempt appearance of volunteers. It appears in a derisive context as Yankee Doodle who "put a feather in his cap and called it Macaroni."[62] The term *Macaroni* applied to an outlandish style of male dress then popular in Europe. A writer in the *Oxford Magazine* wrote in 1770, "There is indeed a kind of animal, neither male nor female, a thing of the neuter gender, lately started up amongst us. It is called Macaroni. It talks without meaning, it smiles without pleasantry, it eats without appetite, it rides without exercise, it wenches without passion."[63]

Colonial Americans were generally tolerant, conservative, hard working, and hard fighting; and Yankee Doodle ultimately became a national symbol that also generally portrayed the rudiments of these qualities. Two decades later, the colonials gleefully assumed the identity of Yankee Doodles, or just plain Yankees, during their quest for independence. Yankee Doodle was no pomp and bluster member of the dandified gentry, nor was he a so-called *spruce prig*, who dressed the part of a gentleman in order to ingratiate himself with his betters while planning to rob them blind. He was the salt of the earth, not quite the British equivalent of middle class, but the embodiment of a nascent and exceptional identity that cast off the last vestiges of being Anglo-American for just being American.

During the tea crisis, there was an immense gulf between the Yankee Doodle gentlemen who planned and directed the protest program and the detritus of colonial society that formed the mobs that acted out in the streets. In the 18th century, it was difficult for different social classes, occupations, and business interests to sustain any form of unity on a particular topic. This fact makes the cohesion of the tea protests somewhat unique. In a social hierarchy based on birth, family connections, and occupation—if one needed to work at all—the long-term interests of one set of persons often came into conflict with the short-term interests of any coalition that attempted to span the entire population. Moreover, the relationships between the people and their home colony, and of each colony and London, were not the same. Boston, for example, was a hotbed of sedition with a history of dissent and obstinacy, whereas New York or Philadelphia were more evenly split in their pro- and anti-Crown sentiments.

One of the most important tasks of these Yankee Doodle gentlemen was to direct and control the Sons of Liberty, who ultimately established a form of mob rule in the streets that was stronger than that of the magistrates in their legislative chambers. Many prominent Patriot gentlemen, made bitter by the ongoing crisis, voiced a preference for mob rule over the arbitrary rule of Parliament, but deep in their hearts they retained a certain social distain for the lowest classes of American society. Among these was a very young New York gentleman born in Nevis in the West Indies, Alexander Hamilton who deplored the present situation of the better class of colonials who were being forced to live outside a proper government.[64] Another gentlemen wrote to friends in London that the street demonstrators seemed like a "trained mob" that bullied and terrorized, tarred and feathered, and paralyzed all government "as if under orders."[65] James Hawker, a British naval captain noted, "The . . . militia drums beat to arms, not to quell the mob collected in defiance of all law and allegiance to their sovereign, but to increase it."[66]

Just who controlled the mob was a matter of speculation, but it was suggested that Sam Adams and John Hancock could call out a mob of hundreds at a moment's notice.[67] More to the point, gentlemen such as Joseph Pearce Palmer—who had dressed as an Indian at the Tea Party, but was an artisan in the 18th-century sense who had been educated at Harvard—acted as a brake on the seamier components of the mob. Boston had been peaceful for one night and day of protest at least, but New York had been ripped apart by several waterfront riots. Significantly, these disruptions had been powered by the energies of unemployed seamen and led by ruder maritime personalities, such as Captain Isaac Sears and the privateer Alexander McDougall. It took all kinds to fashion a revolution, but the gentlemen planners among the activists in Boston eschewed the involvement of vagabonds and strangers.

It is easy to dismiss the behavior of the mobs of the American Revolution. When a mob of American colonists threw the private property of British merchants into Boston Harbor in 1773, it was a good mob—good enough to name a political movement that exhibits a great deal of order and harmony more than two centuries later. Yet, as orderly as the Tea Party of 1773 was, it was just a mob to the British merchants that absorbed the loss of their property. When a businessman was made to ruin his livelihood and to burn his vessel simply because it carried tea to Annapolis, or when rough treatment was administered to an aged doctor that caused a heart attack and his accidental death during a "carting" in Philadelphia, or when Tories in New Jersey were purposely hanged in their doorways because they believed in a different politics, these were also, for the victims, less than harmonious outcomes—the consequences of bad American mobs. Regrettably, the reader may need to take a closer look at the mobs that populated the streets of America during the crisis of the 1760s and 1770s and rid themselves thereby of some romantic notions concerning them.

There was an almost bottomless supply of willing local demonstrators in Boston. In 1757, the top 10 percent of Boston's gentlemen and genteel ladies owed 80 percent of the town's wealth, and by 1763 one in eight of the seamier population was on poor relief suffering from the consequences of the collapse of the Puritan welfare state and the chronic economic instability that followed the close of the French and Indian War. Moreover, there was a large fraction of the matrons of the town who had been left widowed during the several French conflicts (1739–1748 and 1754–1763). With the crop of relatively young widows came fatherless children, adolescents, and young adults—prime candidates for inclusion in any street demonstration—who lacked the direction and control of a father's presence while growing up. Another cause for economic distress, and a sea of unemployed men, was the fact that Boston had lost its premier place as a fishing port to surrounding towns.[68] Benjamin Barnes, the congenial collector of the port of Boston, had formerly given an official wink and nod to many of the illegalities and irregularities of local maritime practice. Charles Paxton, an incorruptible and more efficient customs administrator, had recently replaced Barnes and dramatically increased the seizure of suspect vessels. Consequently, many mariners had gone unemployed. The cutthroat aspects of Boston's clandestine maritime trade thereafter left a cruel contradiction between the adventurously rich and the desperately destitute.[69]

Most 18th-century Anglo-Americans considered any person worthy of being called a gentleman, even without a title, to be part of *their* aristocracy. Yet, a too great an inequality of wealth, influence, or social position threatened that too few citizens living in opulence might overawe too great a multitude of ordinary citizens living in misery. In the previous century, philosopher John Locke had placed the ordinary people in the caring hands of gentlemen, "for if those of that rank are by their Education once set right, they will quickly bring the rest into Order."[70]

Nonetheless, liberally educated and made thereby fit to do nothing of practical value, dozens among the highly placed leaders of the protests of the 1770s—themselves fitting the qualifications of gentlemen—disparaged the ordinary people among their own followers as physically and psychological different from the better classes calling them "grazing animals," "herds of cattle," "sheep," "vulgar," "ignorant," and "narrow-minded and bigoted." The arrogance of one group of leaders among the Patriots produced an abasement of the others who protested in the streets. So much for a tradition of egalitarian democracy and polite political rhetoric that was supposed to characterize a democracy! Among those who are known to have looked down on the humbler sort were not only the older generation of men like George Washington, Sam Adams, Landon Carter, and Gouverneur Morris, but also relative youths in their 20s, like Alexander Hamilton, Henry "Light Horse Harry" Lee, and Thomas Jefferson.[71]

This should not be surprising. In the 18th century, the common people were taught to fawn and cringe in the presence of those of higher than ordinary rank in order to make clear that they realized their own inferiority and subordination. Deference to persons of rank and noble birth was a cherished tradition that Americans inherited from their English forbearers. A 25-year-old apprentice and his 50-year-old father

The threat of tar and feathers overhangs a disaffected American forced to sign the Associators' Pledge. Public signings were a propaganda device used to great effect to undermine opposition. They attracted large crowds of people and were not so violent as to warrant interruption by the army, the government, or those who might secretly sympathize with the victim. (Library of Congress)

visiting the home of a gentleman of an age between them, say 40, were both expected to stand with eyes fixed to the floor and cap in hand during any interview.[72]

The Southern planter aristocracy, though often burdened with crushing debt in order to maintain the gentrified trappings of refinement and learning, believed themselves worthy of precedence among any assembled group of gentlemen especially if they came from New England. The better sort among the richer urban merchants of the towns, together with the lawyers, ministers, and physicians, were considered gentry and acquired a natural ascendancy over the small farmers, tradesmen, and crafters among whom they lived. Yet, tea drinking seemed to provide an artificial rallying point for a number of these seemingly disparate groups. The commonality of tea was perhaps the unique factor that sustained the protests. From hence were the origins of Mr. Yankee Doodle, Gentleman.

DOWNRIGHT CONSERVATIVE

Although innovative forms of protest opened the doors of the political arena to many persons who had never before desired to be involved in forming the policies of government, it also exposed a wealth of hitherto unrecognized political thinkers among the colonials. The constitutional arguments and legal logic of subscribers to the non-importation agreements and of the anonymous authors of letters of protest to the editor, pamphlets, and broadsides often rivaled in their substance the offerings of the best lawyers and parliamentary scholars to be found in London. These protestors were no mere provincials attempting to save a 3penny tax on a pound of tea. Among them were those who were well read and politically sophisticated. England had its Samuel Johnson, Thomas Hobbs, and John Locke, but America had its Samuel Adams, Thomas Paine, and John Dickinson.

The most radical among the protest leaders in America often suppressed their anger, their passion, and their natural recklessness in order to redeem their constitutional rights as Englishmen. Of these Adams and Paine stand out as exceptions. Most others, like Dickinson, undertook to regain the former structure of British society, not to transform it. Indeed the cause for which they acted was in their eyes "downright conservative."[73] The cause proclaimed liberty tempered with piety and virtue. Those who gave in to lesser objectives or their more violent inner demons, like Sears and McDougall, are generally not ranked high among the Founders of America. Yet, in its outcomes, the revolution that the moderates undertook was as radical as any that followed thereafter in that it transformed America from a limited monarchy to a constitutional republic.

The idea of America was totally new, completely untried in the modern sense. Dickinson probably would have been chosen to write the Declaration of Independence, but even he, the so-called pen-man of the revolution, found it impossible to support such a radical move at the time. He continued to support the American cause, however, and wrote the first draft of the Articles of Confederation, a dull and uninspired document that served as the structure of the infant United States until it was found wanting. By way of contrast, in the pamphlet *Common Sense* (1776), Paine transformed the language of politics. Previously *republic* had been a slightly disreputable term that haunted the relic halls of Greece and Rome. Paine made it the utopian ideal for modern popular governance. *Common Sense* appeared at precisely the right moment in the American crisis; it was a game changer that killed any hope for reconciliation with Parliament. It was the most printed of the Revolutionary pamphlets, going through 25 editions in 13 cities and selling 150,000 copies in its first year—this when printed editions of other works usually ran only in the dozens.[74]

Had Americans tried to govern using the political platitudes contained in the Declaration of Independence or the Articles of Confederation rather than the more pragmatic forms of governance written into the Constitution and the Bill of Rights, they would likely have failed to produce a viable nation. They might have mimicked the weak pseudo-republican union of the independent Dutch principalities in the 1580s or devolved into the calculated atheism, systemic cruelty, and bloody chaos characteristic of the each man his own democracy attitudes of the French Revolution in the 1790s. Instead, they created a unique political, religious, and economic environment that freed entrepreneurs, businessmen, commercial interests, and the people themselves from the overwhelming restraints of British-style mercantilism, established religion, and arbitrary government control. Yet, there were several other probabilities that could have followed in the wake of the incident on Griffin's Wharf.

HANG TOGETHER OR HANG SEPARATELY

It is indisputable that many of the principal leaders of the tax protests and tea boycotts were still in hopes of a reconciliation with the Crown, and the war was regarded as one against the unlawful acts of the king's ministry rather than one involving disloyalty to the king's sovereignty. It should be remembered while reading this history that the period of crisis before the revolution was one of great secrecy and personal jeopardy for those who protested the actions of the Crown. Many of the most active characters in the prerevolutionary period, therefore, committed little or nothing to paper contemporaneous with the events, or wrote under pseudonyms in order to avoid charges of sedition, disaffection, or treason. Consequently, it is difficult to precisely reconstruct from the available sources the genuine attitudes and reactions of many common Americans during the crisis over tea. Anglo-American protestors were correct in fearing the retribution of their government during this prewar period.

The British Crown had an uneven and difficult set of experiences with protestors. In little more than 150 years, the British people had beheaded a king (1649), had deposed the son of a dictatorial protector (1660), had led an armed popular rebellion in Virginia (1675), had replaced a legitimate monarchial line with that of a childless Dutchman (William III and Mary II, 1689), had overthrown an attempted royal takeover of the governments of New England, New York, and New Jersey, had begat a new royal line with foreign roots in the German states (Hanover), and had raised two major Jacobin rebellions in Scotland (1719, 1745). As will be shown, those who supported or resisted these movements more often than not paid a heavy forfeit.

The allegiance that a subject owed the king was a personal and individual obligation, and the colonials where certainly *subjects* in all sorts of social, cultural, and political ways that modern American *citizens* can only surmise. Breaking fealty with the king often demanded equally personal and individual punishments, some of which were cruel and unusual in a humanitarian sense. Hanging, beheading, branding, and quartering were out of style in 1773, but not out of living memory.[75] The British courts of the 18th century, unlike those of the United States today, recognized and used the concept of *constructive treason* when dealing with disloyalty. In other words, it was treason to merely speak or write to encourage disloyalty in others even when taking no active role in a rebellion.

The Hanover dynasty, of which George III was a scion, had a clear record of exploiting this concept to suppress both dissent and opposition, especially in Scotland in the most recent rebellion of 1745–1746, where hundreds of prisoners had been summarily hanged or shot by the paternal uncle of George III (the Duke of Cumberland).[76] All those badly wounded on the battlefield were put to the sword or dispatched by the bayonet. The heads of the leaders were placed on spikes atop the gates of Scottish cities. Fortunately for America, the Duke suffered a debilitating stroke that ultimately led to his death in 1765 before the blossoming of the American crisis. Therefore, it is no wonder that Benjamin Franklin warned his fellow signers of the Declaration of Independence, "We must hang together, gentlemen . . . else, we shall most assuredly hang separately."[77]

PERNICIOUS WEEDS

The American population had its roots in a potpourri of religious dissenters; but also among them were displaced Scots, Welch, and Scotch Irish with recent quarrels with the king; Germans, Moravians, and Swiss foreigners with no history of loyalty to the British Crown; former Royalists and Roundheads whose immediate ancestors had been pitted against one another; a self-aggrandizing landed gentry and coarse commoners; plantation aristocrats, gentlemen merchants, and yeomen farmers; black slaves, freemen, and freedmen; apprentices and indentured servants of many races and ethnic origins, many of whom had left the homes to find some greater degree of liberty and prosperity than they had experienced in Europe. In 1773, half the Americans outside New England had no English roots and those in New England were largely at odds with Old England. The diversity of American thought and circumstances may have caused the tea protestors to rise up in a unique alliance to overcome the perceived threat of a despotism that affected them all.[78]

The prerevolutionary period and the revolution itself was filled with the *disaffected*, those who were less than fully committed or even hostile to the cause of independence. These so-called Loyalists and Tories are an important part of the story that follows.[79] It was not in the nature of the most politically conservative—the most *English* among them, if you will—to act as radicals and agitators, but Sam Adams feared them nonetheless. He wrote to another Patriot, Dr. James Warren: "If measures are not soon taken, and the most vigorous ones, to root out these pernicious weeds, it will be in vain for America to persevere in this glorious struggle for the public liberty."[80]

Some of the most ardent supporters of the Crown lost all they owned to the looters or to the Patriot bonfires, including in some cases their very lives. One historian has noted, "The formation of the Tory or Loyalist party . . . its persecution by the Whigs . . . and the banishment or death . . . of these most conservative and respectable Americans is a tragedy but rarely paralleled in the history of the world." At least 100,000 Loyalists fled to England or Canada during the course of the revolution, but many waited until the last minute to take ship with the last redcoats evacuating New York in 1783, hoping in vain for a positive turn in British fortunes that never materialized.[81]

CHAPTER 2

The Empire of Goods

I am a hardened and shameless Tea drinker, who for twenty years diluted his meals with only the infusion of this fascinating plant. . . . Tea amuses the evening. . . . Tea solaces the midnight. . . . Tea welcomes the morning.

—Dr. Samuel Johnson, London, 1757

The necessities of life are obtained with great certainty by the use of the simplest means. The luxuries are more difficult to obtain; the means to procure them are more intricate, and less certain in their results.

—Reverend Charles Finney, 1835

NOT JUST GOODS

By the middle of the 18th century, the economics of trade had become truly global. Englishmen drank French wine and brandy when they could get it; Frenchmen used spices imported from the Dutch East Indies; Hollanders cooked with Spanish olive oil; and Spaniards ate salted cod from New England. Sugar, chocolate, and ginseng moved from the New World to the Old; woodland furs, fragrant sandalwood, Asian silk, and India cloth were sold in markets from Italy to Philadelphia; Indigo dye moved from the east coast of Africa to the south of

England; and human beings were torn from their homes and forced to labor in the wilderness of America.

Englishmen in Britain and America—and other persons of many nationalities—drank tea from China, but the extent of the British imperium represented more than could be found in the bottom of a teacup. Economic historian T. H. Breen noted, "The goods of this expanding marketplace were never just goods . . . they were the stuff by which a society . . . sorted itself out."[1] The roster of imported items available to citizens of the British Empire suggested that it was truly an empire of goods. A list of duty-bearing imports to Anglo-America taken from the *Boston Town Record* at the time of the first non-importation agreements includes both luxury and mundane items, and reads as follows:

> Loaf Sugar, Cordage, Anchors, Coaches, Chaises and Carriages of all Sorts, Horse Furniture, Men's and Women's Hats, Men's and Women's Apparel ready made. Household Furniture, Gloves, Men's and Women's Shoes, Sole Leather, Sheathing and Deck Nails, [embedded] Gold and Silver and Thread Lace of all Sorts, Gold [brass] and Silver [white metal] Buttons, Wrought Plate of all Sorts, Diamond [ware], Stone and Paste Ware, Snuff, Mustard, Clocks and Watches, Silversmiths' and Jewelers' Wares, Broad Cloths that cost above 1 s. per Yard, Muffs, Furs and Tippets, and all Sorts of Millenary Ware, Starch, Women's and Children's Stays, Fire Engines, China Ware, Silk and Cotton Velvets, Gauze, Pewterers' hollow Ware, Linseed Oil, Glue, Lawns [a cloth], Cambricks [a cloth], Silks of all Kinds for Garments, Malt Liquors and Cheese.[2]

By the 18th century, rare spices and unusual fragrances from the East could be found in most upscale markets in the West, and many wealthy families had collections of Chinese porcelain, lacquered ware, and various other Oriental items like rugs, draperies, and wallpaper arranged in special rooms "a' la Chinoise." There was also a Hindustani fashion craze that took root among the socially elite. Gentlemen lounged about their homes in banyans (a quilted full-length robe) and exotic caps or head wrappings, and women donned turbans, saris, and other India styles for social affairs. Intellectuals and scientists, in particular, seemed to make a point in the mid-18th century of having a portrait painted wearing their banyans instead of normal everyday clothing to help to communicate the intellectual or spiritual character of their endeavors. Encyclopedist Denis Diderot, Dr. Benjamin

Rush, and Dr. Benjamin Franklin were all depicted seated, resting on an elbow, and in a studious pose to "exemplify the ways in which portraiture of the learned imbued intellectual endeavors with the markings of gentility."[3]

The women's sari was a length of cloth measuring 13–26 feet long and about 4 feet wide (depending on quality and cost), which was draped around the entire body covering at least one shoulder and sometimes veiling the head, which was more appropriate for women than wearing a man's turban although they did so. Pajamas were worn in England as lounging wear by both men and women as early as the late 17th century and were sometimes called Mogul breeches. The word *pajama* derives from the Hindustani *epai-jama*.[4]

The exotic clothing was not costume in the sense of a masquerade or the wardrobe of a play. It was fashion, freely worn indoors or in the streets, for men over their shirt, breeches, and waistcoat when receiving visitors or addressing neighbors. The Hindustani style was more widely adopted by men than women. Moreover, many influential families dressed their black African slaves and servants in India attire.[5]

THE FUSS OVER TEA

The Greeks and Romans had traded with India through a complex system of ocean and land routes, and the west coast of the subcontinent supported more than 40 trading stations in the second century AD.[6] It is important to note that the people of India needed very little from the West, trading almost exclusively for gold, silver, and necessary technical metals like tin, zinc, and lead. In the culture of India, a woman's wealth and security was accumulated in the golden jewelry that she wore on her wedding day. Consequently, it was gold which parents sought for their daughters and gold for which India traded.

The quest for spices, porcelain dinner services, and oriental fashion may have driven the initial exploration of the world's sea-lanes, but it was tea—shipped from China to India and from India to the West— that was the first foreign commodity to produce worldwide repercussions in the 18th century. The boycott of tea was one of the most popular endeavors of the Patriots during the years leading to the Revolutionary War, but the tea protests did not begin or end with the Boston Tea Party of 1773. Eschewing tea had become a badge of honor among many colonial households from the time of the first Townshend Acts in 1767.

Although it was not always easy to abstain from this popular beverage, hundreds of families throughout the colonies pledged to forgo the use of the unjustly taxed leaves. Newspapers waged campaigns against tea. "If you touch one grain of the accursed tea you are undone," was the sentiment most often conveyed.[7] To dissuade people from using the brew, some boycott leaders and Patriot pamphleteers circulated stories that tea was a poisonous brew, responsible for stomach ailments and nervous disorders. They asserted that tea bred head lice and fleas. It was even suggested that the tea was prepared for export by being pressed into its container by the bare, dirty feet of Chinese workers.[8]

In January 1770, almost four years before the Boston Tea Party, a group of 426 women of Boston signed an agreement not to drink any tea until the tax upon it (then 6d.) was repealed. Even nine-year-old Susan Boudinot embraced the pledge. Some time later, while a guest in the home of New Jersey's Loyalist governor, William Franklin, the young girl was offered a cup of tea. Susan accepted the refreshment, curtsied, raised the cup, and threw the liquid out a nearby window. The reaction of those in attendance was not recorded.[9]

In March 1770 (ironically on the same day as the Boston Massacre), Parliament decided to repeal the hated Townshend Acts, retaining only a reduced tea duty (3d. instead of 6d. per pound). Faced with only a partial victory, Sam Adams and other leaders of the non-importation movement continued to condemn the use and purchase of tea from Britain, but with little added effect. Although a great deal of tea still came to the colonies from illegal Dutch sources, the price differential with British tea had shrunk appreciably making it less attractive to smugglers. The population of Philadelphia decried the local scarcity of tea, and shopkeepers raised their prices on Bohea from 2s. 3d. to a remarkable 3s. 6d. as stocks of smuggled Dutch tea dwindled. Month after month, Americans continued to buy and use British tea, and the burning opposition of the Continental Associations seemed to have cooled. All this was to change in the summer of 1773.

The protests that led to the Boston Tea Party in December 1773 formed around a number of different rumors propagated by certain friends of America living in England who heard murmurings of plots and designs echoing from Whitehall during the previous summer. Actually a street name, Whitehall lends its name to an area of London near Westminster. The name was taken initially from the approach to the Palace of Whitehall that was destroyed by fire in 1698. In the 18th century, the area around its former location was filled with government offices. Hence, *Whitehall* became a euphemism for government used in similar manner to the *White House* or *Capitol Hill* when speaking of the government of the United States.

In 1773, there was widespread belief among the expatriate Americans that the ministry in London was plotting to use the acceptance of the reduced tea tax as a precedent for laying other internal commodity taxes on America in the future. The amount of the tea tax was of little importance because America was totally dependent on all sorts of imported commodities. It was also widely believed that the EIC, once established in a tea monopoly in North America, would soon assert itself in all the foreign commerce of the colonies and by its overwhelming size and political influence drive out smaller colonial businessmen from the lucrative trade in oriental goods. Many merchants also feared EIC intrusion into the profitable fur trade with the Native American population—a trade for which many Americans had fought the French. Either or both these eventualities would have drawn off any hard coin Americans might accumulate leaving them in perpetual debt to their creditors. These suppositions were privately communicated in letters to family, acquaintances, and business associates in America.

Informants in London friendly to the Anglo-American position were among the first to suggest that there were infamous plots among the underlying economic plans of the administration of Lord Frederick North, who had become prime minister in 1770. North was considered an inveterate political schemer. Largely through the mechanism of personal correspondence, word of these supposed schemes crossed the Atlantic and slowly made its way through the colonial population. No one source could precisely articulate the operative details of the tea proposals, and the language of the proposed Tea Act itself was ambiguous enough to allow for a great deal of demagoguery on the topic.

Opposition Patriot Whigs in Parliament fed the rumor mill of colonials visiting London in order to further their own purposes, and much of what was reported as absolute truth in the tea parlors of London and in the colonial press was actually bits and pieces of unconfirmed speculation and downright lies. Parliament, it seemed, needed to implement the act for the colonials to find out what was in it outside the environment of distortions and rumors. This might sound familiar to T.E.A. Party members today, emphasizing the idea that the more things change the more they stay the same. Even Edmund Burke, one of the most vociferous advocates for America in Parliament, was confused by the actions of the government: "Experience and the nature of things . . . prove . . . the utter impossibility of obtaining an effective revenue from the colonies. . . . You keep up the revenue laws, which are mischievous, in order to preserve trade laws that are useless. Such is the wisdom of our plan in both its members."[10]

Among the available sources of information considered most reliable in America was the intercepted correspondence of Governor Hutchinson with William Palmer, a London tea merchant, concerning the cancellation of a tea consignment to the Hutchinson sons in Boston that had been concluded before the Tea Act had been passed. The governor attempted to sell a previously agreed upon load of tea in England and to arrange, for the sake of added profit, for his sons to become consignees for a replacement cargo of the newly duty-free tea that was to arrive in Massachusetts under the act.

Unfortunately for his reputation, in these letters Governor Hutchinson also vented his spleen and set himself squarely against the population of his own colony. He advised altering the founding charters of the New England provinces, separating Maine from Massachusetts, and closing the Grand Banks fisheries to New England mariners. He suggested the establishment of a garrisoned citadel in Boston to help enforce martial law, the stationing of a fleet in its harbor to strengthen the customs service, and the transportation of American "incendiaries" to England for trial for treason. At the same time he entreated his correspondents in England to keep his opinions secret, which they did not do.[11]

In a more businesslike manner, Samuel Wharton, an American trader and acquaintance of Ben Franklin then resident in London, had written to his brothers in Philadelphia that he had successfully concluded their nomination as consignees for the duty-free tea in their colony. For reasons of their own, the brothers apparently released excerpts of the letter to the *Pennsylvania Journal*, although it is difficult to see the advantage to themselves. It has been suggested that it was through the Hutchinson and Wharton letters—reprinted throughout the colonial press—that Americans first learned of the intentions of the EIC with respect to the tea. As corroborative reports of the underlying purposes of the Tea Act flooded into the colonies in the form of provocative letters from Patriots living in England, resistance to the landing of the tea in America increased.[12]

A pamphlet was published in New York and circulated through the colonies called *The Alarm* and signed by an enigmatic "Rusticus." One issue made clear by this anonymous writer was the ill feelings of some colonials concerning the EIC, England's largest and most successful corporation, and its behavior around the world:

> Their [the Company's] Conduct in Asia, for some Years past, has given simple Proof, how little they regard the Laws of Nations, the Rights, Liberties, or Lives of Men. They have levied War, excited Rebellions, dethroned lawful Princes, and sacrificed Millions for the Sake of Gain. The Revenues of Mighty Kingdoms have entered their Coffers. And these not being sufficient to glut their Avarice, they have, by the most unparalleled Barbarities, Extortions, and Monopolies, stripped the miserable Inhabitants of their Property, and reduced whole Provinces to Indigence and Ruin. Fifteen hundred Thousands [1.5 million persons], it is said, perished by Famine in one Year, not because the Earth denied its Fruits; but [because] this Company and their Servants engulfed all the Necessaries of Life, and set them at so high a Price that the poor could not purchase them.[13]

As will be discussed later, a catastrophic famine of four years duration (1769–1773) afflicted the EIC holdings, and the Company failed to respond with any but profit-seeking policies that raised taxes and demanded the production of export cotton and opium rather than food.

Yet the EIC-sponsored marketplace offered an infusion of consumerism in the 18th century that brought about unexpected lifestyle changes for the more affluent among the rising middle classes. It meant the acquisition of a wide variety of luxury and decorative household items in formerly simple homes and a whole new set of household chores that had nothing to do with parsimonious colonial living. Silverware had to be polished, ornate furniture dusted, and company entertained with some elegance of manner. Meals, rather than simple one-pot affairs, became elaborate processions of courses that were guided by books of etiquette that detailed the symmetrical placement of serving pieces and the sequential use of flatware. All this spawned new domestic strategies (like hiring additional servants and cooks with specialized talents) and required more food preservation, careful shopping, and knowledge of fashionable society.

Americans exhibited a great liking for sophisticated imports of all kinds. Among these, they consumed annually 75 tons of pepper and other spices and more than 1.5 million bushels of salt. They imported each year more than 50 different fabrics, a quarter million hats, and an untold number of shoes, boots, silk garters, laces, and fans. Almost 100 different drugs and medicines have been identified among the most common imports as well as fine china, wallpaper, dyes, pigments, files, saw blades, tools, hinges, cutlery, gun parts, and manufactured items of many descriptions.[14]

Historian T. H. Breen noted that the wives of tradesmen and small businessmen—living on the very edge of affluence in an emerging market environment—could ruin their husbands by demanding "silk gowns and scarlet cloaks." Young daughters "must go forth in the newest fashions, so spruce and neat that they may get husbands," even if they undid their parents' finances. The young men's fashion known as the *Macaroni* was equally "absurd . . . a parcel of young fellows, dished out in their tie wigs and ruffles." And the husbands—the husbands, free falling toward certain bankruptcy—could take their solace in having "chocolate or tea or coffee for their breakfast."[15]

GENIAL ADDICTIONS

For 2,000 years, only a few religious communities in Asia drank tea, and it took almost 1,000 years for it to become the common beverage of the Chinese. However, in the last 500 years of the modern era, tea drinking has spread across the world. Its global consumption now (2012) equals the combined total of all other manufactured drinks—coffee, chocolate, carbonated sodas and seltzers, sports drinks, and all alcoholic beverages. It is second only to plain water in accounting for the liquid intake of human beings.[16]

The Atlantic colonies of Anglo-America were blessed with fairly good sources of drinking water by European standards. Water scored well in the areas of hydration, low cost, and general availability, but it scored very poorly in most places in the world on good taste, satisfaction of consumption, and a surrounding mystique. These qualities were among the characteristics that drove consumerism in the era of foreign trade. The most lucrative profits realized by the empire proved to come from the genial addictions, "a quiet smoke, a nice cup of tea, a sweet tooth . . . exotic rarities converted into cravings." The money to be made in supplying items to fulfill these cravings was almost unlimited.[17]

There were three non-alcoholic drinks offered to consumers that were produced by infusing parts of plants in water usually by boiling or soaking. The three great caffeine-bearing drinks of the period—coffee, chocolate, and tea—each originated in a different region of the globe, Africa, America, and Asia, respectively. All three arrived in Britain within a single decade. Two of these, coffee and chocolate, were extracted from a bean and both were very bitter without the addition of sugar—an additive that could be prohibitively expensive when used in large amounts. Tea was innocent enough to drink unsweetened; was both mildly stimulating and elegantly relaxing; and was thought—even today—to possess special health benefits. The tea leaf (*Camellia sinensis*) was cheap to grow and process for shipment and was easier to prepare than either coffee or chocolate. Even today, coffee requires roasting and grinding, and chocolate requires extensive and detailed processing, much of it still done by hand. Tea's greatest disadvantage, however, was that it required long-distance transportation as it grew naturally only in central China.[18]

As a beverage, tea has become one of the great genial addictions of history. From its domestication in southwest China in the fifth century AD, tea initially passed from an aid to focusing the mind of Buddhist monks to a common part of the sophisticated pharmacopoeia of medicinal plants and herbs used to deal with complaints of the head, heart, stomach, or bowels. The views of the 18th-century medical profession concerning the effects of tea on the human body varied. Some claimed that it was an anti-depressant and anti-stress agent, others that it was a sexual aphrodisiac or that it simply enhanced all pleasurable activities. It was further highly prized for "the virtues of relieving fatigue, delighting the soul, strengthening the will, and repairing the eyesight." A Chinese emperor is supposed to have said, "Tea is better than wine for it leads not to intoxication, neither does it cause a man to say foolish things and repent thereof in his sober moments."[19] It is almost certain that when King Charles II had finished his first cup of tea in 1660—the gift of the newly reinvigorated EIC—no fortune teller was at hand to peer into the monarch's cup to read from the dregs of the tea leaves the dire disasters to the realm that were hidden among them.[20]

A possibly apocryphal story places the first coffee brewer in England at Oxford University in 1647 and the first coffeehouse in the same town in 1650. Chocolate, a derivative of American cacao, came to England during the protectorate of Oliver Cromwell. Roundhead forces captured the island of Jamaica from Spain in 1655 and found cacao plantations already flourishing there. Thereafter, the island became the primary source of chocolate for Britain. By 1657, it was being widely advertised in conjunction with coffee as "an excellent West India drink" that cured and preserved the body from many diseases.[21]

Experts suggest that tea first arrived in Europe through the agency of the Dutch East India Company, or VOC (Vereenigde Oost-Indische Compagnie), first in 1610 at Amsterdam, then in 1630 in France, and finally in 1657 in England.[22] In this last year, commonly recognized as the date of its first appearance in Britain, Thomas Garway published a broadside in London advertising the beneficial effects and virtues of the tea that he was offering at his coffeehouse. Tea spread slowly at first, being considered a luxury item on the typical coffeehouse menu alongside coffee and chocolate. In this manner, the ubiquitous English tea was introduced to the empire by way of the smoke-filled coffeehouse rather than the refinement of the ladies parlor.

Garway's tea was made from a solid brick of the stuff—somewhat like an unappetizing brick of fireplace peat—chipped and ground to a powder before being added to boiling water. The brick, rather than the more ubiquitous dried leaves of later decades, was easier to transport by ship and was thought to better resist the deterioration of its qualities. Although it was almost impervious to the damp in the hold of a ship and less likely to absorb unwanted odors while at sea, tea made from a brick proved a good deal less aromatic than its leafy cousin. In 1717, Thomas Twining first began to sell tea by weight. The tax on tea was so high at this time that unscrupulous black market sellers sometimes extended their teas with "smouch," ash leaves steeped in copperas (green iron sulfate crystals) and sheep's dung.[23]

Coffee, and particularly the sugar needed to make it palatable, was expensive. Although the retail price of a pound of tea was about £2 sterlingat the end of the 17th century, the cost dropped precipitously soon after direct trade with China was opened. Tea was sold to wholesale merchants in London at auction, and the price varied widely depending on the its availability at the time of sale fluctuating between 7d. and 74d. per pound.[24] The middle-class London family allotted about 7d. a week per person for tea and sugar, but the better part of the cost was for the sugar. Once weaned from the need to sugar tea as copiously as other drinks, its economic benefits became evident. It was soon realized that a pound of tea could make between 200 and 300 cups of tea, and the humblest man or woman could afford to have their unsweetened tea twice a day (breakfast and afternoon) just like the rich and prosperous in their mansions. The historical chronology of its acceptance indicates that by 1730 use of tea had spread throughout the entire British population.[25]

TEA AT THE COFFEEHOUSE

In a discussion of the Boston Tea Party, it is easy to underestimate the role of the British coffeehouse in spreading the popularity of tea and other exotic items of trades during the 17th and 18th centuries. Coffeehouses became meeting places where business could be carried on and news could be exchanged. A new commercial press brought newssheets to the coffeehouse that were passed around among the patrons. The coffeehouses most often frequented by merchants were in the area of London near the Bank of England and the Royal Exchange, and many of these coffeehouses were named for the colonies. The New England Coffeehouse was on Threadneedle Street. The Virginia and the Maryland were in Newman's Court. There were also in separate locations near the commercial center of London New York, Georgia, and Carolina coffeehouses, but Ben Franklin obviously favored the Pennsylvania Coffeehouse in Birchin Lane. He would have gone there to write letters, pick up his mail, and generally network with the hundreds of American businessmen who walked the streets of London.[26]

One *dressed* to go to a coffeehouse. It must be remembered that coffeehouse customers in the 18th century were not grabbing a latte in a cardboard cup in a modern Starbucks with a negligent look of disconnection on their faces. In the 18th century, having a break in the coffeehouse was a time-consuming experience during which one sat for some hours and observed or conversed with others directly. In this way, they picked up items of news, discussed politics and the economy, and made the personal connections necessary to successfully do business. The agents for Pennsylvania, one of whom was Ben Franklin, seem to have been particularly effective in seeking out and making the best connections. In the coffeehouse they saved 2d. a week in Gazzettes and had their news, business office, entertainment, and coffee for the same charge (about 2d. per cup).

New Englanders in London were often accused of dressing in too rustic a manner for the great city, and, as provincials in sturdy and practical dark broadcloth suits, they stood out in this regard from their more fashionable cousins from the other colonies who better blended into the background of English gentry with their polished cottons, silks, and brocades. It must be remembered that the cultural dividing line in Anglo-America was not the North and South or the slave state and free state of the 19th century. It was New England versus virtually everyone else in America in the 18th century.[27]

In London, gentlemen of like interests and like society tended to gravitate to the same establishments. There were scores of business meetings held every day at places like the Carolina Coffeehouse in Birchin Lane, and the great maritime insurance association, Lloyd's of London, had its origins among the business-minded patrons of the coffeehouse in Lombard Street run by its propietor, Edward Lloyd. In its formative years, Lloyd's made much of its money insuring ships in the slave trade. More than 1,000 slave ships were lost at sea during the 18th century and the trade would not have been profitable without the protection of insurance.

The coffeehouses were also great social levelers, open to all men— women of good reputation generally avoided appearing therein or were banned from entering. Although persons of like minds tended to frequent the same places, such establishments in Britain were generally indifferent to the social status or politics of their patrons. Coffee never truly became a target of boycotts. The names of coffeehouses in America, however, often gave a clue to the politics of its clientele. As a case in point, in 1769, the Royal Coffee House in Boston had become a favorite gathering place for officers of the British army and navy as well as that of noted Tory sympathizers and government officials. Having been accused recently in the Tory newspapers of treasonable activity, James Otis burst into the Royal Coffee House demanding an apology from the patrons. Arguments ensued, tables were overturned, and a sword cut was administered to Otis' head. The deep cut was thought to have set the man into one of his fits bordering on madness, but John Adams had noticed a previous change in Otis' demeanor. The fateful wound healed, but in a short time Otis' increasing madness caused him to be confined and carted away. Once the Tories abandoned the city, the Royal Coffee House was, with little imagination, renamed the American Coffee House.[28]

TEA IN THE PARLOR

If men had their coffeehouses, women had their afternoon tea in the parlor. Tea was a required social function that was strictly governed by convention. Teas not only upheld a woman's social position, they enhanced that of her husband. Such visits were necessary to maintain good feelings between the members of society, and they were required by the custom of the age. In order to maintain the integrity of the family structure, the female relations would periodically gather for tea (or chocolate) sipping infrequently while tracing the family tree from long before the rise of the Stuart kings.

Women hosted teas that required a number of ancillary items in addition to the teakettle, teapot, and teacups. Serving required the right tea table, canisters, bowls, saucers, spoons, strainers, a milk or cream pitcher, sugar container, sugar tongs, and slop bowl. Elaborate tea nips were used to break off pieces of sugar from their cones. The hard sugar was held between the teeth as the tea passed over it. Custom even dictated the arrangement of the serving pieces and varied in accordance with the shape of the serving table. On a round table, the cups and saucers would be arranged in a circle. On a rectangular table, the drinking vessels would be lined up in rows. In either case, the teapot was the centerpiece of the arrangement, flanked by the sugar and creamer on one side and the slop bowl on the other. Teas were also an opportunity for women to show off their fine clothing, their furniture and furnishings, and the competence of their household staff.[29]

Prior to the boycott of the Continental Association, tea was commonly served in the morning as part of breakfast or in the late afternoon as a social event. Colonials preferred their tea strong and brewed it dark. Bohea was so popular that the name came to be used as an eponym for tea itself—like the word *Kleenex* for tissues. Lighter teas, such as Souchong and Hyson, comprised only about 10 percent of the colonial imports. The tax on tea fell more heavily on affluent colonists, to whom tea drinking had become a social ritual, than on ordinary folk.

On October 25, 1774, Mrs. Penelope Barker organized 51 women against the tea tax in Edenton, North Carolina. In the parlor of one of the ladies, they crowded together and formed an alliance wholeheartedly supporting the American cause. The so-called Edenton Tea Party gained much attention in America and significant ridicule in England. According to Arthur Iredell, a Tory who was then living in London, the incident was not taken seriously, because women led it. He sarcastically remarked, "The only security on our side . . . is the probability that there are but few places in America which possess so much female artillery as Edenton." The Edenton women were cruelly satirized in a political cartoon published in London in March 1775. Even though the Edenton Tea Party was ridiculed in England, it was praised throughout the colonies.[30]

Of course, there were those who could not or would not deny themselves the use of tea—drinking it clandestinely behind closed doors, in garrets, or in isolation; preparing it in coffee pots and chocolate

This anti-American cartoon by Philip Dawes,
*A Society of Patriotic Ladies at Edenton in North Car-
olina*, was published in London in 1775. (Library
of Congress)

pots to deceive the eye; and resorting to any subterfuge in order to indulge in the use of their favorite beverage. "These people, when found
out, did not fail to receive the condemnation of the patriotic men and
women, who, from principle, abstained," noted an observer. Theophilus
Lillie, who was selling tea contrary to the agreement, found just how
threatening his situation could become. One morning, he found a
wooden post planted before his door in the manner of the torture
stake of the Iroquois, upon which was a carved head, with the names of
some tea users and sellers on it, and underneath it all, a hand pointing
toward his shop.[31]

FOR THE SAKE OF GAIN

It is ironic that the widespread export of tea from China to the West started near the end of the Ming dynasty (1368–1644), a period during which China became a more inward-looking nation and more closed to foreigners than previously. The trade in tea and other items was, therefore, carried on through Asian intermediaries, such as Hindus, Malaysians, Koreans, or other Indonesians, and almost all the Chinese trade (the so-called junk trade, named for their vessels) was redirected to Europe through other places. Generally, at the time of the EIC, tea went first to India for simple transshipment; but items like raw silk went there to be spun, dyed, and woven by Indian rather than Chinese hands before being exported.

The China trade of the 18th century actually involved about a half dozen major trading destinations other than China in the Far East. Traders visited hundreds of small ports and isolated islands in their quest to complete a cargo of rare goods and bring them to the British factories in India where they were paid for in gold or opium. Many of these were transshipped thereafter to England, where British law required all legal cargoes to touch for the purpose of taxation, and then to America (or Europe, North Africa, or even Turkey) for distribution. Unlike the Dutch, who maintained a presence in many island nations, the British controlled their far eastern trade from a limited number of outposts in India—in the period of the American crisis mostly from the city of Calcutta. Ironically, this made India the economic center of the so-called China trade.[32]

The discovery that Englishmen could make enormous profits by carrying goods by ship from the Far East to Europe was first made late in the reign of Queen Elizabeth I. Some of the first trading fleets of the Honourable East India Company (HEIC; after a merger in 1708 just the EIC) to leave London under the business-friendly auspices of Elizabeth I (Tudor) returned to England after several years absence to find a less entrepreneurial and more financially restrained James I (Stuart) on the throne.[33] The accession of the Scottish dynasty to the throne of England upon Elizabeth's death in 1603 is commonly used to mark the unification of England, Scotland, and Wales into Great Britain, but the political environment of the early 17th century was also very fluid with the ruling families of Britain constantly vying for power and precedence, and the Scots continually stressing their independence.

The directors of the HEIC feared that Stuart sycophants and rival merchants (the Muscovy Company of 1555 and the Levant Company of 1581, for instance) would cause their trading licenses to be revoked. The directors thought that to continue such risky voyages without the promise of a trading monopoly was impossible. English trading vessels leaving in twos and threes were often gone for three years when making a cruise. Added to the political and financial uncertainties were the common dangers of merchant seafaring. In an era when one in seven common trading vessels leaving Britain was never heard of again, returning from a voyage to the Far East was considered very fortunate indeed.

At the bidding of those among his nobles who thought the oriental trade important to the kingdom (and their pocketbooks), James extended the license not for 15 years but permanently, as long as the monopoly it granted proved profitable to the Crown. Under extreme conditions, the Crown could rescind the license, but it had to give the company a three-year warning if it did so. Although previously the aristocracy had eschewed investment in such a risky business, the newfound confidence engendered by the extension of a permanent monopoly on Far Eastern trade attracted them to invest. Soon the directors of the company were accepting subscriptions for trading fleets from aristocrats and Members of Parliament who actively sought out the society of mere merchants in order to assure an acceptance in the membership of their joint-stock company. The social world in Britain was thereby turned upside down, with aristocrats begging the patronage of influential merchants.

The English stock market, capitalism, and empire were all born together in Exchange Street, London. The first joint-stock companies involved in overseas trade targeted to North America were the conjoined Virginia Company of London (London Company) and the Virginia Company of Plymouth (Plimoth Company), which King James I chartered in 1606. The former company was responsible for the founding of Jamestown, Virginia, in 1607, but the latter would need more than a dozen years to plant a settlement in Massachusetts. The defeat of the Spanish Armada in 1588—and the failure of Spain (and its ally Portugal) to recover from it completely—made voyages to the Americas possible.

Spain's ultimate maritime impotence was not only a symptom of a general decay but an inevitable consequence of the Spanish attempts to rule a global empire without an increase in its commercial shipping. Maritime historian Alfred Thayer Mahan blamed the abandonment of commerce, manufacture, and trade by both Portugal and Spain, on "the mines of Brazil . . . [and] those of Mexico and Peru," respectively. "The English and the Dutch were no less desirous of gain," wrote Mahan, "[but] Spain and Portugal sought it by digging gold out of the ground." He noted that "all manufactures fell into insane contempt," leaving the Dutch and the English to provide both Spain and Portugal with clothing, merchandise, and all other commodities, "even to salted fish and grain."[34]

Although the EIC is closely associated with India, each voyage was almost a self-directed venture and each vessel traveling in consort for safety was separately funded by a subscription of stock. One of the earliest English voyages established an outpost on the Indonesian island of Bantam in 1603 from which pepper and other spices could be drawn, but the Dutch arrived in the same year. The two companies fought a continuous series of small island wars there for decades, enlisting the natives as allies on one side or the other. A trade monopoly assured the company that it would avoid the competition of other Englishmen, but it did not stop the companies of other nations from trading, nor did monopoly guarantee it a profit. Moreover, many English companies had interlocking boards with sometimes incompatible goals. Sir Thomas Smythe, his attention split between two ends of the globe, for instance, administered both the HEIC trading in the East Indies at Bantam and the Virginia Company that instituted the settlement at Jamestown in America in 1607.

Captain William Hawkins led the first voyage of the HEIC directed specifically to India and sailed into the principal northwest Indian port of Surat in 1608 with a chest of gold coins and a personal letter to the Mughal emperor from the king seeking trade concessions. Hawkins persisted there for more than two years but returned to England empty-handed, largely because of the interference of influential Portuguese traders. Although the company established a post on the Coromandel coast of southeast India in 1610, King James I threatened to cancel the charter of the HEIC if it showed no greater profit to the kingdom. But voyage after voyage, while financially profitable, failed to wrest any concessions from the Mughal emperor.

Captain Thomas Best in the armed trading vessel *Red Dragon* led the 10th and potentially the last voyage of four trading vessels to Surat in 1612. Coincidentally, a squadron of 16 Portuguese trade vessels appeared there at the same time, and the fleets arrayed for battle. At the Battle of Swally (1612), Best decimated the Portuguese almost single handedly, the armed pinnace *Ozeander* aiding in spraying the enemy decks with canister. The relatively small but decisive naval battle—coupled to outstanding Portuguese losses as dynastic allies of the Spanish Armada of 1588—marked the beginning of the end of Portugal's former commercial monopoly over India and the beginning of the ascent of HEIC presence in the subcontinent. It also convinced the HEIC of the need to establish a small local navy of its own to safeguard its commercial interests.

The factors of the company quickly established a base for four warships at Swally and formed an alliance with the local Mughal (a.k.a. Mogal) ruler. In 1615, Captain Nicholas Downton, attacked by a Portuguese armada at Surat and again greatly outnumbered, beat them off no less decisively than Best. The actions of Best and Downton served notice on the maritime powers of Europe that the English sailor was to be taken seriously. However, these so-called fierce little battles with the Portuguese alone could not establish the English traders with the powers that ruled India. The Mughal emperor of India exhibited a profound lack of interest in commerce with England, and the servants of the HEIC soon learned to be diplomats as well as traders.[35]

As a result of careful posturing from 1615 to 1618, an English representative of the Company, Sir Thomas Roe, was able to devise an advantageous agreement with Emperor Jahangir (said to be Roe's drinking partner), giving the Company "free leave to trade at any port in the Mogul empire, on the east coast as well as the west [and] also the privilege of paying customs once but thereafter no further duties . . . on the same goods." In this regard, the emperor refused to be bound by a formal treaty, but he deigned to issue a set of imperial orders that produced the same effect.[36] In 1640, Sir John Banks of the HEIC had arranged with the Mughal emperor for a permanent source of saltpeter to be available to England every year at an annual price paid to the emperor of £30,000 sterling. This important arrangement guaranteed a renewable supply of gunpowder to Britain that placed it at a strategic advantage over other European nations, especially France, which was scraping pig droppings from Provencal barnyards and human night waste from Parisian privies to produce saltpeter. In 1668, the Portuguese trading factory on the island of Bombay was transferred from King Charles II (Stuart) to the Company, and HEIC commissioners were sent down from their outpost at Surat to take over the island. Charles had little interest in the place, which had been part of his wife's (Catherine of Braganza) dowry in 1661.

With vast sums now available from subscribers in England, the directors of the HEIC decided to build their own fleet of trading vessels—the ubiquitous ships known as an East Indiamen—rather than to

continue to lease or buy inferior vessels. The first three such vessels—
Darling, Peppercorn, and the immense 1,100-ton *Trades Increase*—were
launched near London with the king in attendance, fêted on a sumptuous meal served on a near-priceless set of China import plates. No set
of circumstances better served to exemplify the exalted position of the
HEIC and its directors.

In 1708, the HEIC formally became the EIC (see below). Notwithstanding the fact that the original purpose of the broad military powers given to the Company was to safeguard its commerce from attacks
by the Spanish and Portuguese, at its height the Company had 150 mer-
chantmen, 40 corporate warships, and more than 10,000 mercenary
soldiers in the field—a greater force than many independent nations.
While the EIC land forces were chiefly composed of indigenous mer-
cenaries under the command of European officers, the lumbering East
India trading vessels (Indiamen) of the 18th century were moderately
armed with between 20 and 30 guns and well crewed and officered
by stout bodies of British mariners. Most Indiamen had a sufficient
weight of metal (firepower)—sometimes on two decks spread among a
compliment of medium-sized cannon and swivels—to ward off pirates,
privateers, and the smaller naval warships of belligerent nations. They
looked more formidable than they actually were and often tried to disguise themselves from a distance as Royal Navy warships. The merchant crews of 90–100 mariners made the Indiamen tempting targets
for Royal Navy commanders looking to impress a few seamen, however. Yet the loss of just a few seamen left the trading vessels critically
understrength. Moreover, the directors of the EIC exerted great influence on Royal Navy policy, and the EIC sea officers were often given
precedence over naval officers of similar rank in social circles.

The EIC directors generally hired the Indiamen, but in 1708 the
Company banned the practice due to a growing potential for corruption. The Company thereafter began maintaining its own shipyards
and shipbuilding facilities in England, employing more than 500 shipwrights besides nearly 1,000 trading employees in London. The EIC
also maintained dockyards with building facilities at Bombay from
which its vessels patrolled the Indian Ocean, the Java Sea, and the
Persian Gulf.

The Royal Navy entered the American Revolution in 1775 with approximately 250 vessels of war of all types. Given the complimentary
existence of the Royal Navy and almost 200 vessels of the EIC armed
merchant service, Britain seemed, and was, the unchallenged ruler of
the seas, fearing no combination of the navies of any two maritime

nations on earth for most of the 18th century. The American Revolution would change this perception as the French, Spanish, and Dutch
fleets, and a handful of American warships combined to frustrate a British Royal Navy that at the time had no maritime allies.

THE GROWTH OF THE EIC

In 1708, there had been a major amalgamation of rival English trading
companies that left the newly formed EIC in ascendancy. The HEIC
had developed a powerful lobby in Parliament, yet under pressure from
ambitious tradesmen and associates of private trading firms in India,
a deregulating act was passed in 1694. This allowed any English firm
to trade with India, and it set off a free-for-all. In 1695, Parliament
initiated an investigation into a scandal over the quick fortunes made
through bribery and insider trading. This led to the dismissal of the
leader of the House of Commons, the impeachment of the lord president of the council, and the imprisonment of the governor of the
Company.[37] In 1698, a second East India Company (the English Company Trading to the East Indies) had formed with state funding of
£2 million. This new concern initially sought to act in parallel with
the old HEIC. The powerful stockholders of the old company quickly
raised £315,000 and invested in the new concern gaining a majority
position. Confounded by old HEIC directors serving on the board
of the new entity, it quickly became clear that the original Company
would dominate the competition and that a monopoly would be more
easily policed than a gaggle of independent companies.

The companies merged in 1708 as the United East India Company
during the period of reformation of the maritime laws of Britain under
Queen Anne. The new venture involved both companies with the state
under the excuse that maintaining the saltpeter trade was a national
priority for the armed forces in the Britain, America, and elsewhere.
The new Company, simply know as the East India Company (EIC)
ultimately became the single largest player in the global marketplace,
reserving for itself an influential position in setting government policy
in Britain and around the world.

By 1720, fully 15 percent of British imports were from India alone,
almost all of which passed through the holds of Company ships. In
1730, the monopoly was prolonged and guaranteed inviolable until
1766. It was the initial hope of British merchants that good English
woolens could be traded in the India market for cottons and calicoes,

which in turn could be traded for Chinese silk without the need to drain the British kingdom of gold.[38] The textile mill owners in England initially appreciated the increased supply of cheap India cotton, but they also began to lobby the government to tax India cloth imports and allow British-made woolens sole access to markets in the subcontinent. Cheap cotton calico prints imported by the EIC were threatening the superior position of English woolens at home.

Several acts of Parliament were passed in the first half of the 18th century to prevent the importation of dyed or printed calicoes from India, China, or Persia. This caused the so-called grey cloth (woven, but unbleached and unfinished) to be imported instead. The grey cloth—the British favored a light tan background, the native Indians a darker shade, but it was not actually gray in color—was then overprinted in southern England with popular patterns. Supposedly to protect the jobs of British weavers, an additional law was passed that fined any person caught wearing any calico printed or stained outside Britain excepting that used for neckcloths and linings. This attempt at protectionism failed as linen-cotton (fustian) combinations and so-called silk calicoes were imported in contravention of the law. Silk-lined capes and greatcoats became fashionable. Early India calicoes were produced through a painting technique, but London manufacturers used a block printing process similar to that used in making wallpaper.

HEADY FRAGRANCES

Asian spices like peppercorns, cinnamon, nutmegs, and cloves had begun the race to the Far East. These were the big four among the fragrant spices brought overland to the Mediterranean for many generations and made available by Arab traders. So desirable were these spices that a pocketful of peppercorns was at times valued the same as so many grains of gold. After the eastern and southern coasts of the Mediterranean came under the control of Muslim rulers unfriendly to Europe, the land-based trade in spices almost ceased due to the high duties they demanded. This made the sea routes to the Far East more and more desirable and potentially more profitable.

So many of these rare spices originated in the islands of the Molucca Sea, near New Guinea, that the group came to be known as the Spice Islands. It was said that the smell of the spices produced a heady fragrance at sea when vessels were downwind of the islands. Although steps were taken to isolate the source of the spices to these islands, ultimately plants and seeds were smuggled out to other areas in the tropics where they could be grown. By such means, India became a source of pepper and ginger; the West Indies and Brazil sources of cloves; Zanzibar and Madagascar producers of black pepper; and Nigeria and Sierra Leone traders in ginger.

The small island group known as the Banda Islands were the only known sources of nutmeg and mace. At first this source was a closely guarded secret. In the 17th century, the Dutch and English waged bloody and genocidal wars among the islands for their control. Not until the Napoleonic Wars were the English able to move rootstock to Zanzibar and Grenada. The dried fruit of a tree native to the Caribbean and parts of South America (*Pimenta dioica*) came to be known in England as Allspice because it was thought to simulate in fragrance a combination of cinnamon, nutmeg, and cloves. Allspice was a major ingredient in Jamaican cooking. The fragrance of this fruit helped lead Columbus to the mistaken notion that he had reached the Spice Islands in the late 15th century.

JUST PLAIN CHINA

Chinese porcelain and stoneware reached the Near East during the Tang dynasty (7th–10th centuries AD), but the technology that produced it reached its pinnacle during the Song dynasty of the 12th and 13th centuries. They did not become available in Europe, however, until the 16th century (Ming dynasty). Japanese and Chinese lacquered wares were also admired and ultimately were being imitated by European craftsmen. Direct trade in the blue and white Ming porcelain was established between Europe and the Far East in the latter half of the 16th century, first by the Portuguese and later on by Spanish, Dutch, Swedish, and English ships.

During the 18th century, porcelain was regularly imported because the best examples in the world were made in China, and it could be had at attractive prices. The Chinese process for making it was a closely guarded secret. Imari porcelain—named for the red and blue Japanese version but produced in China and Korea as well—was quite popular, and thousands of blue and red fragments of this China have been unearthed at American colonial sites by archaeologists. By the middle of the 18th century (ca. 1756), Chinese Imari porcelain production had eclipsed that of Japan. Export porcelains for the European trade often imitated authentic blue and white wares or made use of enamel colors over underglazes of cobalt blue and iron red. Foliage, flowers, and more traditional decorations slowly gave way to ship and port motifs thought to be better suited to European markets. Gilding was not uncommon. To make genuine Imari, each piece was fashioned by hand, painted, and fired in the kiln as each color was applied. The finished product was hard, translucent, and it rang with a clear tone when tapped. The unglazed base of the plates often had a gritty texture that helped to authenticate its origin.

These imported Chinese wares made a deep impression on European craftsmen, especially the potters, who tried to duplicate the hard Chinese porcelain but could only copy shapes and patterns from China on tin-glazed earthenware made in Holland, France, and England. Named for the tin oxide that was added to the lead glaze slip, the European process produced a white opaque surface sometimes known as creamware or pearlware that could be used as is or overglazed and refired with color, but nothing comparable to actual Chinese porcelain. On these white glazed ceramics, European potters used cobalt blue to imitate Chinese figure scenes, flowers, birds, and other common patterns from late Ming and Kangxi porcelains. The imitations became known conventionally in English as *faïence*, in French as Saint-Porchaine ware or *faïence blanche*, and in Dutch as the familiar and ubiquitous blue and white *delft*. German potters may ultimately have come closest to producing porcelain similar to that of the Chinese, but they also kept their processes closely guarded.

The result of all these attempts to produce non-Chinese porcelain was a flourish of decorative potting technology in Europe. Nonetheless, European copies did not have the resonance, hardness, or luster of the Chinese originals. It is known today that this was due to the lower kiln temperatures (about 1000°C) used by European potters as compared to those used by the Chinese (between 1200°C and 1400°C). Moreover, the Chinese added aluminum silicate found in a mineral known as mullite to the slip, which became glass-like at higher temperatures and added translucence to the finished product. Ironically, the most common source for mullite in Europe was later found to be on the nearby Island of Mull off the coast of Scotland.

THE JUNK TRADE

Both the Dutch and English attempted direct trade with China in the 17th century, but most of the goods that reached Europe came to the holds of European vessels indirectly by way of the southeastern junk trade. The Dutch were the most successful of the early European traders in arranging terms with the junk captains. Initially, the island of Formosa (Taiwan) showed promise as a place where direct trade with the Chinese might be possible, but ultimately it was found that merchants in the Chinese port of Canton were almost always offering better deals.

China was a trading nation. For centuries Chinese junks had carried goods all over the Far East to the Philippines, Malaysia, Sumatra, and India, and brought back products and profits to their home ports. The Chinese merchants advertised their wares in their shops with bright red characters as they had for hundreds of years. The Chinese government was largely unconcerned about regulating the trade of its own people, but became concerned when the first European vessels arrived carrying Jesuit missionaries. Virtually every imperial edict regarding foreign traders in China thereafter described them in derogatory terms.

Although they remained suspicious of all foreigners, in 1683 the new Chinese government (Qing dynasty) adopted the idea of expanding its foreign trade, and the ships of many countries were encouraged to tie up at Chinese wharves. Islamic sea traders from India were already actively trading with China when the vessels of the French and British companies made their first appearance. The Ostend General India Company followed in 1717; the Dutch VOC in 1729; the Danish Asiatic Company in 1734; and the Swedish East India Company in 1734. There were also occasional vessels from Armenia, Prussia, Italy (Venice), Austria-Hungary (Trieste), and Spain. Few legitimate American vessels appeared in Canton in these early days because the British Board of Trade absolutely prohibited Anglo-American colonials from trading in China before 1783.[39]

The Chinese viewed the increase in foreign influence in its ports with apprehension and feared that western ideas might corrupt the country as a whole. In 1760, they took the first steps to isolate the common Chinese people from western influences. They closed all their ports to foreigners save Canton where they were restricted to a quarter-mile square area bounded by streets called Hog Lane and Old China Street and closed off to the local Chinese by a fence.[40]

The first western vessels to deal directly with Mainland China came from Portugal, and they were granted a trade monopoly in the port of Guangzhou, which the Portuguese called Canton or Cantao. It is through these Europeans rather than the Chinese that words like

Cantonese, Cantonware, and their complements derived their common use. The major Chinese merchants at Canton, known as Hoppos, controlled the upriver flow of trade to Macao through the auspices of the Chinese government. The Hoppos were quick to take steps against recalcitrant foreigners, but with time and increasing foreign knowledge, these methods of controlling the traders became less effective.

This was especially true of the linguists needed to translate Chinese into European languages. Without translators, foreign traders were significantly handicapped in making arrangements outside those sanctioned by the government in Beijing. Chinese linguists at Macao, capable of speaking local Cantonese and the official Mandarin, initially needed a passing knowledge of only Portuguese, but by the 1730s pidgin English had replaced all other foreign languages as the medium of communication. Occasionally, a foreign company or trader might employ a Jesuit or other knowledgeable European to translate or deliver messages in Chinese, but any communication that bypassed the established protocol was generally looked on with great disfavor.[41]

The resident employees of the various European nations lived in a row of wharf-side buildings known as factories although no manufacturing took place there. The factory buildings of the 18th century were combination warehouses, business offices, and residences for the factors, merchants, and staff. These buildings with their sloping roofs and whitewashed walls ultimately reached two or three stories and had been built by the national companies that first established a significant volume of trade at a particular location. The most imposing factory in many ports was usually that of the EIC.

Virtually all of the Chinese servants and vendors in Macao and Canton were permanent employees of the factories, some serving the same company for their entire lives. They maintained the factory buildings and apartments during the trading off-season and acted as gardeners, cooks, and house servants when the factors were in residence. Their wages were usually paid to a local *comprador* (vendor) who arranged their employment and oversaw their work. The compradors often became trusted associates of the company and loyal friends to the factors.

The duties of factory compradors and those who supplied the ships were somewhat different. Ship compradors were constantly on the move in their small fleets of sampans and often employed their own family members to help them. Their basic task, beyond providing the ship's stores for a return sea voyage, was to keep the crews provided with fresh food and water while the cargoes were unloaded and loaded. This could take several months.

The desire for spices and authentic Chinese or other Oriental products drove the China Trade, and skippers lined up to get command of trading vessels destined for the western and southern Pacific, the Indian Ocean, or the South China Sea. Sea captains made good use of the prevailing winds when making these voyages. In an era dependent on sail, the seasonal monsoons provided a reliable source of propulsion. Moreover, a good run to the east could be made "in the westerly winds of the southern latitudes" and "a fair slant . . . to Canton" could be enjoyed in the northeasterly trade winds.[42]

COMPETITION, THE SPICE OF LIFE

The trading companies that did business in these ports had several common characteristics, but in the 18th century the EIC had largely displaced most of the trading nations in India save the French. It had then fought and won dominance over the French in the Seven Years War and attempted to overawe the majority of local governments in much of the subcontinent. Although the Portuguese, Dutch, French, and Germans had stations in the region, to some extent the organization and operation of the EIC in the 18th and 19th centuries has come today to dominate the concept of Far East trading.

Portugal had been the first European nation to attempt trade in the Indian Ocean, but early on, the Portuguese effort had largely exhausted itself. Only a few of their isolated stations remained by the end of the 18th century. The burden of supporting a Far Eastern trading empire with ships and garrisons was just too much for so small a country so far from home. The French trading firm Compaigne des Indies Orientales, active in the 17th and 18th centuries, would collapse in the 1770s, and the national effort would be further devastated by the demands of the French Revolution and Imperial Wars of the 1790s and 1800s. Nonetheless, its trading stations in the Far East remained largely in the hands of French nationals. The Dutch VOC retained a stranglehold on the profitable Spice Islands of Indonesia, including Sumatra and Java, and the Spanish controlled most of the trade from the Philippines from its base at Manila.

Americans did not come on the scene in their own right—that is, independent of Great Britain—until 1785, and then they were largely considered interlopers. Eighteenth-century economists promulgated the idea that the common people could not handle the temptations of an unregulated free marketplace and urged government to protect them from it by restricting their access to it.[43] A number of the earliest American mariners to enter the trade, therefore, had engaged in the equivalent of smuggling and piracy under British rule. The British in particular, but also other Europeans, found that they could not curb the sale of bargain merchandise and trade goods offered by the New Englanders.[44]

The Board of Trade was the connective tissue that held America to the rest of the trading empire. In 1696, King William III had appointed eight paid commissioners to promote trade in the empire. Formally known as the Lords Commissioners of Trade and Foreign Plantations, they were commonly known as the Board of Trade. The board carried on the work of controlling all the colonies and trading outposts of the empire through the appointment of governors and regional military commanders, as well as through the setting of policy. Although it had virtually no control over the Royal Navy (which was directed through the powerful office of the Admiralty), the Board of Trade carried out its job with dexterity, but it also experienced long periods of relative inactivity. Unfortunately, it devolved into chaos under George III, failed to respond effectively to the American crisis, and was abolished in 1782 by an act of Parliament under the Rockingham administration.

CHAPTER 3

Consumers and Providers

With our eyes too firmly fixed on the Puritans, we fail to see that hundreds of thousands of immigrants were rounded up and persuaded to come to America by men moved by secular motives of empire and profit.[1]

—*Richard Hofstadter, historian*

One fact is undoubted, under Parliament the state of America has been kept in continual agitation. Everything administered as a remedy to the public complaint . . . is followed by a heightening of distemper.[2]

—*Edmund Burke, Minister to Parliament*

FOUNDATIONS OF EMPIRE

It was an Anglo-American population with as complete knowledge of British history and manners that laid the foundations of empire in the New World as schoolchildren have of the culture of the United States today. The Anglo-colonials were familiar with proper parliamentary procedures as practiced in their town meetings and colonial legislatures as well as the relationship between their assemblies and the governor, and the colony with the Board of Trade and the Crown. Nonetheless, in the first 100 years of settlement, all but the most stalwart religionists had internalized the basic fundamentals of an emerging nation-state based on jurisprudence rather than on scriptural morality. Moreover, the considerations of an emerging global trading empire were threatening the vestiges of feudal politics and subsistence strategies. By 1760, however, a revolution in commerce had by-passed and shoved aside economies based on an unwilling and permanent peasantry ruled by feudal overlords as well as those based on the utopian expectations of early Puritan socialism.

The British trading empire was founded on the principle of mercantilism, which history suggests was a necessary signpost on the road to industrialism, capitalism, and the free market. Formulated in the 17th century, mercantilism theorized that colonies existed chiefly to benefit the parent state. This benefit was realized in two ways. Real wealth was to be measured by the store of precious metals a nation held, and the state that accumulated the greatest store of silver and gold was thought to be the richest. Second, any nation that could maintain a favorable trade balance with its neighbors could always settle the difference by demanding payments in gold. Freedom from foreign trade deficits, therefore, was considered a measure of commercial strength and economic health.

The vitality of the British economy and the structure of the empire itself had initially been founded on the monopolies granted to chartered trading companies, which brought wealth into the empire through their operations. Profit margins from foreign trade were two to three times what a merchant could expect within Britain, and on some commodities, such as betel nut (areca) from Bengal and tobacco from Virginia targeted for European markets, profits in the 1760s were routinely 75 percent or better.[3] The betel nut—like the stronger coca leaf used by South American natives and controlled and taxed by Spain—was used as a mild stimulant as part of ritual and tradition throughout southern India, Indonesia, and China, but the English adopted betel simply as a means of acquiring a mild buzz. So much for our sober ancestors.

The EIC was unquestionably the most successful of the trading companies, valued at £21million sterling in 1775. As the Industrial Revolution dawned in Britain, however, a highly self-contained and independent domestic manufacturing economy evolved, and this came to better characterize the quintessential mercantile state of the later 18th century. Both the raw materials and the markets for all the finished products of a robust manufacturing economy had to remain inside the empire for the state to be successful. "It is the consumption of our products, as well as the manufactures of them," noted a contemporary English observer, "which gives bread to the hungry, circulates trade, brings in money, and supports the value of our lands."[4] Accordingly, Britain sought to remain the center of manufactures, banking, and military resources, whereas the colonials were confined to the dual roll of providers of raw materials and consumers of British manufactures—yet being strictly prohibited from fashioning their own manufactured goods.[5]

The profits from colonies could be precarious, but tobacco and sugar proved reliable sources of income for both merchants and government. Sugar had many uses. The thick sap of the sugarcane plant could be heated to make molasses and in turn distilled into rum. Moreover, tea was initially thought to require sugar to make it palatable. The British, therefore, highly valued their outposts in the West Indies because of their output of sugar, and they stationed troops and warships to defend them long before a single redcoat was stationed in the Anglo-American colonies. The defense of the tobacco plantations and forest wilderness of North America was left to the colonials.[6]

In 1748 and much to the consternation the Anglo-Americans who had secured it, the British had returned Fortress Louisbourg (a.k.a. Louisburg) on Cape Breton Island, Canada, to the French for the single city of Madras in India. Massachusetts' troops had taken the lead in capturing the troublesome French citadel, which had supplied and directed raids by their Native allies on the New England frontier. Numerous colonial volunteers had lost their lives fighting the French and their Native American allies, especially the Abenaki. Anglo-Americans would be asked to do so again. It was obvious that the ministry in London had greater concern for the welfare of EIC outposts half a world away than for its Atlantic colonies. When news broke of this distressing event, the population of Boston—primed to lash out by an ongoing financial crisis involving the so-called Land Bank—rebelled. Onrushing Bostonians surged through the streets, the crowd swollen to more than 1,000. The province found itself facing what resembled at least a civil crisis, if not an armed insurrection. At that time, Governor Jonathan Belcher had moved decisively to quell the uprising—imprisoning the leaders and using all the forces at his command to keep the royal government in power—all for possession of a city thousands of miles away in India. There can be no doubt that the bitterness engendered by this circumstance was one cause of the revolution. Parliament voted, thereafter, to ransom Louisbourg from the colonies. The sum coming to Massachusetts was in excess of £138,000 sterling.[7]

Yet in less than 20 years the situation had changed. While the peace treaty of 1763 was being negotiated, a bitter debate arose in Parliament over whether France should be made to cede to Britain all of Canada and the Ohio Country or the sugar island of Guadeloupe in the Caribbean. Guadeloupe would have been an immediate and valuable asset. However, the Crown wished to rid itself of the French presence in North America that was interfering with the normal flow of commerce with its Atlantic-facing colonies. The list of important raw materials from continental North America had grown with its economy. In order to soothe the loss of the sugar island felt on Exchange Street in London, Parliament immediately fostered the establishment of English-owned fisheries in Nova Scotia.

There was never a thought in London of dividing the vastness of Canada and the Ohio Country into an assortment of new English colonies in the interior. The existing set of English provinces had proved frustrating enough. It seemed easier to administer Canada as a single entity, unhampered by the political activities of white settlers. This resulted, in part, in the Proclamation of 1763, of which more will be said later. London would simply reaffirm the mercantile role of the coastal colonies as a source of raw materials and a market for manufactures. The opinion of the Board of Trade was that opening the interior to further settlement might "divert [his] Majesty's subjects in America from the pursuit of these important objects." The Board further noted that its policy was "to confine [the] settlements as much as possible to the sea coast and not to extend them to places inaccessible to shipping and consequently more out of the reach of [British] commerce."[8]

ACROSS THE POND IN LONDON

Britain may have given birth to the Anglo-American colonies, but by the middle of the 18th century, London had also taken on the unmistakable look of America. "Plants, products, people, and exotica from the New World filled the taverns, streets, theaters, and even the [Royal] Court of the centre of empire."[9] American trees and plants adorned the public parks as well as the gardens of the gentry. Curiosities—animals, weapons, tools, and Native Americans themselves—were gathered in fashionable homes, collected in museums, and illustrated in British books and paintings. American settings and characters began to appear in written works and stage plays. American sugar, chocolate, and tobacco had become common, if expensive, and American rum threatened to overtake gin as a favorite alcoholic beverage for London's masses.

Even though ocean travel was dangerous, slow, and uncomfortable, Anglo-Americans often passed back and forth between Britain and North America. Certainly most persons never returned to the home islands, but merchants, seamen, artists, university students, children attending boarding schools, clergymen, colonial lobbyists, agents, representatives, and speculators were all willing to *cross the pond* to complete some important business or personal quest in London. Edward Tighman of Maryland noted, "It would be impossible to enumerate all the benefits to be acquired in London . . . more is learnt of mankind here in a month than can be in a year in any other part of the world."[10]

The schools in London were reportedly better than the tutors and small group instruction available in the colonies, or at least they were thought more suitable for those Americans who desired to be considered a legitimate part of the English landed gentry. Many colonial fathers took advantage of a trip to Britain to expose their children to what was thought to be missing from provincial society. A stay could last more than a year, or several years, and the experience was thought to be of greater educational value than any missed schooling at home.

Young men, scions of wealthy colonial families, were likely to visit the city or take their education there, and many found it difficult to return to provincial living. One-third of the 56 signers of the Declaration of Independence had visited London, most of them having taken their education there as adolescents or young adults. Moreover, there was no place in the English-speaking world better suited than London for daughters to find a husband of independent means or at least genteel refinement. There were rarely fewer than 1,000 wealthy mainland Americans and West Indians to be found in London all the year round. The city was, after all, the capital of the empire and one of the largest urban centers in the world. Nonetheless, every person of influence seemed to know the business of every other person of influence. It should be emphasized that while America was remote from Europe, it was not cut off from it.[11]

The flow and counterflow of Anglo-Americans across the Atlantic Ocean was driven somewhat by events in Britain. The plague of the mid-1660s and the Great Fire that burned much of London in 1666 stifled this movement. In 1702, Cotton Mather had written *Magnalia Christi Americana*, a two-volume work describing America as a Puritan utopia. Written in English and widely sold in London book stores, this work is generally credited with increasing English immigration to New England during the reign of Queen Anne. It has been estimated, however, that the greatest absolute number of colonial Americans to visit London did so in the 1750s and 1760s, two decades before the War of Independence. The desire to visit the Old World to drink in the culture of England overcame many political disputes between the two places, but most visitors did so due to some underlying matter involving business.[12]

For example, Lawrence Washington visited London in 1749 as an agent for the Ohio Company, a land speculation company. He also sought out medical advice at this time for his chronic ill health probably due to advancing tuberculosis. As boys of age 11 and 10 years, Lawrence and his younger brother Augustine Jr. had been brought to London and enrolled at the Appleby School in 1729 to receive their formal education. It was from his half-brother Lawrence that George Washington inherited Mount Vernon.

All young, respectable women were expected to begin seeking out a marriage partner appropriate to their social position as soon as they left adolescence, and London was not only a good place to get an education and some social polish, it was also a fine place to seek out suitors, especially among the hundreds of American expatriates there doing business or receiving their own educations. Parents hoped for a son-in-law with a sugar, tobacco, or indigo plantation in his future, but they greatly feared romantic entanglements that could not clearly lead to an appropriate marriage because even the hint of unseemly behavior could create a sexual scandal that would leave a daughter unmarriageable. Any young woman with whom scandal became associated was quickly shipped home. While the natural calendar of childbearing seems to have been the fundamental reason for considering marriage, wealth was the primary factor in arranging a particular pairing or choosing a husband. Maintenance of one's social position was a close second. Cousin marriages were common in the American South, but almost unheard of in New England where there were many more unrelated families.[13]

Those men who chose to follow one of the three professions known as the black graces—law, medicine, or religion—found that the best place to study or improve their credentials was in Britain. Most students would attend college for a term or two without advancing to a degree. This may have been due to the general irrelevance of academic degrees as they did not secure any added social position for the upper classes of society and could not be afforded by those of humbler origins. The study of law in Britain was fairly well developed in the 18th century. Law might be studied at London's prestigious Inns of Court, or the Temple Bar, an imaginary entrance to legal learning marked with a monumental archway designed by Christopher Wren. Religion could be had at any number of Schools of Divinity, but medicine was just beginning to regiment its protocols. Many young men found it difficult to readjust to life in the colonies after experiencing the excitements of England, passing from one area of study to another in order to remain in Britain.[14]

There were no formal schools of law in the colonies and most colonial lawyers learned their profession as apprentices. Most of the deputies to the Congress were lawyers and six of the signers of the Declaration were self-taught. After tracts of popular devotion and religious doctrine, books on the law were the largest number imported to the colonies. Nearly as many copies of Blackstone's commentaries on law were sold in America as in England.[15]

The Anglican Church was responsible for all schools of higher education in London. These included universities at Cambridge and Oxford. By the middle of the 18th century, there had been a remarkable change in the strict authority of religious institutions that had not yet affected the precincts of religious education. The Church of Scotland, which under the Act of Union of 1707 was independent of the Anglican Church, had its theological seat at St. Mary's College of the University of St. Andrews. The Church of Scotland is a Kirk, a national church but not a state church, and does not recognize the monarch as its head.[16]

In the colonies, Puritan influence was strongest at Harvard. The immediate goal of the founders of the school in 1634 was to produce a new generation of orthodox preachers, "dreading to leave an illiterate ministry to the churches when our present ministers shall lie in the dust."[17] Zeal to produce an educated ministry prompted the founding of many colleges. Yale (the Collegiate School, 1701) in Connecticut was a haven for those Congregationalists who were less dogmatic than their Puritan brethren in Massachusetts. Moved to New Haven with the help of EIC money, Yale would become a hotbed of radical thought during the revolution, and Congregational ministers (who Loyalists called the Black Brigade) would be among the most steadfast supporters of independence.

Medicine in the 18th century was mired in an intellectual wasteland. Pharmaceuticals were also in an infancy and plagued by unfounded beliefs and speculative protocols. Almost all 18th-century medicines were botanicals—infusions of herbs and stems, flowers and seeds. Some of the most widely read medical books were essentially catalogs of plants—where they grew, how to prepare them, and what they did in a medical sense. Tea fit nicely into these protocols.

Most body functions lacked precise medical explanation in the 18th century. Each school of medical thought had its own simplistic version of the cause of the ills that tormented the human body, and many were thought to be due to maladjustment of the body's system of humors—phlegm, black bile, yellow bile, and blood. Methods of treatment, like bloodletting, emetics, and purges, were aimed at expelling a harmful surplus of a particular humor.

Nonetheless, in 18th-century England, the Greenwich Seamen's Hospital was a pioneering medical facility established under the authority of the Admiralty. Blood pressure was discovered and measured for the first time, and it was noted that exposure to pure oxygen brightened the color of blood. Transfusion had been attempted, the lymph system was discovered, and the mechanics of blood clotting noted. Public health and hygiene received greater attention than previously. Doses of mercury (a bad idea due to its side effects) were given by mouth to dispel the outward effects of syphilis and other sexually transmitted diseases. James Lind, a Scottish naval surgeon, in his *Treatise of the Scurvy* (1754) identified the cure for this dangerous disease of sailors. Individual captains and admirals took note of this, but it took many years for the Admiralty to accept his findings and order regular supplies of lemon juice and whole limes to its ships as preventatives. Although Edward Jenner had pioneered a crude form of vaccination against smallpox (known as variolation), the true cause of many epidemic diseases, general infections, and gangrene (putrefaction) were largely unknown.

In America, the Pennsylvania Hospital was opened in 1751 through the cooperation of Benjamin Franklin and Thomas Bond, a physician, but there were no schools of medicine in the colonies before the opening of the Medical College of Philadelphia in 1765. Thereafter, in 1767, a department of medicine was founded at Kings College in New York, which awarded the first American medical degree in 1770. However, there were many prestigious schools of medical science that Americans could attend in Britain, especially in London and in Edinburgh, Scotland. In the 18th century, more than 100 Americans are known to have graduated in medicine from the University of Edinburgh. At the time of the revolution, it has been estimated that there were not in all the colonies 400 physicians who had received medical degrees, yet there were probably more than 3,500 medical practitioners. Physicians were distinguished from barber surgeons and surgeon apothecaries by the possession of a university medical degree (MD or MRCS).[18]

In 1764, during an outbreak of smallpox, the town selectmen of Boston had committed the population of the city to a regime of variolation. Although many persons refused to be treated, the decision of the selectmen was justified. The epidemic was brought under control and of the 4,977 inoculated only 46 had died (less than 1 percent), while of the 699 that had acquired the disease in the natural way 124 had died (almost 18 percent). All the troops of Washington's Continental Army were variolated against smallpox in this manner.[19]

BEN FRANKLIN'S LONDON

Significant among the learned visitors to London was Benjamin Franklin, who presented himself at the Court of St. James in 1757 as a representative of Pennsylvania, a scientist, author, and wit, dressed by design in a frontier fur cap that could easily have graced the head of a frontiersman. At the time Franklin was considered the greatest American scientist of his day, and he had also earned a wider international reputation through his experiments with electricity. These went far beyond flying a kite in a thunder storm—which he did do—and included the designation of + and − for electric charge, the invention of the electrical capacitor, and the use of the lightning rod. Retired at age 42, Franklin had syndicated his printing business throughout the colonies providing money, presses, molds, and type to printers up and down the Atlantic coast for a share in their profits and assuring a network for the dissemination of his work and writing.

Although the quintessential colonial Anglo-American, Ben Franklin would live 25 years of his long life in Europe, with a great number of these being as a middle-aged adult in London (1757–1763 and 1764–1775) and a half dozen more years as an elderly ambassador to France (1777–1783). He spent much of his time in London living in a terraced Georgian townhouse in Covent Garden where he rented rooms, but his only surviving historic home stands nearby on Craven Street where he lived with his young son, William, from 1757 to 1758 while serving as a lobbyist for the Penn brothers who lived literally around the corner. The elder Franklin was an urban creature thoroughly at home in London, and his son may have forged psychological connections to Britain and the Crown in these formative years of his life.

Scholars have long wondered about Ben Franklin's personal life during the many years spent in London away from home—there certainly were some scandalous escapades with younger women during his later years, but it is more certain that he frequented the many coffeehouses that flourished in London in his free time. Among these, the King's Arms, the Pennsylvania, the George and Vulture, and the St. Paul's have been identified.[20] From a cultural standpoint, coffee houses served as centers for social interaction—places in which to talk, write, read, discuss, or simply pass the time drinking coffee, tea, or hot chocolate (or sherbet in summer) while munching on biscuits. Notwithstanding this veneer of civility, at nightfall many coffeehouses transformed themselves from quiet places of business and introspection into dens of iniquity and gambling where high-priced prostitutes plied their trade and high-stakes wagering was on the menu.

THE OPPORTUNITY OF PEACE

With the humiliation of the French in the Seven Years War (1756–1763) and the signing of the Peace of Paris in 1763, the number of people passing to and fro between the Old and the New Worlds once again increased. The public welcomed the prospect of an extended peace on both sides of the Atlantic. Towns were illuminated with fireworks, feasts were held, and congratulatory addresses and sermons were given. London began a house-building boom, and prosperity and optimism broke out almost everywhere. After the peace of 1763, many among the colonial gentry took advantage of this first opportunity offered in a quarter century to visit London with their families in relative safety. There were seldom fewer than 1,000 wealthy Anglo-Americans in London, and in any given year after the peace, the number might approach 5,000. Many of these colonial visitors took residences in London. Although rented rooms in good neighborhoods were very expensive, they would not be outdone with regard to their accommodations, and they generally sought out each other's company by forming small enclaves within London's better precincts. A small community of southern planters, mostly from the Carolinas and Virginia, coalesced each season among the terraced townhouses near Kew Gardens, Whitehall, or St. James Park with Buckingham Palace standing across the green, and most of their children attended the same few boarding schools. Many offspring of these colonial families were tutored at home as children and sent to England to complete their education.[21]

Unless they were in London strictly on business, most of these travelers came in family groups. "All of these [visiting] families were members of the wealthy elites of Britain's American empire . . . well-to-do colonists, whose trade and social networks crisscrossed the Atlantic." Only the New England colonies were underrepresented, possibly due to their innate sense of parsimony, possibly due to a lingering distrust of royalty, but more likely due to a general lack of personal wealth.[22]

Americans blended well into London society, and though known to be colonials, the Laurens family was considered English and took care to look and sound like Englishmen. The group surrounding Henry Laurens (who would be the second president of Congress) included several older children and a black slave named Scipio who was brought along to serve as the youngest boy's body servant while at Mrs. Clarke's boarding school in Chelsea. London had the largest black population of any city in the empire, estimated at more than 15,000 persons. There were many times fewer slaves than black freemen in London. Nonetheless, absentee American planters, their families, and their black slaves were common enough in the city.

With the exception of West Indian sugar growers, white southerners, like the Laurens, were among the wealthiest of Anglo-American visitors. Some were wealthier than their opposite number on the social scale among the residents of London. The total wealth of the southern plantations (estimated at £86 million) was four times greater than that of New England (£19 million) and two and half times that of the middle colonies (£30 million). The far less numerous Americans living on the fabulous income of sugar plantations in the West Indies were 10 times richer in terms of personal income than the average southern plantation owner. In this way, the meaning of average wealth for an individual in Britain or America was somewhat confounded by the greater mass of poor people and the tiny number of wealthy ones.[23]

Having returned to the colonies, the repatriated visitors to London went to great expense to bring English styles and motifs to America by building Georgian mansions, formal country gardens, and fashionable townhouses in rank imitation of what they had seen in Britain. The city of New York, for instance, had a mixture of newer and older sections—many of the latter built of wood.[24] Buildings along lower Broad Street (Broadway) were generally in the old Dutch style with gabled ends, but the new English-style construction of the gentry was mostly of three-storied red brick with shuttered windows and handsome doorways and façades that mirrored those in the better sections of London.[25]

A coach with matched team and black footmen in colorful livery was considered a social necessity even within the limited confines of tiny American towns, some with a single unpaved main street. Southern plantation owners planned country mansions that required artisans unavailable in the more remote parts of the colonies. Consequently, Italian masons and plasterers were brought in to build and decorate these plantation houses, and small communities of Italian-speaking immigrants settled in the American South.

The personal experience of life in London and acceptance in its social scene among the English nouveau riche were crowning achievements for the southern colonial aristocracy in particular. The gossiping buzz of the London drawing rooms, the elegance of the fine houses and the fashions, and a passing glance at the royal coach taking George III and Queen Charlotte on the way to the opera were thought to leave a metropolitan polish on those who experienced them.

ANGLO-AMERICAN TRADE

As the English colonies in America grew so did their volume of trade. Between 1720 and 1750, the colonial economy of the early decades that focused on domestic food production changed to a trading economy focus on making a profit, and the volume of colonial imports and exports with Britain doubled. Although this circumstance should have been greeted as evidence of a growing and prosperous British empire, the colonies were trading with other countries as much as they were with England. South Carolina traded one-ninth of all its rice production directly with the countries of the Mediterranean for wine, fruit, and salt. In like manner, Connecticut traded its vegetables; Maryland, its wheat; Pennsylvania, its corn; and New York, its flour. Massachusetts and much of coastal New England clandestinely traded cod with the French islands in the Caribbean in return for salt or molasses. Moreover, colonial merchants and shipowners were becoming active everywhere within the colonies being "fully in command of the coastwise commerce" in America and extending their more clandestine operations into the Caribbean and Island trade. It soon became obvious to the Crown that its North American colonies were slowly approaching economic independence.[26]

The American colonials liked sophisticated imports. Anglo-America had become a consumer marketplace capable of absorbing ever-larger quantities of British manufactured goods. While many of these were

necessities, others among them made life warmer, easier, or more
comfortable. For the growing middle class, many of these items simply made life more enjoyable. The newspapers carried advertisements
for Prussian linens, India ginghams, ebony and ivory fans, looking
glasses, mahogany picture frames, wallpaper, kidskin and lambskin
gloves for men and women, all imported through London.[27] "Suddenly, buyers voiced concerns about color and texture, about fashion
and etiquette, and about making the right choices from among an
expanding number of possibilities."[28] The commonality of desirable
imported goods tended to unite the colonials from Maine to Georgia
in a consumers marketplace. In many cases, their social, religious, and
geographical differences were moderated by their common buying
experiences.[29]

The businessmen of the colonies north of Maryland seemingly had
little reason to quarrel with the British commercial and financial regulations of the period before 1760. There were powerful ties of interest that bound the colonial businesses of New England to the mother
country. The most comprehensive regulations affecting the distribution of goods in the southern colonies was the requirement that European manufactures imported into the colonies had to be loaded in
and shipped from England. Early in the 18th century, the hardships
that this restriction imposed on colonial commerce were theoretical
rather than actual. Most desirable goods came from England, in any
case. There was a change in the wind, however, as the most fashionable and profitable items increasingly came from the Far East and India
rather than the East End of London. American skippers began to com-
plain of having to share their profits on India goods with English middlemen simply because the law required their cargoes to touch land in
Britain before moving on.[30]

THE TRIANGULAR TRADE

Parliament, under George II, had attempted to reassert its authority
over trade practices in Anglo-America with the Molasses Act of 1733.
The heavy import duties on molasses imported from non-British Caribbean islands should have eliminated the trade. Instead they seemingly made both the colonials and their foreign suppliers more eager
to work together, and the contraband rum industry flourished. This
patently illegal trade was extremely lucrative, surviving even the outbreak of several wars between the French and British monarchs.

Although many historians remain fascinated by the three-way traffic in molasses, rum, and slaves, it was the fisheries of the Grand Banks that provided the dried cod used to feed the slaves on the island sugar plantations that fundamentally supported the Triangular Trade. Only 5 percent of American rum was used in the slave trade. Without the cod, the islands would have been unable to support the large number of slaves needed to produce sugar and molasses. Nonetheless, profits were to be had with every exchange made on the trading triangle. Rum distillers in New England made tidy profits changing the molasses into liquor for domestic consumption, and the indigenous slave traders of Africa used their scant portion of rum as both a consumable and as an item for further trade. The ubiquitous New England skippers and shipowners took their share of the profits by carrying the cargoes, including human ones, on each leg of the trading triangle. Profits from this business helped New England to offset its considerable deficit in commodity trading with Britain that amounted to nearly £1.5 million in the decade before the outbreak of the revolution.[31]

REORGANIZING THE EMPIRE

There is little doubt that London intended to prohibit the colonials from following the natural pathways of geographical expansion and economic growth that lay before them. The consumption of British goods would not be promoted by new settlements in the American interior, "which being proposed to be established at the distance of fifteen hundred miles from the sea . . . [will] probably lead [the colonials] to manufacture for themselves."[32] London had restricted the development of colonial manufactures to protect its own domestic industries, but it made few prohibitions against the development of colonial maritime industries because it was thought that they strengthened the empire. Soon after the Peace of Paris in 1763, Americans began to revitalize their natural interests in the sea.

As early as 1720, the shipping that traded between England and the colonies in America was estimated to carry possibly one-third of the total tonnage from England to all foreign countries.[33] No longer needing the protection of the Royal Navy at sea after the defeat of the French, American trading vessels, whalers, fishing vessels, and slavers inundated the ports of the world. Of the 20 largest cities in Anglo-America only one (Lancaster, Pennsylvania) was not a port. New England was soon providing almost half of British shipbuilding capacity worldwide. Colonial shippers and merchants made their profits by moving raw materials to England and returning finished goods to the colonial markets. The government took its part of the wealth generated by this activity in the form of taxes, port fees, and customs duties. This system was thought fair, if not perfectly so, until Parliament attempted to tilt the economic playing field in favor of its friends in the EIC.[34]

Almost all that the government did in the decades before the revolution had led to increased government regulation and involvement in American business, and increased government intrusion in the daily lives of the people. The EIC, its agents, and its friends in Parliament viewed compliance with these regulations in a solely commercial light as being good for the Company's business, and few observers supposed that the Americans would view them on the grounds of abstract principles, like lack of representation in Parliament, infringements of personal liberty, or the imposition of tyranny. Of course, some of what Anglo-Americans claimed as violations of ancient and fundamental principles was hyperbole.

A quarter century before the advent of this crisis of governance, there were strict provisions enacted by Parliament regulating the sale of tea with a view to its keeping the market supplied with a sufficient quantity to answer the demand in Great Britain and to prevent prices rising above those prevalent in other countries. Among these provisions was one requiring the EIC to keep a stock of tea on hand, at least equal to one year's consumption according to the demand of the preceding year, and the Company was authorized to import tea from other sources in Europe in case of a threatened deficiency. This well-reasoned policy was initiated to buffer the tea supply from spikes in price and unforeseen shortages.

Acts of Parliament in 1767 under George III required American merchants re-exporting tea acquired in London to do so without breaking bulk—that is, in the same packages in which they had been sold by the EIC. A prior act in 1748 had also required the tea to be exported from London in quantities no smaller than the *entire lot* in which the Company sold it. The size of an entire lot was often as much as the entire cargo of a ship, or as little as a few dozen chests. The penalty for doing otherwise was forfeiture of the tea and the packages containing it.

There was good reason for such regulations. Once landed and removed from its packaging, smuggled tea was impossible to differentiate from legal tea, hence the need to maintain the original packaging. Documents claiming importation from Britain were easily falsified, and legitimate documents could be reused to cover illegal shipments. An unanticipated outcome of these provisions, however, was to discourage English merchants and traders from exporting tea to Ireland and the American colonies where the demand for such large quantities of legitimate tea was not warranted. Unable to assume the risk of dealing in large quantities, small businessmen were virtually squeezed out of the legal trade and many turned to smuggled tea. The Townshend Act of 1767 eased this stricture somewhat, substituting a requirement that the tea should not be exported in quantities less than the whole of the contents of any one chest or other original package in which it had been sold at the public sale held by the Company in London.[35]

Subsequent to the imposition of the Tea Tax of 1773, the Company departed from its established mode of disposing of its teas by public auction to the merchants and wholesalers in London ("by the candle" as previously required by law) and adopted a new system of becoming its own exporter and wholesaler to the colonies. A select group of American merchants was chosen to act as Company consignees to four colonial ports—Boston, New York, Philadelphia, and Charleston. Each of these had been nominated by a London merchant who gave his bond that his American counterpart would remit the required funds and duties to the EIC in London. This policy represented a great reduction in the price of quality tea in America that had hovered around £1 (240d.) per pound for the best type. The arrangement covered all the costs of the tea (shipping, warehousing, etc.) as well as the Townshend duties retained by the EIC and a generous profit fixed at 6 percent to be evenly divided between the colonial consignees and their London sponsors.[36]

Those engaged in the tea trade with America—many of whom lived in the colonies—did not welcome such a powerful competitor as the EIC. Such competition incurred the opposition of the merchants and dealers who purchased tea in the colonies and assumed all the risks of its subsequent disposal on the retail market. Moreover, the plan would not have necessarily forced smugglers out of their black market in tea. Illicit traders purchasing Dutch tea could still realize a profit both from its lower base price and the avoidance of the duty. The non-payment of an additional 3d. per pound in Townshend duties alone represented a relative profit to the smugglers of almost 13 percent. Moreover, the factors in Holland were more willing than those in London to offer attractive credit terms to American skippers.[37]

It can be seen in the case of tea—certainly a symptom of a wider crisis in the government's concept of central control of the economy—that the government ministers in London willingly sacrificed the profits of its small businessmen and the developing free market system on the altar of regulated trade and price controls in a number of areas that favored what would be called big business today.[38]

In the decade straddling 1770, the nature of colonial trade in North America had changed more than anywhere else in the global trading empire. North America had evolved a more modern form of industrial economy than any other region outside England and under British control. Although agriculture remained their preeminent occupation, Americans were increasingly employed as tradesmen, artisans, crafts-men, and skilled manufacturing workers. The populous coastal cities quickly became the focus of colonial wealth and talent. In the environs of the two largest urban centers—Philadelphia and New York—tech-nology, science, and industry had become so well entrenched that most of the population did not practice the self-sufficiency characteristic of their rural cousins in the backwoods. The latter were constantly pos-sessed of numerous supposed slights and genuine political grievances at the hands of their city cousins. Quarrels among those living on the frontiers and those living in the more urban settings of the major cities—and among the colonies themselves with respect to conflicting land claims and policies concerning the Native tribes—were symp-tomatic of a very uneasy colonial unity under any circumstances.[39]

Moreover, the Atlantic colonies remained the major overseas mar-ket for British goods even as late as 1774. Although the non-importation agreements resulting from the Stamp Act crisis lowered imports from Britain somewhat from 1765 to 1768, in their aftermath imports rose almost 47 percent from their pre-crisis levels being valued at an aver-age of £3.7 million annually in each year from 1771 to 1774. The col-lapse of the non-consumption movement after the victory over the Stamp Act, especially in major cities like New York and Philadelphia, led many in the business community to incorrectly forecast a more conciliatory relationship between America and London for the re-mainder of the century.

Nonetheless, most Americans still lived off the land divorced from the maritime trades and the details of seaborne commerce. The ag-ricultural nature of the southern plantation economy and the subsis-tence farming of the frontiers were still highly visible. In the 1780s, Benjamin Franklin noted that the great business of America was farm-ing, and historians down to the present have kept the notion alive. However, outside the South, skilled trades, craftsmanship, fishing, and shipbuilding had actually overtaken agriculture as the leading commercial activities in terms of the value of their annual production before the revolution. Skilled tradesmen like shipwrights, joiners, metal smiths, metal founders, furniture and cabinet makers, cartwrights, saddlers and shoemakers, stone and brick masons, wigmakers, and printers—known collectively as mechanics and artisans—were ascending the economic ladder to prosperity and financial security in a manner undreamed of by their equals in Britain.[40]

Financially fortunate Americans desired many of the luxury items available in Europe, but they did not want to pay the duties and taxes that government required on all imports, especially when these items were being produced in Britain for British subjects. They resented being treated as foreigners. The unceasing demand for these items engendered the internal development of a number of colonial manufactures that were not envisioned under the concept of mercantilism, such as glass and ceramic making, iron and brass founding, gun making, printing and book publishing, and other colonial industries. The establishment of some of these industries in the colonies was considered illegal, and many craftsmen, actually producing new manufactures, resorted to the fiction of serving as repairmen or of reworking finished items imported from Britain in order to do business.[41]

Those colonials practicing subsistence farming on the frontiers rarely experienced a lack of the basic necessities of life. An enterprising farmer might make a few shillings each season by selling deerskins and furs at the trading post or by splitting out roofing shingles and cutting firewood for sale in the towns. From this, he could clothe his family in something other than animal skins. Yet, the common residents of frontier communities, scraping a living from among the stumps of the newly cleared forests, would not realize a marketable surplus of agricultural produce for decades. Thereafter, almost all the wealth accumulated by years of labor resided in their livestock, the land, and the improvements that they made on it, such as barns and fences.

Southern agriculture in the tidewater regions revolved around the largely autonomous plantation economy, which came to depend on race-based slavery. Tobacco and rice were the most important export crops in prerevolutionary America. The production of lumber and indigo helped to supplement plantation income. Very little of the valuable variety of long-staple cotton was grown in this period except in the Sea Islands region of South Carolina, and the more common short staple variety was used domestically. Linen made from the thread-like inner part of the flax plant was a much more common fabric. Sugar production was almost entirely reserved for the islands of the

Caribbean. The largest crop grown in the South in terms of its volume was corn, which was food for both man and beast.

Dyestuffs were an important commodity in the 18th century. Natural dyes extracted from common organics like onionskins, sage leaves, and walnut husks, had provided yellows, greens, and browns since medieval times; but the more brilliant colors of the 18th-century fashion palette required dyestuffs from outside the colonies. Fustick (bright yellow), madder root (pinks–red), Brazil wood (red), logwood (dusky blue), and cochineal (scarlet–crimson) were all imported from the West Indies or Central and South America; and each came under the taxing regime of the Board of Trade. Logwood and cochineal were brought to Europe as part of the American treasure on Spanish galleons. Turmeric (yellow), safflower (yellow), and indigo (blue) were native to Asia. Greens were made by overdying yellow cloth with blues or boiling yellow cloth in an iron pot with iron filings. A combination of logwood (or indigo) with a ferrous sulfate mordant (color fixer) produced a colorfast black used in the formal clothes of ministers, magistrates, and mourners.

Eliza Lucas Pinckney is commonly credited for advancing the production of American indigo as a profit-producing commercial crop. True blue indigo dye came from Asia where it was used to dye textiles and particularly silk for centuries, and it should not be confused with blue natural dye substitutes like woad or knotweed. The extraction of the indigo dye was difficult and distasteful work requiring exposure to strong solutions of caustic lye. The indigo color is generally that of today's blue jeans, but has many shades. The color could be so vibrant that physicist Sir Isaac Newton used it to describe one-seventh part of his rainbow in 1701, "visible yet immaterial, the color purest in meaning, with the power to negotiate the two spheres of God and man."[42]

Fortunately, in her early life before her marriage, Eliza had been an excellent experimental botanist, creating a process that made the production of indigo much more profitable. She also had considerable business sense, having assisted her own father with the management of three plantations while still in her teens. As an adolescent girl, Eliza had experimented with ginger, cotton, and alfalfa as profit-making crops for her father's upland acres. Ultimately, she settled on indigo, cultivating and improving the strains of the dye-producing plant with the help of an indigo worker of African descent. Using the improved seeds from her crop of 1744, Eliza, who at age 20 was obviously a gifted promoter, convinced her neighbors to plant it. The output of American-grown indigo exploded. The volume of indigo exported in

1745 was 5,000 pounds and that of 1748 had risen to 130,000 pounds. The cultivation and processing of indigo dye accounted for one-third the value of all colonial exports before the revolution. In 1774, cubes of the blue dye were passing as currency in South Carolina, and exports worth £1.1 million were being shipped to Britain.[43]

WEALTH

Southern planters generally lacked true aristocratic bloodlines, but they formed an aristocracy of their own devising by applying their wealth and social status to the wheels of colonial government. Yet, most plantation owners were cash poor and constantly in debt. They could, however, support themselves through the annual agricultural cycle with the products of their own plantations. When their crops were sold, they experienced a glut of money with which to pay their debts or buy luxury goods. Thus, the agricultural cycle drove much of the business cycle in the southern colonies.

The wealth generated by mercantilism was not evenly distributed among all Americans. It has been estimated that the average free white person in British America in 1770 had a net wealth of £74 after balancing the differing values of colonial currencies with that of silver coin. This figure represented only an average distribution of a total wealth (buildings, farmlands, slaves, livestock, cash, and personal belongings) in all the colonies estimated at £150 million. New England residents averaged a mere £33 in personal wealth, those of the middle colonies £51, and those from the agricultural plantations of the South £132. By comparison, the far less numerous whites living on the fabulously wealthy sugar plantations of the West Indies averaged £1,200 each.[44]

While most of the labor force of the South was composed of slaves, whose value was added as wealth, a much greater proportion of the labor force in the North was composed of free whites. Moreover, much of the wealth in the northern colonies came to reside in the hands of just a few fortunate colonial merchants, tradesmen, and shippers. The slow pace of wealth accumulation may have contributed to the general dissatisfaction with the mercantile-style economy expressed by many working-class colonials in New England.[45] A writer to the *New York Journal* in 1767 asked, "Are our Circumstances altered? Is Money grown more plentiful? Have our Tradesmen full Employment? Are we more Frugal? Is Grain cheaper? Are our Importations less?" Another noted cynically that the leaders of the protests seemed to be drawn heavily from those who had no property to lose.[46]

WAGES

In the British trading empire, wages for laborers varied between 9s. and 12s. per week, with 10s. (1/2 pound, £25 per year) being one of the most common rates found in business records from the period. Evidence submitted to British authorities in London in the 18th century suggests that an average day laborer could expect to earn between £25 and £40 annually if fully employed, but colonial wages are generally accepted to have been nearer the higher amount. This is somewhat misleading, as many laborers were not fully employed for an entire year and the value of various colonial currencies confounds a precise estimation. By way of comparison to manual laborers, an unmarried countinghouse clerk had a reasonable expectation of earning a steady wage amounting to about £50 annually without regard to the season of the year, and most analysts used this as a benchmark for wages.

The wages of textile workers were generally below those of other laborers, and they were often charged for the use of the employer's looms or stocking frames.[47] This may help to account for the large number of Patriot recruits who identified themselves as weavers—second only in most documents to farmers. Those workers with special skills, such as masons, or those who provided their own specialized tools, such as leather workers, may have made as much as 15s. per week. However, determined and skillful employees doing piecework might briefly increase their weekly earnings to £1 or even £2. These wages were difficult to sustain in a colonial economy driven by seasonal spurts of agricultural productivity. Particularly well-to-do artisans, like the makers of jewelry, of optical and musical instruments, of clocks and carriages, or of fine furniture, might increase their annual earnings to more than £100 by the employment of apprentices and journeymen.[48]

The term *Artisan* conveyed a greater notion among workers of artistic talent and independence from an employer. It was used to describe those skilled craftsmen and handcrafters who, usually through serving an apprenticeship of some kind, had the right to view their skill as a kind of intellectual property to be used by themselves to make a profit. Artisans like jewelers, silversmiths, and engravers could work in their own shop or put out their skill to an employer. They were often formed into guilds or trade organizations that policed their members as to their level of skill or their right to practice their trade. A great number among the planners of the Boston Tea Party were recruited from this portion of the working population, most notably Paul Revere.

Women throughout the colonies were expected to work and contribute to the family income. Mainstream Puritan thinking, the basis of New England society, was particularly devoted to "an especially draconian hierarchy of the sexes in which the woman's role was that of obedient, quietly devoted helpmate." Sole authority in matters economic, religious, and political resided in the male head of the household. Women were responsible only within the bounds of "huswifery." On the other extreme, the Pennsylvania society dominated by the Quaker religion, co-founded in Britain by Margaret Fell and George Fox, was one in which women were given greater authority in child-rearing, in women's matter, and even in the church.[49] The aristocratic mistresses of large plantations in the South were charged with managing the entire household. They budgeted the family income, dealt with merchants, and supervised a number of household servants and slaves. Finally, frontier women everywhere were not generally confined to gender specific roles, doing any task that furthered the subsistence and survival of their families.[50]

Many laboring-class women hired out for charring, washing, cooking, sewing, and nursing services. They often manned market stalls in the town square or hawked wares in the streets from carts or baskets. The work of dispensing food and drink often fell to younger females, who tended customers as serving girls or tavern wenches filling the same niche that many young people do today as waitresses, waiters, and buss persons. Young men often worked as stable hands, horse handlers, and manual laborers. The widows of tavern and shopkeepers often continued the business long after the death of their husbands, and a remarkable number of licensed establishments seemingly had no male proprietor that anyone could remember. The wives of these men were also their business partners helping to run the establishment, providing food and clean clothing for the workmen or boarders, and sometimes maintaining the accounts. A mid-18th-century source noted, "None but a fool will take a wife whose bread must be earned solely by his labor and who will contribute nothing towards it herself."[51]

The real value of the weekly wage in terms of the purchasing power it brought to the wage earner is difficult to pin down largely due to the paucity of records, the bartering of goods and services, swings of deflation and inflation, and the wide variety of currencies and exchange rates characteristic of the American colonial economy. The reported expenses for the family of a married man with two or three children vary widely in the available estimates from 8s. 3d. to more than £1 weekly. They include the cost of food and drink, clothing, rental housing, and fuel. These estimates are viewed with some suspicion by students of the period as being "miscellaneous and incidental" in nature, but generally a shilling (1s.) a day of income would just barely keep a family alive on a strict budget. Under such a circumstance, each person in a family bringing in any extra earnings, no matter how paltry, increased the comfort of them all. Fuel—essentially firewood— was much more available in the colonies than in Britain, but many salaries—especially those of ministers, teachers, and town clerks—were paid in so many cords of firewood rather than in cash money. This could be used, sold, or bartered for other items. However, it is clear that the income of most colonial laborers was barely enough to sustain their families, and the common wage did not allow for the accumulation of much in the way of personal wealth or possessions.[52]

PAPER MONEY

The colonial governments substituted paper currency, each of their own devising, in an attempt to solve the problems caused by a lack of coins. Maryland produced the best form of paper currency before the revolution. The sterling silver conversions for a Maryland paper dollar were clearly printed on its reverse using symbols for crowns, shillings, and pence that aided in its circulation and helped to maintain its value. The 1767 Maryland issue, designed with the help of Benjamin Franklin, became the basis for the new Continental currency of the American revolutionary government in 1776.

The value of paper currency varied from colony to colony. As long as the specie coins circulated freely, the paper maintained its value. As the coins disappeared from circulation, as they did from time to time, the paper currency depreciated. The value of the paper usually reflected that of the Spanish silver dollar. At midcentury, £100 sterling silver in London was worth £160 in local paper in New York and New Jersey, £170 in Pennsylvania (including Delaware), £200 in Maryland, £800 in South Carolina and Georgia, and £1,400 in North Carolina. The reader will note the absence of the New England colonies from this list. There is good reason. The paper bills issued by the New England colonies were known as bills of credit or fiat money; that is, they could not be exchanged for fixed amounts of gold or silver coins on demand. They were generally retired through their acceptance as payment for local taxes. The paper bills, outside New England, were worth no more than Monopoly money outside the confines of the board game. The Currency Act passed by Parliament in 1751 restricted only the paper money in New England. It allowed the existing bills to be used as legal tender for public debts (i.e., paying taxes) but disallowed their use for private debts, such as purchases from merchants. A second act in 1756 restricted paper currency in all the colonies.[53]

In 1749, Parliament granted Massachusetts a payment of more than £138,000 for its expenses fighting the French four years earlier. The payment to Massachusetts came in the form of 650,000 ounces of Spanish silver and nine tons of copper halfpenny and two-farthing pieces. Thomas Hutchinson, who had broached the idea with the colonial office, thought the copper coins would be useful in stimulating colonial commerce. The silver was to be used to retire the outstanding Massachusetts paper, an idea opposed by both Samuel and John Adams. The coins had scarcely come into circulation in Massachusetts when it was found that the paper currencies of nearby colonies were suddenly and heavily depreciated. Five years later in 1754, the colonial office in London introduced thousands of copper coins into the middle and southern colonies to help free up their commerce. The copper coins, actually 1 and 2 farthing (1/4d. and 1/2d.) tokens (not lawful money) prepared by British mining companies, were sacked, boxed, and shipped at a cost to the colonial governments of 6 percent of their face value.

The silver, having intrinsic value, remained in circulation only briefly. The useful copper tokens were not immediately absorbed into the colonial economy, but like water in a sponge they disappeared with time. The colonials themselves were largely at fault for removing hard currency from circulation. Coins from England were melted down into flatware, tea services, and candlesticks, or were hoarded, hidden behind wallboards, or buried in gardens by apprehensive and economically unsophisticated colonials attempting to put aside an old-age fund for themselves or a valued inheritance for their children.

The Sugar Act of 1764 required the payment in specie coin of all public debts and duties, and the Currency Act of 1764 effectively made all paper money then in circulation worthless. All of the colonies except Massachusetts, which had redeemed most of its paper obligations, faced financial ruin as the value of their outstanding paper evaporated.[54] Americans like Benjamin Franklin believed that a free flow of capital in the provinces would keep interest rates low and help facilitate trade. However, the natural flow of hard currency (coin) under the system of mercantilism was purposely tilted toward the parent country, and the resulting balance of payments continually removed coins from the colonies. Although Parliament was actually attempting to formally stabilize the monetary systems of all the colonies, the colonists assumed that the coins paid in duties and taxes would be shipped to England, leaving them nothing in which to make the payments of trade balances. In fact, the British ministry intended to keep the coins in the colonies to help pay for the thousands of troops that it had authorized for colonial protection. Some of this would have found its way back into the colonial economy.

A fear of the resultant drain of hard currency from North America gripped all the colonies, but it particularly affected the cash-dependent and currency-starved merchants of New England. Colonials foresaw a future of perpetual debt unpayable regardless of how hard they labored or how successful were their businesses. The fundamental problems surrounding the colonial monetary system were never rectified, and the cash provisions of the acts of 1764 remained in effect until the eve of the revolution serving as an undercurrent to the general discontent that the colonials had formed for British trade regulation.[55]

In 1775, Alexander Hamilton estimated that there was close to £7 million in genuine coinage in the colonies. This represented about £2 14s. per free white person. This might seem an adequate stock of coin when a single shilling commonly bought a meal at an inn, a room for the night, and stabling and feed for a horse.[56] However, adequate quantities of money did not necessarily translate into a stock of currency capable of sustaining normal business transactions. Many coins and paper issues were not "denominated" in terms that allowed them to "circulate as freely and easily as they might have," making it easier to pay a year's rent with a single gold coin than to find the few coppers needed to purchase a side of bacon once a week.[57]

SMUGGLING

Americans began evidencing a general dissatisfaction with the intrusive nature of British rule in their daily lives as early as 1764. There were many areas of contention prominent at the time, but the one point that struck sparks with the Crown was the colonial passion for avoiding customs duties by smuggling. Although smuggling was an old and widespread activity practiced throughout the empire, American smugglers proved particularly adept at evading the customs, especially with respect to trade with the West Indies, southern Europe, and the west coast of Africa.

Smugglers were criminals, but like the rum runners and speakeasy owners of the era of 20th-century Prohibition or the dealers in illegal drugs and marijuana today, they enjoyed a certain prominence in colonial society, largely because they provided manufactured goods and luxuries at much lower prices than could legitimate sources. Many highly born and well-respected men in America dabbled in the black market of contraband wines, brandies and rum, tea and coffee, fine fabrics, glass and dinnerware, alloyed metals such as brass and bronze, finished metal objects, tools and machines, printer's type, and other goods manufactured outside Britain. The greatest year for tea smuggling—estimated as a proportion of all tea imported into the colonies—was 1750. The price of legal tea thereafter decreased markedly making smuggling less profitable. Regulations promulgated in 1767, however, increased the tax on tea (6d. per pound) raising the price of legal product once again.[58]

The port of Boston was constantly abuzz over the landing of smuggled goods. John Hancock, a respected Boston merchant and member of the colonial social elite, was held to be one of the most notorious smugglers in colonial America. When his sloop *Liberty* was seized with a cargo of smuggled Madeira wine, a riot broke out among the good people of Boston in his support.[59] "The Boston people are run mad," reported Thomas Hutchinson. "The frenzy was not higher when they . . . hanged the poor witches."[60] Respectable citizens were horrified at the flagrant and unashamed manner of the smugglers. Yet, informers to the customs agents, if found out, were beaten, dragged through the streets, or tarred and feathered. Similar occurrences were recorded in New York, Newport, and Philadelphia. Two royal customs officers in Philadelphia who had seized a shipment of wine were set upon by a mob that assaulted them and then stole the wine.

Smuggling, taken together with illegal manufactures, and a determined and unrelenting resistance to properly constituted authority disrupted the well-founded underpinnings of the British trading empire. The stockholders of legitimate trading companies, apprehending the loss of a large proportion of their profits to the colonials, complained bitterly to London about the lack of enforcement of legitimate trade regulations. The loss of revenue for the government was also considerable. The Exchequer estimated the losses due to smuggling alone at almost £40,000 sterling each year. In response, the customs officials were ordered to fit out a number of lightly armed sloops and schooners to patrol the American coastal waters and halt the smuggling. These vessels were generally known as revenue cutters.[61]

It should be noted that contemporary reports of widespread evasion of the customs among Americans might be overstated. From 1765 to 1767, customs officials made only six seizures of contraband in New England waters, and only one of the cases brought against the supposed smugglers was won by the Crown.[62] On the other hand, Americans simply may have been expert at avoiding detection by customs officials. Many smugglers created large fortunes for themselves by nosing their craft into the coastal shallows and small rivers where the revenue cutters could not follow.[63]

Previously, customs vessels were required to focus their patrols to within two leagues (approximately four miles) of the coast, whereas vessels of the Royal Navy were generally restricted to patrolling out of sight of land. In 1764, the Admiralty approved the purchase of six sloops and schooners, ironically built in America, for the purpose of patrolling inshore waters, and it endowed its naval officers with the powers of revenue agents. This was a change in protocol equivalent in the eyes of colonials to declaring martial law on land—like replacing constables with soldiers. Each of these vessels was provided with a crew of British Jack Tars, a file of Royal Marines, and a cadre of young Royal Navy officers. The cutters were named *Chaleur, Hope, Magdalen, St. John, St. Lawrence*, and the infamous *Gaspée*, and their appearance engendered protests and demonstrations everywhere.

It seems that the vigorous enforcement of the regulations rather than the actual financial burden of the taxes was the cause of much of the colonial alienation. The colonials viewed the new measures as violations of fundamental constitutional principles rather than as the simple enforcement of established trade practices by government bureaucrats. Colonial customs officials, in particular, seem to have become "tactless, arbitrary, and mercenary" in the performance of their duties.[64]

Admitting that any system, poised to control global economic affairs, would inevitably be highly complicated, the colonies were actually affected by only a handful of regulations. In the 17th century, the basic navigation acts were designed to protect the British economy from foreign competition. Americans did not consider themselves foreigners, hence their calls for the protection of their rights as Englishmen. Additional policies were adopted to funnel enumerated colonial products through British ports; to encourage specific industries by the use of bounties; to promote the production of certain raw materials; and, finally, to directly prohibit new industrial endeavors that would compete with those already established or promoted by other legislation.[65]

Initially, the Navigation Acts were "not a source of serious complaint by the Americans."[66] In most cases the regulations had neither a positive nor negative effect on colonial prosperity. Rather than being oppressive, certain aspects of the acts were actually an important source of colonial wealth.[67] Colonial planters could accumulate large fortunes in only a few years by growing enumerated crops, such as rice, tobacco, and indigo. Moreover, restrictions placed on the colonial iron, hat, and shipping industries did "not materially hamper" their development.[68]

The Sugar Act of 1764 was the first of the new measures designed to reorganize the empire and raise revenue from America. The act not only put a small 6d. tax on each gallon of molasses but it also contained more than 40 provisions for changes in the customs and commerce regulations, thereby affecting an unprecedented change in the status of the colonies "amounting to a constitutional revolution."[69]

Documentation and regulatory paperwork was vastly increased, and enforcement was extended to almost all coastwise traders including the smallest intercolonial shippers who might move cargoes only a few miles along the shoreline. The skippers of vessels greater than 10 tons were required to obtain documentation of their cargoes before they were shipped out and to do likewise when they were landed even if going from one colony to another. "If any goods are shipped without such sufferance . . . the officers of the customs are empowered to stop all vessels . . . which shall be discovered within two leagues of the shore of any such British colonies or plantations, and to seize all goods on board."[70]

The Townshend Acts of 1767 thereafter created the so-called Writs of Assistance (general search warrants), which were widely regarded in America as unconstitutional and damaging to personal liberty. Vessels and cargoes could be condemned on the most technical grounds, and the regulations were to be enforced in the admiralty courts operating under a system of law different from that used in the local colonial court system. This was a particularly noisome part of the act to the colonials, somewhat like having a present-day parking ticket judged by a military tribunal.[71]

No course of action by the government in London could have been calculated to more arouse colonial resentment. Many Americans claimed that the customs officials tried "to use the revenue laws as a cloak to set up in America a centralized authority over domestic and foreign commerce."[72] Hostility toward "a plundering revenue service" was especially strong in those localities in which bureaucrats most vigorously prosecuted enforcement of the regulations in terms of harassment, excessive fees by the courts, and the seizure of vessels and cargoes by the navy.[73]

In 1773, Benjamin Franklin described the nature of the enforcement problem and its consequences in a piece titled *Rules by Which a Great Empire May Be Reduced to a Small One*. Herein he paints a picture of Gestapo-like tactics better attributed to a repressive and despotic tyranny than a society of free citizens living under a constitutional monarchy, a theme echoed by many radical publications of the period:

> Convert the brave, honest officers of your navy into pimping tide-waiters and colony officers of the customs. Let those who in the time of war fought gallantly in defense of their countrymen, in peace be taught to prey upon it. Let them learn to be corrupted by great and real smugglers; but (to show their diligence) scour with armed boats every bay, harbor, river, creek, cove, or nook throughout your colonies; stop and detain every coaster, every wood-boat, every fisherman; tumble their cargoes and even their ballast inside out and upside down; and, if a penny-worth of [dressmakers'] pins is found unentered [on the cargo manifest], let the whole be seized and confiscated. Thus shall the trade of your colonists suffer more from their friends in time of peace than it did from their enemies in war. . . . Oh, this will work admirably![74]

It is unlikely that the regulations alone imposed so serious a burden on the colonial economy that it caused the Americans to disrupt one of the greatest trading empires of the 18th century simply to redress trivial inconveniences.[75] Nonetheless, it must be admitted that the Sugar Act, Currency Act, and other regulations produced considerable organized opposition in New England and the Middle colonies and less in the plantation South. The linkage between these acts and the protests is unmistakable.[76] Nonetheless, the representative attitudes of Americans— merchants, shippers, gentry, clergy, and their political supporters—as presented in journals, sermons, newspapers, broadsides, pamphlets and other contemporary literature supports the idea that the regulations were enforced in such a manner as to erode the historic loyalty to the Crown of a great number of Americans. The ill feelings engendered by the regulation of trade and the enforcement of the customs quickly evolved into a wholly new ideological argument, which denied the right of Parliament to legislate for the colonies.[77]

In *The Wealth of Nations* (1776), political economist Adam Smith wrote, "Though North America is not yet as rich as England, it is much more thriving, and advancing with much greater rapidity to the further acquisition of riches." Similar sentiments were expressed two decades ago with respect to Japan or Korea and are being expressed today concerning the economic growth of China. Like Americans today, Anglo-Americans two centuries ago, with their rugged self-sufficiency and entrepreneurial spirit, were poised to leap forward economically, but only in a manner most profitable to themselves. Old ideas, restrictive legislation, or slow-moving bureaucracies could not hold back such people.[78]

CHAPTER 4

Seedbed of Discontent

I am sincerely one of those . . . who would rather be in dependence on Great Britain, properly limited, than on any other nation on earth, or than on no nation. But I am also one of those, too, who, rather than submit to the rights of legislating for us, assumed by the British Parliament, and which late experience has shown they will so cruelly exercise, would lend my hand to sink the whole island in the ocean.[1]

—*Thomas Jefferson*

THE STAMP ACT CRISIS

The French and Indian War created a vast debt estimated by the British Exchequer at an unprecedented £150 million. An additional annual appropriation of almost £2 million was needed for the imperial peace establishment—an army and navy to secure an empire that stretched from Hudson's Bay in Canada to the Bay of Bengal in India, half a globe away. Only £350,000 of this annual expense (approximately 18 percent) was determined to be due to the administration of the American colonies. Although the Parliament expected to pay the lion's share of future expenditures, the ministry of George Grenville decided to extract at least some of the money, estimated at about £60,000 in 1765, from the colonies in the form of a stamp tax on all legal and business papers, newspapers, printed forms, playing cards, wall paper, and licenses. Stamped printers stock and newssheets were also made available.[2]

In the 18th century, an income tax was unthinkable, even for the revenue-starved British Empire. Many people in Britain and America opposed an income tax, on principle, believing that the disclosure of personal income was an unacceptable intrusion of government into their private matters and a potential threat to their personal liberty. Moreover, in Anglo-America, the legislation laying *internal taxes* had always come from the local colonial assemblies. Anglo-Americans were familiar with paying taxes, but even the imperial ministers of the Crown had not proposed the modern expedient of a profit-killing, economy-enervating tax on personal income.

The stamp protests were the most widespread and effective of all actions taken against the Crown prior to the revolution, and they set the protocols and character of the tea protests a decade later. "Looking back it is clear that such a tax, being internal instead of external, might raise a storm of protest."[3] Along with the passage of the Stamp Act, Parliament renewed the Mutiny Act, which required the colonial assemblies to house and support the troops sent to America. These provisions of the Mutiny Act were known as *quartering*.

The Grenville ministry sought to minimize the potential reaction to the stamp tax by appointing American stamp agents rather than English ones. The insignificant size of the tax assured many in Britain that any protests would be minimal. Moreover, the Stamp Act was calculated to fall heaviest on the wealthy, who it was thought used more documents than the ordinary people. This would divide any resistance along the lines of social class or sectional interests.[4]

This plan misfired badly. It seems that the Grenville ministry miscalculated both the unforeseen effect of the tax and the breadth of the reaction to it. Frontier farmers rarely dealt with public papers, but they were intimately concerned with the land. Different stamp taxes, above the usual costs of land patents and surveys, were specified for deeds or grants of land of less than 100 acres, of 100–200 acres, and of 200–320 acres. Colonial shippers and merchants were required to take out numerous public documents while conducting business, including bills of lading, clearance permits, insurance policies, rental agreements, mortgages, attachments of property, and all kinds of contracts. The Stamp Act also affected lawyers, newspaper editors, printers, and an army of municipal employees who signed indentures, produced public documents, or ran a licensed business. As many as 70 percent of colonials read newspapers with the stamp prominently in view, and in an economy as regulated as was that of Anglo-America, almost every businessman, craftsman, street vendor, innkeeper, and shopkeeper was required to obtain an annual license and pay the tax. It has been estimated that 1 in 20 Anglo-Americans were required to take out a license or permit of some kind to follow their occupation. The tax on playing cards was particularly irksome as almost everyone played cards as a form of diversion, and the uncoated cards of the 18th century wore out quickly. New decks with the king's tax stamp on the package screamed taxation to every person who played whist or cribbage in a tavern or in a parlor.

THE VIRGINIA RESOLVES

Contrary to the hopes of Parliament, the whole of Anglo-America seemed to unite in opposition to the Stamp Act. In May 1765, seven resolutions condemning the stamp tax were proposed in the Virginia House of Burgesses six months before the act went into effect. The

Although three of the seven resolves were defeated in the Burgesses, the acceptance of the remaining resolutions was cheered throughout the colonies. All seven were published in the colonial newspapers as if they had been passed unanimously. (Author's collection)

Virginia Resolutions claimed that only the colonial legislature had the right to tax Virginians. "Taxation of the people by themselves, or by persons chosen by themselves to represent them . . . is the only security against a burthensome taxation, and the distinguishing characteristic of British freedom." Among the resolves was firmly lodged the concept of consensual government found in the political writings of Thomas Hobbes, John Milton, and John Locke, a foundation stone of American political theory. "His Majesty's liege people . . . have without interruption enjoyed the inestimable right of being governed by such laws, respecting their internal polity and taxation, as are derived from their own consent."[5]

The first reaction in the colonies to the unprecedented Virginia Resolves was one of shock, yet many Americans found themselves in accord with their primary thrust. Soon even the common people began to denounce taxation without representation, and they spoke openly of supporting the rights of Englishmen, of defending American liberties, and of government by the consent of the governed. The argument over specific regulations and stamp taxes had quickly evolved into an all-out battle concerning constitutional principles.

NON-IMPORTATION

The Stamp Act was designed to take effect on November 1, 1765. In October, a Stamp Act Congress met in the city of New York with representatives from nine colonies in attendance. The governors of Virginia, North Carolina, and Georgia prevented any delegates from attending, and the legislature in New Hampshire simply sent word of its support. The Congress prepared a resolution, which it sent to King George III and Parliament, requesting the repeal of the Stamp Act and the Revenue Acts of 1764. The petition also asserted that the basic rights of the colonials had been violated by Parliament's attempt to tax them without their consent. Many merchants pledged not to import British goods until the offending acts were repealed. Those who did not pledge faced open intimidation by the mob, which fashioned itself into a high-sounding Continental Association. Yet even in the face of growing discontent, London went forward with the printing of thousands of stamps and dispatched them to the colonies. For some Americans, the audacity of the government in this regard outraged them more than the legislation.[6]

The non-consumption aspect of the resistance effort took on the form of agreements not to purchase a stated list of imported wares and to lend all encouragement to the domestic manufacture of replacement items. Many of these items were favorites among the middle and upper classes, but the list reflected the general parsimony of the wider community that favored a general reduction of unnecessary expenses and a rejection of conspicuous consumption. Nevertheless, the effort did not escape the criticism of many among the wealthy friends of the government who felt that their lifestyles were being sacrificed on the altar of political protest.

The resistance to the Stamp Act was more active and more physical than many history texts would suggest, and the tea protests pale by comparison. For this reason, the appointment of colonial stamp agents turned out to be a crucial mistake that insured the failure of the stamp policy. Colonial stamp distributors, their property, homes, and families were simply too vulnerable to the displeasure voiced by their neighbors in the mob to carry out their obligations. This factor caused most of the agents to resign their posts as soon as the level of protest over the stamps rose above tavern mutterings to become street demonstrations. No polite political rhetoric was to be found here. Government officials on the Crown side of the stamp issue faced an outraged, outspoken, and resolute populace, who engaged them at every possible opportunity, both public and private. Hidden among the catcalls, insults, and mockery were some well-reasoned arguments, solid constitutional points, and appeals for the protection of the rights of Englishmen.

One month after the imposition of the non-importation agreements, the Stamp Act took effect. In some colonies on that day, all business was suspended. In others, the law was ignored or rendered unenforceable. Almost everywhere, colonists refused to permit the landing of the stamps on American shores, and frightened government employees placed those that were landed under protective custody. Those Stamp Act agents, who had not already resigned their posts, hid in their homes and refused to appear in public. In Massachusetts, many fled to the protection of the provincial troops in Boston. In New York, violence broke out when a mob gathered to burn the royal governor in effigy and harassed the troops with a surprising lack of regard for their own safety. Several homes were invaded and looted. Windows were broken and fires set in the streets. Only the restraint practiced by the soldiers and their officers prevented an exchange of gunfire. It must be noted that at this time these were colonial troops (provincials) under the command of the governor or files of Royal Marines seconded from the navy, rather than red-coated regulars. The regulars would not arrive in large numbers until 1768, and then they would be sent to intimidate Boston, not New York.

The Royal Navy played a significant roll during the height of the stamp crisis. With the legislatures and many of the governors on the side of the colonials, the ships of the Royal Navy were often the only practical instruments of British authority left in the colonies. However, it should be noted that the Admiralty gave its naval commanders much greater freedom of action than the Board of Trade allowed its governors or army commanders. Moreover, the naval and military commanders, the customs officials, the stamps agents, and the governors were not part of a continuous chain of command. This was one of the weaknesses of the empire's bureaucracy, with each reporting to his own distinct superior. All that was expected of them was polite cooperation between the services and the branches of colonial government.

The pattern for resistance to the stamps was set in Boston, and it was in Boston also that the Royal Navy attempted to fashion a practical response to the problem presented by the protests. When the local stamp agent Andrew Oliver was intimidated into resigning his office, the governor, Francis Bernard, took steps to save the stamps from the populace. This seems slightly ridiculous to us today, but the governor was aware that the mob had designs on the paper stamps themselves for the purpose of propaganda. Turning the stamps over to the colonials, or allowing them to be destroyed, would have been "greatly humiliating and derogatory to His Majesty's government."[7]

Governor Bernard asked Captain Thomas Bishop of HMS *Fortune*, then the senior naval officer in Boston, to take the crates of stamps aboard his ship and secure them until they could be unloaded at Castle William on an island in the harbor. He also asked that the navy intercept any ships from England carrying additional shipments of stamps for other colonies. Several days later, the merchant ship *John Galley* arriving from London was intercepted with additional packages of stamps for Rhode Island, which were also deposited at Castle William. No one dared to even open the packages for inspection.

By way of contrast, the colonial protests against the stamps and the stamp agents in Rhode Island quickly turned violent, even though the stamps had not arrived. At the time, HMS *Cygnet* (commanded by Charles Leslie) was the largest warship in the harbor at Newport. The local stamp agent, Augustus Johnston, the chief customs agent, John Robinson, and several of their friends retreated to the warship in fright when riots broke out. Leslie ran out *Cygnet*'s guns and made a great show of clearing the ship for action and preparing to repel

The hated tax stamps came to the colonies in sheets of different values to be affixed to documents, like the postage stamps of today. Printers were also required to purchase stamped paper stock or affix the stamps with glue. (Library of Congress.)

boarders by raising the nettings and distributing cutlasses and pikes to the crew. This ploy kept the rioters at a distance.

New York was always a hotbed of antigovernment protest. The struggle for political dominance in New York, however, was no unevenly matched contest between mobs of like-minded citizens and a few customs officials as it was in Boston or Newport. No place in America was so evenly split in its loyalties. From first to last, Patriot sympathizers and government Loyalists were in constant conflict and turmoil. Even the colonial legislature was split between the powerful pro-Loyalist DeLancey and pro-Patriot Livingston families.[8]

Captain Archibald Kennedy was posted to New York as its chief naval officer on HMS *Coventry*. He was himself the son of a customs collector from New York, and his property became a pawn in the hands of the mob led by New York radicals, like Isaac Sears and Alexander McDougall, former privateers and Sons of Neptune, who now became leaders of the Liberty Boys, or Sons of Liberty. The New York stamp agent, James McEvers, immediately resigned, leaving the colonial lieutenant governor, Cadwallader Colden, responsible for the stamps until the newly appointed governor, Sir Henry Moore, should arrive. Colden was sure that the Liberty Boys intended to seize the stamps, which he had Kennedy shift to Fort George at the tip of Manhattan Island.[9]

Meanwhile, on November 1, 1764, the Liberty Boys in New York staged a particularly effective demonstration, massing several thousand protestors and penetrating the outer defenses of Fort George. This protest gave Colden great concern, and he immediately deliberated with the City Council and decided to hand over the stamps to representatives of the mob before their persistence brought on a bloody conflict with the garrison of the fort. The protestors burned 10 boxes of stamps as an example to the government of their power and then retired. This incident was a major blow to royal prestige in New York and elsewhere in the colonies.

The stamps for South Carolina and Georgia reposed for some time in the hold of HMS *Speedwell* (commanded by Robert Fanshawe). Thereafter, South Carolina's stamps were permanently deposited at Fort Johnson in Charleston never to be used. Upon receipt of Georgia's stamps, however, Governor James Wright actually attempted to issue them and put the Stamp Act into practice. Wright was notable as the only governor to actually have issued documents with the stamps attached. Although Fanshawe supported the governor with a detachment of marines, Wright backed down as soon as a mob of protestors appeared before his home. The stamps were returned to the hold of Fanshawe's ship.

In every colony the stamps spent at least some time under the protection of the Royal Navy; and, with the exception of those few stamps burned in New York and a handful issued in Georgia, no others were destroyed or taken. The navy had done its part during the crisis, but the Stamp Act had been a total failure as a source of revenue and as a government policy. Although the act had failed miserably everywhere in the colonies, London considered what happened in New York the worst failure of the whole Stamp Act affair. In March 1766, after being warned of a possible armed revolt, Parliament repealed the Stamp Act.

The Stamp Act protest united all the colonies from Maine to Georgia, was successful everywhere that it was employed, and experienced very little domestic opposition. It is with great difficulty that researchers can unearth expressions of support for the stamps from among any but Crown officials. Finally, it was eminently successful in backing down the stated objectives of Parliament and of embarrassing the ministry. The king dismissed Grenville shortly thereafter.

The Grenville government had passed the Stamp Act, but the Rockingham administration that followed inherited all the troubles that it had caused. Parliament's repeal of the Stamp Act was greeted with great rejoicing in the colonies. Both spontaneous and deliberate celebrations were initiated, and nighttime illuminations and bonfires were held in many cities. The *New York Mercury* reported that more than 1,000 Liberty Boys met in celebration in New Jersey at the Sussex County courthouse.[10] However, the vigor with which the colonials had responded to the stamp tax caused an unfortunate reaction by the Rockingham ministry.[11]

PIN MONEY

On the same day that it repealed the Stamp Act, the Rockingham administration passed the Declaratory Act, which stated that Parliament had the total right to legislate any laws governing the American colonies in all cases whatsoever. Seen as a face-saving device, the Declaratory Act seems to have produced little colonial reaction at the time, and the boycott of English goods was generally relaxed. However, at least some of the more radical thinkers in the colonies saw the Declaratory Act as "a statue, laid up for future use, like a sword in a scabbard."[12]

In 1766, Charles Townshend became Lord of the Exchequer, the department of government that levied and collected taxes and duties. Townshend was directly opposed to any policy of caution or moderation with respect to the colonies. He proposed a series of revenue measures to help pay for the administration and security of the colonies and thereby relieve the burden on the British taxpayer in England.

The demands made on America might not have been as great had London extended these measures to the entire empire and tapped its resources in India. However, Townshend was a champion of the charter rights of the EIC and a friend to many of the directors of the Company who also served on the Board of Trade. *He declared all revenues derived from India to be the property of the company and free from taxation.* He further materially reduced the tax burden on landlords in Britain, who he considered "harassed country gentlemen." These decisions further increased the portion of the revenues to be derived from America. No course of action by the government in London could have been calculated to more arouse colonial resentment.[13]

There was a good deal of resistance to the passage of the bill in England, and although Townshend died suddenly in 1767, the Townshend Revenue Act "stole through the House; no man knew how."[14] The duties were reissued and expanded in 1769 over the protests of a vociferous Patriot Whig minority, which generally supported the colonial position on taxation for its own political purposes. The duties set taxes on a vast number of "goods and commodities of growth, produce, or manufacture of the British Colonies." These fell into two groups, distinguished as enumerated or non-enumerated. Those enumerated items included "tobacco, cotton, wool, indigo, ginger, fustick, or other dying woods; pitch, tar, turpentine, hemp, masts, yards, and bowsprits; sugar, molasses, rice, tea, coffee, pimento, cocoa nuts, and raw silk; beaver skins, hides, deerskins, and leather; copper ore, whale fins, and potash."[15]

The list of enumerated items encompassed almost all the yield of colonial production on the North American continent and in the islands of the Caribbean. A number of the articles—tobacco, indigo, ginger, dying woods, and cocoa—were subject to duties even when they were simply shipped between colonies. In theory, a paper of dressmakers' pins moved by rowboat less than a mile across the Hudson River from Manhattan to New Jersey was subject to duty, and if undeclared at customs was considered smuggled goods resulting in prosecution, a fine, and seizure of the vessel and all its cargo. One can only surmise that the authors of the law in London were grossly unaware of its implications in the colonies. Perhaps they did not read the bill before they passed it. Modern readers can better appreciate the inconvenience experienced by their forbearers if they imagine having to produce tax receipts for all the goods in their automobiles every time they crossed from one state to the next.

There were also enumerated items that were subject to duties when imported directly from Britain. These were largely comfort items desired by the affluent and nearly affluent, and they included Spanish,

Portuguese and all other wines except French ones, which were prohibited; all teas; red and white lead (used in house paint); white, red,
and green glass; dressmakers' pins, all sorts of paper; and artist's colors. The non-enumerated items, mostly iron and builders lumber,
could be shipped to Britain without a duty. However, the shipper had
to post a cash bond in silver coin of twice the value of the cargo, and
he was subject to forfeiture of the bond, his vessel, and the cargo if he
landed them, even by accident, in any part of Europe except Britain
and specified parts of Ireland.[16]

Reams of paper were made so expensive by the duty that colonial
newspapers resorted to making their newssheets physically smaller.
The *Pennsylvania Chronicle* noted that a simple paper of dressmakers'
pins had gone from 10d. to 2s. (24d.), a 140 percent increase, "and
other articles were equally high in proportion."[17]

It is obvious why the increased price of paper turned many printers and newspaper editors against the government policy, but the high
cost of pins was much more effective in raising the temper of America's
women. Ben Franklin specifically chose common pins as an example
when he condemned the duties as destructive of good government in
1773, and the First Continental Congress took note of the increase in
their price and recommended a boycott of pins to the public in 1774
(*New York Gazette*, October 6, 1774). If the level of protest against tea
seems extreme, the protest over pins seems incomprehensible unless
the reader knows its context.

The production of pins and sewing needles was absolutely prohibited outside of Britain, yet it was the type of small business enterprise
that Americans were willing to do and were capable of performing. In
a letter to her husband John in Congress in 1775, Abigail Adams wrote
that she especially needed pins, and she would give $10 (Continental)
for a thousand. There were 6,000 pins in a common merchant's bun-
dle. Besides their obvious use in sewing, pins (along with tapes and
ties) were essential to the arrangement of fashionable 18th-century female attire. A paper of 100 pins would have been an appropriate gift
from a young man romantically interested in a young woman, and a
small pillow with a sentiment wrought in pins was a nice gift for a wedding couple or the birth of a child. The request for pins between John
and Abigail Adams is used as a repeated metaphor for their love in the
Broadway musical *1776*. Patriot women made a great fuss over their
pins and sewing needles and might spend an entire hour on hands and
knees searching for one that had dropped to the ground. Many women
resorted to using the spiny natural thorns from the Hawthorn tree as
a substitute for pins out of doors.

Economist Adam Smith opened his famous *Wealth of Nations* (1776) with an analysis of the types of labor required in a pin factory—as suggested by an entry he read in Diderot's illustrated *Encyclopedia or a Systematic Dictionary of the Sciences, Arts and Crafts* (released in separate progressive volumes between 1751 and 1762). Smith noted of the process, "The important business of making a pin is . . . divided into about eighteen distinct operations, which in some manufactories are all performed by distinct hands, though in others the same man will sometime perform two or three of them." For Smith, a pin factory was no trifling industry. Had pin manufacturers adopted his concept of *division of labor*, they might have produced thousands of pins a day instead of hundreds.[18]

London expected the Townshend duties to produce £40,000 per year of revenue, but their enforcement was likely to require a greater amount of expense. As enforcement of the acts increased, "the colonists resisted with greater stubbornness." Legitimate imports from Britain fell from £2.2 million to £1.3 million in a single year (1768–1769). In Philadelphia, imports from Britain were cut in half from £400,000 to £200,000, and in New York they fell from £500,000 to a mere £75,000. Not only was the royal exchequer denied its increased revenue, but merchants, manufacturers, and ship owners throughout the empire were denied a great deal of business. The result of raising taxes was a severe depression of the British economy that added to unemployment and underemployment, especially among the maritime workers on the waterfront, and it increased the call for political change and enhanced economic opportunity elsewhere. Sound familiar?[19]

By the winter of 1767, colonials everywhere were searching for new methods to oppose or confound Parliament, and many chose to resurrect the boycotts. A chief oversight of the non-importation agreements used to force the repeal of the Stamp Act, however, was to provide against the drinking of tea, one of the imported articles on which a large sum was spent annually by all classes of Americans. Colonials purchased on average 500,000 pounds (by weight) of legal tea every year and probably as much again of the smuggled variety.

Beginning in December 1767, a number of women's groups agreed among themselves that they would use no foreign teas for a year. The genesis of the movement seems to have been truly organic, beginning in ladies' parlors, spoken of in town meetings, and spreading by means of reports in the press and through private correspondence. The women argued that the non-importation effort against tea should begin modestly and amongst themselves because "the Gentlemen at Taverns & Coffee Houses . . . drink scarcely anything but Wine and

Punch," whereas "among the Ladies at those useful *boards of trade* [italics added] called Tea Tables it [doesn't] cost half so much to entertain half a dozen Ladies a whole Afternoon, as it [does] to entertain one Gentlemen only one Evening at a Tavern."[20]

QUARTERING—A MATTER OF MONEY

The quartering bill was part of the Mutiny Act, which established a standing army for the protection of the empire, but its provisions were to cause a great deal of trouble with the colonial assemblies. Quartering placed additional stress on the already strained finances of the provincial legislatures, but it had little direct effect on individual citizens. Generations of American school children have left history classrooms believing that through quartering Britain had forced colonials to take red-coated troops under their roofs, eating and sleeping in their homes. This was not the case. Quartering was about money, not living space. Under the quartering provisions, the Parliament could extract a great part of the expense of "defending, protecting, and securing" the colonies without seeming to violate the constitutional principle of external taxation by simply obliging the provinces to pay the bills that the regulars accumulated while in America.[21]

Opposition to the Mutiny Act, which was a minor grievance during the Stamp Act crisis, now began to surface. The center of the storm was the city of New York. During the summer of 1766, violence broke out in the town. The mob, including the Sons of Liberty, was protesting in support of the legislature's continued refusal to comply with the quartering provisions by paying for the food, fuel, and fodder of the regulars. After noting the growing groundswell of disquieting events and fearing a repetition of the Stamp Act resistance, the Crown, with an increasingly ill William Pitt serving as prime minister, suspended the New York legislature for its continued refusal to comply with the quartering law. The ministry may have had the power to suspend the legislature, but most colonials considered that they did not have the right to do so. Understanding that this time London would not be intimidated as it was concerning the stamps, most of the colonies refused to follow New York's lead. Yet only Pennsylvania executed the quartering provisions to the letter of the law. The other provinces granted provisions to the troops through acts or bills of their own devising, thereby preserving the appearances of constitutional principles and their own freedom of action. This raised a cry of outrage and charges of hypocrisy from among the Boston radicals, which prevented any more supplies being voted. Thereafter, much of New England followed Massachusetts' example and ignored the authority of the law.[22]

Colonial opposition to the Mutiny Act created a series of strange alliances in Parliament that joined the liberal wing of the Whig Party and the Tories in an effort to punish the colonies for their ill behavior. This reaction was exacerbated by the illness of Pitt, who failed to control the House Commons from his seat among the Lords. It is here that the continued effect of instability in the post of prime minister can most clearly be seen. Without a strong political head, Parliament seems to have taken on an unwise course with respect to America with little regard for its possible consequences.

The colonials were perfectly serious in their belief that taxation by Parliament—or any legislation that affected the colonies and not the general population of the empire without their consent or at least their sufferance—was a violation of their constitutional rights. The dissolution of the New York legislature seemed to verify America's worst fears of an impending tyranny. However, many in London considered the colonial arguments simple fabrications designed to avoid paying taxes. Using the idea that the Americans would trump up novel arguments against external taxes as easily as they had against internal ones, Tories in Parliament pressed for new bills with unfortunate similarities to the Stamp Act. However, it seems certain that everyone in Parliament understood the need to exercise the right to tax America at this time, and many foresaw the colonial ambition to become a nation of independent states creeping over the horizon. Lieutenant Governor Hutchinson went so far as to suggest the "abridgement" of the "rights of Englishmen" for all colonials who continued to dispute the power of Parliament to legislate for the colonies.[23]

The greatly enlarged customs bureaucracy imposed by Parliament was the feature of these policies that most annoyed the colonials. A Patriot pamphlet referred to the customs officials as "miscreants, blood suckers, whores, and Cossacks."[24] Taxation now became a test of political wills. More than any other issue of the period, this one served to "radicalized such key [American] figures as Henry Laurens and John Hancock." It was becoming obvious that the Anglo-Americans would either throw off completely Parliament's right to tax them or submit to the total sovereignty of the Crown. The middle ground of continued compromise was quickly disappearing, and those who did not choose sides were attacked by both extremes.[25]

THE CIRCULAR LETTERS

In February 1768, the radical faction in the Massachusetts General Court sent a message to the assemblies of the other colonies urging a united resistance to the Townshend duties. This message was called the *Circular Letter*. It was designed to throw up an impregnable defense against taxation by Parliament in every colony and to make certain that colonial liberties were not undermined in the guise of imposing mere trade duties and regulations. The Virginia House of Burgesses followed with a circular letter of its own in March. Most Americans saw no fault with the circular letters as simple attempts to redress grievances with the Parliament, but by June, the Sons of Liberty in Boston, at the instigation of Sam Adams, James Otis, and John Hancock, had mobbed royal officials and rioted in the streets. Many conservative colonials viewed the riots and the harassment of royal officials as intemperate, disrespectful, and disloyal, and the circular letters were widely blamed for inciting the violence. British officials in London were keenly aware of the renewed colonial unrest brought on by the Townshend legislation, and many members of Parliament considered the circular letters "little better than an incentive to rebellion."[26]

Lord Hillsborough, who had become colonial secretary at Townshend's death, decided to take a firmer stand with the colonies by ordering the governor of Massachusetts to dissolve the General Court. He also dispatched four regiments of British regulars to Boston. Knowing of the uproar created by the suspension of the New York legislature, it is a wonder what his thinking was, but it is plain that he expected trouble. The presence of the regulars was clearly intended to intimidate the colonists into submission and to suppress dissent. They accomplished neither of these desired outcomes. Landing in the colony in October 1768, two of the four regiments were immediately detached for service in Halifax, Nova Scotia, leaving the remaining units woefully undermanned and generally incapable of effectively dealing with the insurgent Bostonians who badgered and provoked the soldiers pitilessly.

A warship of 50 guns, *Preston*, was summoned by the customs officials in Boston to enter the harbor to add psychological support to the presence of the regulars, but it had little effect largely because almost no one in Boston thought the Royal Navy would actually fire on the city. Additional warships were added to the harbor fleet with equal lack of success. Some of these vessels, particularly *Asia (64)*, *Somerset (68)*, and *Boyne (70)*, requiring deeper waters than those of the generally shallow harbor, were confined to the deeper shipping channels. They could, therefore, neither maneuver among the marshlands nor get into position to effectively bombard the shore. The total effect of the troops and ships was to make Boston look and feel like a besieged city rather than one under the benign protection of the Crown.

Taking British restraint for license, the unremitting upheaval in Boston had spread to the other colonies. In March 1769, the merchants of Philadelphia joined the boycott of British goods, and in May, the royal governor dissolved the Virginia House of Burgesses for its continued opposition to the acts of Parliament. The burgesses simply met the next day at the Raleigh Tavern in Williamsburg and agreed to a boycott of British goods, luxury items, and even slaves.

In New York in January 1770, the Sons of Liberty clashed with 40 British soldiers over the public posting of antigovernment broadsheets. Violence had erupted when British soldiers hacked down the city's liberty pole, prompting a mob to set on them with clubs and cutlasses. Soon more soldiers joined the fray, charging the crowd with fixed bayonets across a hill and up a slope in a struggle sometimes called the Battle of Golden Hill. Several men on both sides were seriously injured, but none were killed. Parliament retaliated by ordering that all Americans accused of agitating on the topic of taxation be sent to England for trial on charges of treason.

The expectation that the Royal Navy would not fire on colonial cities ultimately proved false. *Rose, Swan,* and *Glasgow* bombarded a number of coastal towns in Rhode Island and Connecticut in 1775 just days after Lexington and Concord; and *Asia, Rose,* and *Phoenix* opened broadsides several times on New York City in 1776. A formal policy of bombarding towns into submission appears to have begun as early as September 1775, but its application was not ratcheted up until after 1779 in response to the French alliance. During the course of the war, British vessels bombarded or burned every colonial seaport of appreciable size with the exception of Baltimore and Salem.

A GLORIOUS FUNERAL

Throughout the winter of 1769–1770, daily life in Boston was marked by numerous clashes between soldiers and civilians in the streets. As yet no one had died in the protests or their policing. Both sides waited for the one incident that would spill over into irreconcilable violence. In February 1770, Ebenezer Richardson, a customs official and friend of Thomas Hutchinson of Massachusetts, killed an unfortunate young Bostonian during a protest, and many thought that the killing was the spark that might ignite the ultimate crisis.

Richardson was a notorious customs informer. As an opponent of the radicals and an outspoken friend of the Crown, he had recently been heard goading the Patriots, "Let 'em come on me. I'm ready, for I've guns loaded." Beyond Richardson's tendency toward bluster, he may have acted in self-defense. A crowd of protestors had surrounded his house adding eggs and stones to a variety of missiles. With all the windows of the house broken, Richardson's wife and two daughters came under attack, and his wife was struck by a rock. At this point, Richardson had decided to arm his weapon, loading it with swan shot (pea-sized pellets) and aiming it at the swirling mass of boys and adults.[27]

Ultimately, he pulled the trigger, promiscuously spraying the crowd with shot. One in the mob was nicked, another slightly wounded, and the last received a mortal wound. This was an 11-year-old lad named Christopher Seider (a.k.a. Snyder and Snider). Among the doctors who rushed to treat him was Thomas Young. He and Dr. Joseph Warren labored until evening to save the boy's life. Seider died soon after 9:00 P.M. Meanwhile, the crowd had multiplied from the insistent tolling of the bell in a nearby church. Only through the intervention of William Molineaux and other radical leaders was Richardson saved from an immediate hanging. He was briskly taken to the relative safety of Faneuil Hall. After some days, Hutchinson allowed Richardson to avoid immediate prosecution by claiming self-defense. The Boston radicals were outraged, and they vowed to wipe out the entire system of customs houses and customs officials. In the wake of the Boston Massacre some weeks later, Richardson was arraigned and jailed until George III eventually granted him a pardon at the request of Hutchinson, an act that further isolated the governor from the population of the city.[28]

Seider was a poor immigrant German who worked in the nearby home of a wealthy woman in the North End. The boy ultimately received a glorious funeral. Sam Adams and the Sons of Liberty succeeded in staging the affair with full pomp. The *Boston Gazette* described the procession as containing "five hundred schoolboys . . . a very numerous Train of Citizens . . . [and] at least two thousand of all Ranks, amidst a crowd of spectators."[29] The Sons of Liberty ordered a board affixed to the Liberty Tree with biblical verses concerning the need to punish the wicked. Even Hutchinson agreed that it was "the largest [funeral] perhaps ever known in America." The killing and its aftermath received widespread notoriety in all the colonies. Newspapers in New York and Philadelphia reported the details of the shooting in particularly gruesome detail, while using the incident to drive home the baseness of the customs officials and the effect of the incident on the rebellious mood of the town.[30]

THE BOSTON MASSACRE

Early in the winter of 1770, a group of soldiers in Boston was accosted by a mob armed with clubs. One soldier received a significant wound from a blow served up with a bit of iron bar, and the mob was driven away only by the discharge of a musket into the air. Excepting the gunfire, the incident was becoming so commonplace as to warrant no further remark.

Thereafter, however, mobs of colonials and Liberty Boys, egged on by radical leaders, roamed the streets spoiling for a fight in the belief that the regulars would not fire upon them. "The soldiers nerves were frayed to a ragged edge," as singly and in pairs they were set upon in alleys or along the darkened wharfs. Colonel Dalrymple, the British regimental commander in Boston noted, "I don't suppose my men are without fault but twenty of them have been knocked down in the streets . . . and no more has been heard of it, whereas if one of the inhabitants meets with no more than just a kick for an insult to a soldier, the town is immediately in an alarm."[31]

Unfortunately, the colonials came to believe that they could harass the troops with impunity. In March, less than two weeks after the Seider killing, a group of radicals headed by a free African American named Crispus Attucks confronted a squad of soldiers near the customs house. Many in the crowd were carrying clubs. The British soldiers, frightened by the threats and taunts of the mob, opened fire on the crowd at point-blank range. Attucks and two others were killed instantly and two more were mortally wounded. The colonials spread the false rumor that a group of small boys casting snowballs had brought on the resulting clash, and Paul Revere quickly issued a less-than-accurate engraving of the event that supported the details espoused in the Patriot propaganda. The victims were buried with great ceremony at the same gravesite as young Seider.

The political leaders of the Boston mob labeled the incident a massacre and demanded the arrest and trial for murder of the soldiers and their commander, Captain Thomas Preston. Consequently, the

**Paul Revere made a particularly effective, if inac-
curate, engraving of the incident that served to
inflame many throughout the colonies. (Library of
Congress.)**

soldiers were confined, but no one could be found to act in their defense. Finally, John Adams and Josiah Quincy of Braintree, Massachusetts, volunteered to act as their attorneys and provided a defense
sufficient to acquit Preston and all his men of murder, save two who
were convicted of manslaughter and branded on the thumb as a punishment. The branding was evidence of the mercy of court given once
and never to be extended to these men again. Thereafter, Hutchinson
prudently requested the withdrawal of the regular troops from the
city streets to an island garrison in the harbor to prevent further
incidents.

THE TEA TAX

One of the odd circumstances surrounding the Boston Tea Party
was the fact that the protest followed a proposed decrease in the tax on
tea. From the time of the Townshend duties, colonials had paid 6d. per
pound tax on tea, which was fixed within the retail price (as are all taxes

passed along by sellers as a part of their cost of doing business). This tax was to be cut in half under the Tea Act of 1773 and given indirectly to the EIC. Moreover, a modern analysis suggests that the individual American colonial was much less taxed on average than his counterpart in Britain who "paid as much as a third of his income to the government . . . in the form of various sales and excise taxes." Of course, there were many more poor people in Britain than in America who had no tax burden at all—the bulk of the taxes in England being paid by the fabulously wealthy landlords, market speculators, and corporate businessmen whereas the burden of taxation in America fell largely on the rising middle class. Yet taxes in America were rising at a rapid rate, and the burden came to reside on a smaller and smaller fraction of the population, particularly those whose meager wealth came from private business and agriculture. "After 1750 the tax burden in New York and Boston almost doubled, and in Philadelphia it rose as much as 250 percent." It was the rapid change made to the economic environment, especially through the strict enforcement of regulations that had formerly been neglected, which caused the level of protest to rise.[32]

In April 1770, under the new ministry of Lord Frederick North, the Mutiny Act failed to be renewed and the Townshend Acts were repealed by Parliament. That is, all the duties were repealed except that which taxed tea, which Parliament, once again, retained as a symbol of their right to tax the colonies. Subsequently, with the repeal, "all except the most radical [of colonials] withdrew from the protest movement." Moderate Americans were willing to pay the new 3d. tax or even the former 6d. on a pound of tea that they had paid for several years, as long as the tax was collected from the merchants in England and not in the colonies.[33]

For the radicals in America like Sam Adams the question of the tea tax was a fairly focused one of due process under the British Constitution, as the consumer would pay the tax in either case.[34] A cynic might suggest that the legitimate economic complaints posed by the tea tax were so inconsequential that Americans chose to couch their protests in terms of violations of their civil liberties in order to justify them. Moreover, the customs facilities, regulations, and the royal officials needed to enforce the collection of duties remained in place. The warships and troops sent to intimidate the colonials also remained on station or in barracks, if not patrolling the streets and the harbor inlets. For little more than a year after the repeal of the Townshend duties, the colonies were marked by an uncharacteristic lack of cooperation among the colonials themselves. Radicals like Adams, Otis, and

Hancock seemed frustrated in their attempts to keep the fires of protest burning at the cost of a mere 3 pennies.

THE BURNING OF *GASPÉE*

In 1772, the uneasy quiet was suddenly changed into overt violence. The Royal Navy cutter *Gaspée*, commanded by Lieutenant William Dudingston, intercepted the colonial packet *Hannah*, commanded by Benjamin Lindsay, in Narragansett Bay. The master of the *Hannah*, inbound to Providence from New York on his regular run, refused to heave to and have his papers examined. Although he had done so many times before, Lindsay, annoyed by Dudingston's arrogant and officious manner in the past, had taken advantage of a fresh wind, an ebb tide, and a shallow draft to avoid the cutter, which ran aground on a sand bar. A frustrated Dudingston sat aboard the stranded cutter, waiting for the flood tide to float it off.

The *Hannah* continued on to Providence where word spread of the revenue cutter's stranding. Eight longboats under the direction of Abraham Whipple and John Brown were launched, each filled with vengeful colonials armed with staves, stones, and a few firearms. In the dead of night, the colonials overwhelmed the crew of the lightly armed *Gaspée* and burned the vessel to the waterline. Dudingston, who was wounded during the encounter, was then arrested on a specious charge and fined by the local sheriff. This almost inexplicable turn of events, wrought upon the hapless Dudingston in the performance of his duty, ended when his admiral paid the lieutenant's fine.

The burning of its vessel and the detention of its officer outraged the government in London, but a special Royal Navy investigation chaired by Judge Robert Auchmuty, Jr. under the authority of the vice-admiralty courts failed to make any recommendations for avoiding similar events in the future. The colonial government of Rhode Island expressed its regrets and sympathy over the incident, and a reward of £500 was posted for information leading to the arrest of the attackers. However, no one could be found to identify the assailants, even though the pledged amount represented several years' income for a common laborer.

The burning of *Gaspée* serves to highlight the deteriorated state of central control and the ambiguous nature of authority that came to characterize colonial government in this period. Governor Joseph Wanton of Rhode Island had positioned himself on the committee

Eight longboats under the direction of Captain Abraham Whipple were launched, each filled with vengeful colonists armed with staves, stones, and a few firearms. In the dead of night, the colonials overwhelmed the crew of the lightly armed vessel and burned it to the waterline. (Author's collection.)

to be able to limit the effectiveness of the naval inquiry and frustrate Auchmuty and Andrew Oliver (Hutchinson's in-law), who also sat on the board of inquiry. While no proof of overt collusion has come to light, it is thought that Wanton conspired with his own Deputy Governor Darius Sessions to provide creative counter-testimony to the actual facts of the case. Wanton also revealed to the colonial assembly a letter written to him from Lord Dartmouth discussing the Crown's intent to have the perpetrators of the attack tried in London and publicly executed for high treason. However, he failed to support independence and was deposed by the assembly in 1775. It still remains unclear in the *Gaspée* incident why so many colonials should have so quickly taken advantage of this particular opportunity to express their resentment toward the Royal Navy, which had patrolled the same waters without a remarkable incident for several months.

COMMITTEES OF CORRESPONDENCE

During 1772 and 1773, many colonials formed themselves into committees, whose purpose was to maintain communications with other towns and cities. The first such *committee of correspondence* was formed at a Boston town meeting called by Sam Adams. The committee had 21 members. Similar groups were formed in Virginia, New Hampshire, Rhode Island, Connecticut, and South Carolina. Many persons, who would come to lead the revolution, were among the initial members. The committees were important because they served as the first mechanism for welding the separate colonies into a unified body.

In November 1772, the committee in Boston, under the leadership of Sam Adams, issued an anti-British publication known as the *Boston Pamphlet*. Bound with a simple thread stitch, as were many such inexpensive publications, the pamphlet categorically attacked the British positions on taxation, standing armies, admiralty courts, jury trials, and support for the established church. The *Boston Pamphlet* was widely circulated throughout the colonies through the efforts of the individual committees of correspondence. The government in London miscalculated throughout both the potential economic effect of its policies and the breadth of the reaction to them. As relations deteriorated between New England and Britain, the Crown repeatedly responded with the worst possible moves. These political counterstrokes caused the level of protest to rise above tavern mutterings to become street demonstrations and violent attacks.

CHAPTER 5

The Marketplace of Ideas

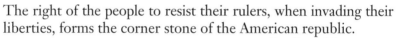

The right of the people to resist their rulers, when invading their liberties, forms the corner stone of the American republic.

—Dr. David Ramsey, 1789

I esteem it above all things necessary to distinguish exactly the business of civil government from that of religion and to settle the just bounds that lie between the one and the other. If this is not done, there can be no end put to the controversies that will be always arising between them.

—John Locke, On Toleration, *1689*

ALL FOR ONE

History teachers are fond of dividing the political parties in America into Tories and Whigs as if they lined up on separate sides of the street during demonstrations and taunted one another. This is not quite right. In the colonies, political factions were much more often aligned in terms of planters versus merchants, shippers versus traders, high-born versus commoner, or any of a number of other party, social, or religious affiliations based on one or more qualitative characteristics.

The political opposition to the Crown considered all those friendly to the king to be Tories, but those who regarded the Sons of Liberty as misguided generally failed to form themselves into a formal party. The majority of Tories in America—outside the few government officials who had some obligation to voice a resistance—preserved for the most part "an arrogant silence toward the arguments of the opposition" and kept their political opinions to themselves. This seems to have been a natural consequence of their innate conservatism. As a result, so-called Toryism was all but eradicated in Massachusetts long before the first shot of the war was fired at Lexington.[1]

Some critics of the protests have observed that Anglo-American politics often pitted the New England colonies against any combination of all the others. When one considers the preeminence of Massachusetts in New England and of Boston in that colony, it often seemed even more pointedly as if it was the politics of the Patriots in Boston versus those of everyone else. In the aftermath of the Boston Tea Party, the Crown seemingly agreed with this proposition restructuring the Massachusetts government, curtailing free speech in its town meetings, filling the council with Crown appointees, and dispatching an army of occupation to Boston under a military governor, General Thomas Gage. As September 1774 ended, an increasingly distraught Gage, having served as governor for six months, wrote of the spreading controversy to Lord Dartmouth, the colonial secretary: "Your Lordship will know from various accounts, the extremities to which affairs are brought, and how this province [Massachusetts] is supported and abetted by the others beyond the conception of most people, and foreseen by none. The disease was believed to have been confined to the town of Boston, from whence it might have been eradicated no doubt without a great deal of trouble, and it might have been the case some time ago; but now it's so universal there is no knowledge where to apply the remedy."[2]

Within a month of Gage's arrival, Thomas Hutchinson was in London pouring additional poison in the ear of the king and demanding death warrants for John Hancock and both Adams. The king was familiar with Hancock and Sam Adams, but had never heard of his "brother" John Adams (they were cousins), except as a defender of his soldiers in the Boston Massacre case. The king suggested the arrest instead of William Molineaux of whom he had heard less favorable reports. The idea of the collective punishment of the whole population of the Massachusetts colony bothered some members in Parliament, and they spoke out against it in frustration as counterproductive. Nowhere else in Anglo-America were such extreme and reactionary steps taken, yet the treatment of Boston united the colonies in defiance. "The attack on traditional rights seemed so excessive, so unreasonable, that to explain Boston's plight, Americans entertained conspiracy theories about evil, grasping rulers in London."[3]

TORIES AND WHIGS

In the politics of the latter half of the 18th century, *Tory* was little more than an unfriendly epithet for politicians or other persons closely identified with the king. In England, the archaic Tory label was applied equally to the Prime Ministers Lord Bute (1762–1763) and Lord North (1770–1782), but only the former considered himself as such. All the politicians who served as prime minister during the American protests, save Bute, considered themselves Whigs. Yet Frederick North, serving as a Whig in cooperation with the Tories in implementing the Crown's policies, became one of the most hated men in the colonies.

It has been noted that the British government went through seven prime ministers from 1760 to 1782. North served for the last 12 of these years, encompassing almost the entire American crisis from the Boston Massacre to the end of the Revolutionary War. Upon the accession of George III in 1760, many of the old political distinctions in government had become obscured. The Whig factions became virtually distinct parties all of whom claimed the appellation of Whig, while the real political difference was between the "King's Friends" who supported the activist role of the Crown and those who generally opposed it. The most conservative Whig faction—the one that most closely mirrored American political thought and demands for a return to English constitutionalism—was the Patriot Whig Party, once numerous but a decided minority in Parliament in the 1760s and 1770s.

Unfortunately, the North coalition in Parliament held an overwhelming majority, and North had not the slightest doubt that Parliament—unlike our own government that supposedly has strict limits on its powers—had the absolute power and unlimited right to legislate for the population of the Empire on *any matter whatsoever*. For a royal government that arrogantly professed to have the power to direct the form of one's religion and the method of communicating with one's God, this proposition was startling and frightening in its potential consequences. Many Anglo-Americans rejected the assertions of Lord North out of hand, as overturning centuries of English constitutional history and legal practice since Magna Carta (1215) and reaffirmed in the English Bill of Rights (1689). Thomas Jefferson warned that if government were allowed to define the limits of its own powers in such a manner the result would be nothing short of despotism.[4]

Americans learned about Lord North and his policies largely from partisan essays and editorials that originally appeared in antigovernment British newspapers, and these made no attempt to report events in an objective manner. Americans concluded from these reports— many of which were supplied by like-minded friends resident in England—that their cause enjoyed broad support among the British people. One political rival observed of North that he was a "profoundly mediocre" administrator and "had no system or plan of conduct, [and] no knowledge of business."[5] Benjamin Hallowell, commissioner of the customs in Boston and possibly the town's second most hated resident official (after Hutchinson), complained that Americans enjoyed too great an access to the speeches made in the House of Commons by opponents of Lord North. He believed that this stream of biased information served only to inflame their passions against the administration. Sound familiar?[6]

During the 1760s, colonial newspapers began to identify particular persons or groups in America as Whigs (the Country Party) and Tories (the Court Party) based on their positions on the political issues of the day. These appellations were extended from those used in Britain, but they generally failed to describe the true political philosophy of either the *Patriots* or the so-called *Loyalists* in America.

In 1679, King Charles II had dissolved what was known as the Cavalier Parliament, which he had first summoned in 1661, a remarkable 18 years earlier. During the last years of this longest Parliament in history, a loose grouping of members, known as the Country Party, had opposed the Court's influence in its deliberations, particularly its attempts to secure votes through bribes and patronage. Those who fought most vigorously against the Court's corruption and its foreign policy also strongly opposed the persecution of Protestant nonconformists while remaining adamantly anti-Catholic. These Country Party members became Whigs. In reaction, a Tory ideology had developed that supported the supremacy of the Established Church, the royal dominance over Parliament, and the Corporation Act that restricted the admission into government of those following nonconforming religions.

A colonial newspaper of the 18th century explained to its American readers that the term *Whig* was first given to the Presbyterian *Whiggamores*, members of the Kirk Party in Scotland during the Wars of the Three Kingdoms (1650–1651), who were forced to survive on but-termilk whig, or whey, when they were persecuted by the established church. The nickname was later applied to those members, headed by Anthony Ashley Cooper, Earl of Shaftesbury (Locke's patron), who demanded the exclusion of James II from the English throne on the grounds of his supposed Catholicism. The term *Tory*, applied to An-glican churchman and their supporters, originally referred to Irish highwaymen who lived by plundering the innocent traveler, as did the established church in forcing tithes from religious dissenters. The ma-jority of Patriots were Protestant but not members of the Established Church (or only nominally so), hence the appellation. "Whig and Tory then are used only with allusion to the originals," disclaimed the edi-tor. "Such as trust to our common dictionaries for an explanation, will only deceive themselves."[7]

SENTIMENTAL TORYISM

The political paradigms that separated the factions among the Whigs in England were significant, yet by the time of the Boston Tea Party, the Tories had ceased to function as a cohesive political party, their power residing in forming ruling coalitions. Rarely throughout its history were the liberties of the common people of the empire ad-dressed among Toryism's foremost principles, in any case. The Whigs drew their political support from emerging industries and merchants, whereas the Tories relied on landed interests and the royal family.

Sentimental Toryism remained strong in both Britain and America, with the established Anglican Church being most closely associated with it in the colonies. Sentimental Toryism was highly traditional in its doctrine, harking back to Richard Hooker who had published a treatise to defend the Church of England against the Scottish Pres-byterianism of preachers like John Knox as early as 1593. Thomas Hobbes (*Leviathan*, 1651) and Robert Filmer (*Patriarcha*, ca. 1640) attacked the more democratic thinking and defended the divinely derived authority of the king, leading to John Locke's refutation of *Divine Rights* and the development of the theory of *Natural Rights*.

Among the influential political philosophies to evolve after the con-clusion of the English Civil Wars was that of Locke, who had been working on his theory of government for some time prior to the pub-lication of his work *Of Civil Government, Two Treatises* (1689). Herein, much of the political philosophy of American Patriots can be found.

Locke's *First Treatise* was a refutation of Filmer's earlier scripture-based thesis supporting the concept of a divinely appointed, unlimited, and hereditary monarchy. Locke's *Second Treatise* established the ascendency of natural law, the right of property (including a justification of slavery), the existence of a social contract between the people and their ruler(s), and the right to revolution when the contract was broken.

The opposing philosophies of Divine Rights and Natural Rights continued to run throughout the 17th and 18th centuries "with devious twists and turns through the labyrinths of respectable opinion."[8] Writing under the pseudonym "Candidus" in general contradiction to American radical thought, Reverend William Smith of Philadelphia published a political tract insisting on the benefits of continued British rule in America. In his argument, Smith referenced the work of Charles-Louis de Secondat, Baron de Montesquieu, to glorify "this beautiful system . . . our constitution . . . a compound of monarchy, aristocracy and democracy." Implacably opposed to independence, Candidus went so far as to claim that "independence and slavery [were] synonymous terms," repeatedly citing the profound and elegant philosopher David Hume against the subversive designs of American radicals.[9] The least the radicals could do was to consult the people before making a leap in the dark toward Independence. "Thus," wrote Smith, "we may be [done] out of our liberties, our property, our happiness, and plunged deeper and deeper into . . . war and bloodshed, without ever being consulted."[10] In an age during which the concept of a 24-hour news cycle was unimaginable, Smith was an able propagandist having speeches recorded in the newspapers, printed in pamphlets, and made available to the public before their inflammatory effects had worn off.

Smith was well read in Enlightenment theory. Both Montesquieu and Hume were among the moderate Enlightenment thinkers whose theories better applied to a Dutch- or Italian-style republic than to the ideological democracy of the radical American Patriots. Yet these same writers unwittingly combined to develop some of the ideas of English political liberalism such as the rights of the individual, the equality of all men, and the artificial nature of the political order.[11] Radical Enlightenment writers rejected British-style constitutional monarchy as a recipe for dividing sovereignty. They preferred what was effectively a modified monarchy encased in aristocracy.[12]

Several prominent British literary figures of the 18th century such as Dr. Samuel Johnson, Alexander Pope, and Jonathan Swift supported Toryism—the last writer producing numerous pro-Tory pamphlets until his death in 1745. Sentimental Toryism could be summed up in the 18th century as supporting—in a strict order of precedence—first, the God of the Anglican Church, then the monarchy in the person of the king, and finally the empire in terms of mercantilist economics. The welfare of the people (individuals) was generally ignored and was thought to be reflected in the welfare of the empire from which benefits supposedly overflowed to the people. "Thus each very opulent man . . . gathers round him a circle of the poorest of the people," wrote Oliver Goldsmith. "What they may then expect may be seen by turning our eyes to Holland, Genoa, or Venice, where the laws govern the poor, and the rich govern the law."[13]

LIFE, LIBERTY, HAPPINESS

Americans proposed an alternative menu to Church, king, and Empire in a series of novel *civil values*, including life, liberty, and the pursuit of happiness for individuals, the last of these firmly rooted in their continued accumulation, possession, and free disposal of their property (wealth). Lawrence Sterne, an observer of the foibles of human nature, noted in 1770 that no one of these three could be enjoyed in isolation, "the desire of life . . . is implanted in a person's nature, and the love of liberty and the enlargement of ones wealth are sister passions to it."[14]

The origin of these three specific qualities was not uniquely American and could be found in slightly altered form repeatedly in the political philosophies of the previous century, especially in the request for peace (safety from imminent execution), liberty, and prosperity in the *Grand Remonstrance of 1641*. The Grand Remonstrance was a long, wide-ranging document that listed all the grievances perpetrated on the people by King Charles I through his governance of both Church and State since the beginning of his reign. A half century later, in "A Letter Concerning Toleration" (1689), Locke also defined the so-called civil interest as including the right to life, liberty, and the possession of outward things. Locke had fled to Holland as a political refugee in 1683, and he returned in 1688 when the Glorious Revolution deposed James II. According to Locke, who was writing in defense of the revolution, it was the duty of the civil magistrate by the impartial execution of equal laws to secure all the people in the just possession of those things belonging to this life. The right to *happiness* so freely expounded by Americans in the 1770s was formerly expressed as a right to *prosperity*, or *property*, or *estate*, but these expressions were

thought to isolate too many persons experiencing no prosperity or
having no property or estate who, nonetheless, supported the idea of a
political revolution.

Locke also carefully wove this interconnection of life, liberty, and
property into the fabric of religious freedom, or at least religious toleration, which permeates all the radical political philosophies of the
period:

> No man complains of the ill management of his neighbor's affairs.
> No man is angry with another for an error committed in sow-
> ing his land or in marrying off his daughter. Nobody corrects a
> spendthrift for consuming his substance in taverns. Let any man
> pull down, or build, or make whatsoever expenses he pleases, no-
> body murmurs, nobody controls him; he has his liberty. But if any
> man does not frequent the [established] church . . . everyone is
> ready to be the avenger of so great a crime, and the zealots hardly
> have the patience to refrain from violence and rapine so long
> as . . . the poor man is, according to form, condemned to the loss
> of liberty, goods, or life . . . [and] deliver[ed] . . . to the executioner
> to be burnt alive . . . burning I say, literally, with fire.[15]

Locke defined war also in these terms as a state of enmity and destruction brought about by one person's (or one group's) premedi-
tated attempts on another's life, liberty, or property. The law of
self-preservation, integral to Locke's appreciation of life, allows that
those attacked may kill the attackers in self-defense and make war or
even revolution. It was this principle of *vital interests* that Americans
used to justify their revolt.

LIFE

Although "Liberty or Death" was widely proclaimed, just how the
empire threatened American lives in 1773, or how death and liberty
became conjoined is somewhat obscure. The essence of this interpretation seems again to originate with Locke. Ultimate sovereignty
according to Locke resided within the individual, not in the external
accoutrements of government or in the king. A man could not part
with his right to life by political compact, or by civil agreement, or
even by his own consent. Locke noted of the Glorious Revolution:
"The throne of our great restorer, our present King William, [was

made] good . . . in the consent of the people . . . being the only one of all lawful governments. . . . No man will have a legislator imposed upon him but whom he himself has chosen."[16]

Sam Adams referred to life inclusively as one with the three inviolable rights: personal security, personal liberty, and private property. Reverend John Allen proclaimed the foundations of American liberty from the pulpit of the Second Baptist Church in Boston in 1772:

> Americans have a privilege to boast of above all the world. They never were in bondage to any man . . . consider what English tyranny their forefathers fled from, what seas of distress they met with, what savages they fought with, what blood-bought treasures, as the dear inheritance of their lives, they have left to their children, and without any aid from the king of England; and yet after this, these free-born people must be counted rebels, if they will not loose every right of liberty, which their forefathers bought, with their blood, and submit again to English ministerial tyranny—O America! O America! . . . But suppose my Lord, that this should be the bloody intent of the ministry, to make the Americans subject to their slavery, then let blood for blood, life for life, and death for death decide the contention. This bloody scene can never be executed but at the expense of the destruction of England.[17]

Unfortunately, when working in concert with the Royal Army and Navy, the colonials had experienced only failure or disappointment. The struggle with France for North America had required the cooperation of the colonials and the British Army to a degree never before experienced. However, the effort was marred by ill feelings created during the initial tactical phases of the conflict. The Crown officials felt that they should have been met with gratitude for defending the colonies. Instead, the provincial legislatures resisted their propositions and treated the British military with disdain, ridicule, and even contempt. The massacre of Edward Braddock and his regulars on the Monongahela River, where only the cool response of the Virginia militia and the decisive actions taken by George Washington saved the majority of the survivors from total annihilation increased Americans' sense of self-importance and lowered the prestige of the royal government and the British military in their eyes.

American seamen, impressed into Crown service, had been ill-used or had sickened and died. Up to 70 percent of the estimated 2,000

American volunteers serving with the fleet in the final French war failed to return, and one-seventh of the thousands of colonials serving in the military land campaigns of the Seven Year's War had died, also mostly from sickness, disease, or privation.

Similar situations had continued in peacetime, especially during the Stamp Act crisis. When Lieutenant Thomas Allen, commanding the cutter *Gaspée*, put into Casco Bay, Maine, in 1764, he and his press gang were attacked by a mob. Lieutenant Thomas Laugharne of the cutter *Chaleur* received similar treatment in New York. When he appeared with his longboat at the city wharf, he was mobbed and made to surrender the handful of men he had pressed. He was then compelled to watch as his own longboat was removed from the water and burned in front of city hall. New York station commander Captain Archibald Kennedy in HMS *Coventry* thereafter recalled all his press gangs and became so chronically short of hands that his own warship was rarely able to leave its anchorage, thereby limiting its effectiveness.

In 1768, ships under Commodore Samuel Hood anchored in Boston where they could provide the most aid to the government and the customs officials. One of Hood's skippers immediately began impressing seamen from merchant vessels entering the harbor. The Massachusetts General Court protested Hood's presence and declared the impressment of seamen in peacetime illegal. Hutchinson proffered his own opinion as chief administrator of the colony that impressment was legal throughout the empire at any time, but even he found these actions ill-advised in light of the tenuous peace that was then holding in the city.[18] The ongoing dispute between the colonial administration and the General Court over the jurists' prerogatives was an underlying cause of unrest in Massachusetts. The dispute with Britain concerning impressment was not resolved in the revolution and would be taken up again as a cause célèbre in the War of 1812.

LIBERTY

Liberty—the natural absence from absolute and arbitrary power over one's life—was necessary to the preservation of human society and individual dignity. Liberty seems to have been distinguished among the writings of theorists from *freedom*, which had connotations involving the absence of bondage, personal responsibility, or legal obligation. Patriots demanded liberty or independence in the streets, but they rarely proclaimed freedom. In a society that recognized slavery and indenture and was structured in definite hierarchies, there was always the threat that calls for liberty and freedom would degenerate into license and undermine the structure of society—a society that still believed in the necessity of a ruling class.

Intellectuals among the Patriots often wrote or spoke of restoring their *political liberty* in terms of legislatures, rights, and privileges. A reader of Locke, Montesquieu, and other enlightened philosophers, Dr. Benjamin Rush of Pennsylvania became an advocate for progress based on a form of liberty, equality, and fraternity in which all men by their nature shared. All persons might be born equal and think of themselves as brothers in a cause, but their equality of station in society, in particular, went further than most Americans were willing to go. Other Americans like John Trenchard and Thomas Gordon argued in *Cato's Letters* (1774) for *economic liberty*.[19] They pointed to an annual imbalance of trade that had risen to £1.3 million sterling, sucking scarce capital and coin out of the colonies and virtually enslaving American business to British financiers through the imposition of regulations and restrictions. Adam Smith viewed economic liberty as the freedom to enter contracts. A free society should have the liberty to open its trade to the world.[20]

Other radicals, especially among the street mobs and wharf denizens, acted in terms of a pseudo-libertarian concept of *personal liberty*—the license to do as they wished supposedly bounded only by a quality that Sam Adams and other leaders referred to as moral virtue. Repeatedly resistance to British officials and the enforcement of customs regulations included the type of crowd action that commonly appeared on the waterfront where, it should be noted, almost all the major demonstrations took place. America's largest cities were all seaports. Sometimes the participants thought in terms of the theoretical concept of political liberty; sometimes they acted in terms of their personal liberty to do as they wished; most times there were several ideas about liberty swirling through their heads simultaneously. "Whatever definitions of liberty appeared on the waterfront, the maritime world's understanding of liberty helped to shape the struggle for American independence." Any effort to restrict trade or limit smuggling threatened the livelihood of a whole segment of the waterfront population, and maritime workers of all types provided the mobs for the earliest calls for liberty in America.[21]

Sometimes religious dissenters among the Patriots espoused *religious liberty* fearing enslavement to the established Church of England that was still strong in terms of adherents in the colonial South. New

England was largely composed of Congregationalists, Pennsylvania of Quakers and Pietists, and the entire frontier region had a majority of Presbyterians and evangelicals, who valued the liberty to worship as their consciences dictated without paying tithes to the established church. The name *black regiment* or *black robe brigade* was occasionally used by British propagandists during the revolution to refer collectively to those dissenting clergymen that assisted in rallying the populace against the Crown. Even the great Liberty Bell in the Pennsylvania State House had a religious inscription from the book of Leviticus, "Proclaim liberty throughout all the land to all the inhabitants thereof."[22]

It also seems certain that religion and liberty were inextricably linked in the political philosophies of the period. Absolute separation of morality from doctrine, rather than church from state, was fundamental to most enlightened radical thinkers. They questioned the status of Providence (if not God) and the place of ecclesiastical authority in the social order as deists or agnostics. Such radicals as John Jebb in England and Thomas Paine in America betrayed a considerable lack of respect for the divinely established order of things in their writings— the more radical Paine going further than Jebb while not quite espousing atheism. Following the remarkable retreat to Manhattan after the disastrous Battle of Brooklyn Heights in 1776, the first great victory of British combined arms in the revolution, Washington reflected this attitude when he noted, "Providence—or some good honest fellow, has done more for us than we were disposed to do for ourselves."[23]

The separation of church and state almost had the status of an afterthought in their arguments against churches—any of the churches structured around a particular religious sect or calendar of essential beliefs. Thinkers like these insisted first on liberating moral behavior and social policy from church-based theology, and then freeing the civil power from the authority of an established church, thus leaving unfettered both human inquiry and individual conscience.[24]

PROPERTY

Locke's philosophy argued for a *labor theory of wealth* (property, including but not restricted to real estate). This was an expansion and explanation of the work of Thomas Hobbs who had combined the ideas that an individual person was entitled to accumulate property due to the labor that he contributed to its production. Thus the charcoal maker came into rightful possession of the value of his product through the cutting, splitting, stacking, and firing of wood, and the potter through the preparation, throwing, and forming of worthless clay. In a similar manner, Americans considered the hauling of fish from the ocean or the clearing of the wilderness and the preparation of the land for production sufficient infusion of their labor into its value to underpin their claims of ownership. Under these circumstances, free and unrestricted possession of property was a sacred right bestowed by nature's God with which the government could not interfere. The two pronged argument—sacred rights and property rights—would be used by American radicals all the way through the crisis to deprecate the claims of the Crown. Moreover, both Hobbs and Locke believed that it was the duty of government to encourage the accumulation of private wealth, not tax it into the hands of magistrates and monarchs. "Lawyers must sanctify it [property], magistrates must protect it and scholars must devise ways to maximize it."[25]

ALL MEN CREATED EQUAL

Locke's defense of slavery under the concept of property was labored, intricate, and not quite convincing. His benefactor, Lord Shaftesbury, is commonly thought to be the coauthor of *Fundamental Constitutions of Carolina*, which in 1669 argued the legality of slavery in the American colonies and the status of bondsmen as chattel (property). This document was widely referenced in the arguments against the abolition of slavery. British jurisprudence did not recognize *race-based slavery* in which the status of a slave was inherited from mother to child, but it did recognize slavery as an individual disabling status, as punishment for crime or in liquidation of indebtedness, and indentured bondage as a consequence of a contract of limited duration as in the case of an apprenticeship of several years or an enlistment (military or naval) of some difinite term. As will be seen, many persons in the 18th century were not free in a modern sense.

Unfortunately, the early history of slavery in North America is poorly documented and inconclusive. It seems certain that none of the founders of the first English colonies anticipated a dependence on black slaves. The Spanish and Portuguese were much more dedicated to the concept of race-based slavery than the English, who initially viewed indenture as the primary method of supplying labor for their enterprises. The Spanish or Portuguese were responsible for more than three-quarters of all Africans brought to the Americas as slaves, and the same nations enslaved the vast majority of all the Native Americans living in the New World.

Throughout the 17th and 18th centuries, colonial laws and procedures progressively abandoned the common-law precedents of English jurisprudence in order to control the bound population of the colonies and appease both the employers of indentures and the owners of slaves. The distinction between free blacks, black indentured servants, and black slaves quickly blurred into a system of race-based perpetual servitude. By the beginning of the 18th century, race-based slavery had firmly established itself in America in place of indentured service wherever large numbers of agricultural workers or menial laborers were needed.

Unlike free white employees, slaves were not free to change their condition should it become too burdensome. They could be physically chastised by their masters for many forms of disobedience, for insolence involving a white person, and for petty crimes. Incredibly, masters did not have unlimited legal power over their slaves. A slave accused of a felony could not be purposely mutilated, maimed, or killed as a punishment without the intervention of a court. A slave defendant was not entitled to a jury trial, but a hearing officer was required to determine the merits of the case and to act as a finder of fact. As the hearing officers came from the community of free white slaveholders, questions of guilt or innocence were often moot. Nonetheless, the slave was allowed to make a defense. In such a case, the defendant needed to rely on his own testimony or the testimony of other slaves. Slaves could not subpoena whites to testify. Both the law and custom gave great leeway to the officers of the court in determining the nature of any punishment.

INDENTURES

In a society where whites were often degraded and treated as brutally as slaves, social distinctions often proved more important than racial ones.[26] Historians have been hard pressed to explain the sudden shift from white indentured labor to black slavery, and many tend to ignore the phenomenon jumping into their analyses of a well-established system of slavery in the 19th century as part of a discussion of the American Civil War. Indentures were less expensive to maintain than slaves, were acquired as young adults and sent off to fend for themselves when they aged, and generally proved more tractable workers. The increasing number of slaves being brought from Africa easily filled a shortfall of indentured workers. Slave markets provided an abundant source of labor that was found to be less restrictive than indentured servitude. Once purchased, slaves were the master's property until death or sale. Indentures were limited by time. At the end of the contract, the bondservant was free to leave. Additionally, while slaves had enforceable legal rights, indentured servants were more likely to bring grievances against their master to the attention of authorities and to seek legal action before a legitimate court.

Not all indentures were servants and the idea of a so-called indentured slave was a contradiction in terms. Indenture was a legal contract, usually voluntary but sometimes one imposed on a child by a parent or on a person of any age by a magistrate as a consequence of a legal proceeding. British law allowed for the *specific performance* of contracted personal services—that is, a person could be forced to labor under the terms of a contract for another. Through a system of bounties, much like those used to enlist soldiers for the military, agents of the colonial proprietors assembled groups of persons who contracted themselves to work for a specified number of years for wages. These were represented to be artisans, mechanics, husbandmen, and laborers by the agents, but many—possibly the majority—were from among the economic refuse of the British Isles or other parts of Europe. The contracted person could buy off the contract with some fixed amount of money, but under English law the sum had to be given in specie coin. Ironically, being indentured provided a stability and predictability to economic life that many unskilled workers sought out because they feared the chronic unemployment that characterized European economies. However, these same persons found that willing workers were a scarcity in America, largely because the frontier offered land to anyone willing to work for himself.

The laws of indenture were also true to some extent of the marriage contract and the protocols that bound families. The domestic services, the labor, and the property of the wife became the property of the husband, and she could be required to fulfill the common sexual role of a wife. The labor of children was the property of their parents until they reached their majority, at which time both the parent and offspring were freed of any financial obligations. Parents often tied their adult children to them thereafter through threats to their inheritance.

Apprenticeship was a form of education usually accomplished under indenture (contract) freely entered into by caring parents. Children who were orphaned, or too numerous and with families unable to support them, could be apprenticed under an indenture to learn a skill. In addition to the obvious trades of joiner (carpenter), blacksmith, or printer, children were also apprenticed to learn farming, reading, and ciphering. A widower with no inclination to remarry might apprentice his son to a trade and his daughter to be taught to read. It is likely that the girl would also learn the skills in which her deceased mother would have instructed her as well.

Financial burdens and single parenthood were not the only reasons for "sending out" children. This custom was particularly popular among the Puritans of Massachusetts, who sent their pubescent children to other respectable homes to learn a skill or apprenticed them to a trade as a matter of course. Samuel Sewall sent out his three daughters—Hannah to learn housewifery, Elizabeth to learn needlework, and Mary to learn to read and write. His son, Samuel, was bound as an apprentice to a craftsman. While the parents' intentions may have been in the child's best interest, apprenticeship was sometimes a painful experience, especially if the master or mistress proved unkindly or unfeeling. Sewall made the following entry upon his departure from his daughter Hannah who he had deposited with a new family: "Much ado to pacify my dear daughter, she weeping and pleading to go [home] with me."[27]

Many laws governed the manner in which the indentured person could be treated. Indentured servants were entitled to a modicum of privacy, a place to sleep and everyday food, and common care during an illness. The time of service lost to sickness could not be held against them. Their contract could not be sold out of the colony, nor could they be cheated out of their freedom dues—those items due them at the conclusion of the indenture. Overall, indentured servants were given a legal status similar to that of wards of the state. Sometimes indentures were promised reading and writing lessons during their tenure. Many women, who were made readers so that they could study the Bible, were not taught to write the polished hand and flawless grammar of the upper classes because common society saw no need for them to do so; but it would be an error to consider most women illiterate. The Pennsylvania colonial assembly passed legislation that gave indentured servants two suits of clothing, a new axe, a grubbing hoe, and a weeding hoe as freedom dues.

Indentures, and servants of all kinds, were usually forbidden to engage in any activity that had the potential to interfere with their work. A mistress could physically discipline her servants, and whippings were not uncommon. Servants were not permitted to drink and certainly not to marry. A female servant who became pregnant was liable to her mistress for the additional costs incurred for a midwife, a nurse, and any subsequent child rearing. Since few servants were in a position to pay for such expenses, their time of servitude was commonly extended from 18 to 24 months. The ratio of women to men in the colonies was such that many female indentured servants easily found husbands upon the completion of their service or disappeared into the frontier population under a married name.

Disputes between indentured servants and masters occasionally made their way into the courts. The most common complaint by servants was that the master or mistress was not properly attending to their physical welfare. There were also specific claims that the master failed to provide proper clothing or food. The majority of charges against servants were for running away or stealing. Advertisements offering rewards for the capture of runaway bondsmen and apprentices pepper the newspapers of the 18th century. Other common complaints included unruly behavior, fornication, profanity, and sexual misbehavior. Penalties for offenses varied from one colony to another and evolved as time progressed. They rarely went beyond added days and mild lashings. Anyone found to be assisting a runaway indenture was required to pay the master £20 damages and an additional £5 to the court as a fine.

By the 1690s, the free-flowing supply of emigrating indentured servants from Europe began to subside and their numbers fell steadily through the remainder of the colonial period. Men were more likely to indenture themselves than women, usually as laborers or farm hands. In the Chesapeake region, an average of only two women per year emigrated as indentured servants from 1718 onward. This was due, in part, to the improving economy in England, which left fewer individuals willing to leave their homes in order to sell themselves into bondage.[28]

The slave, bondsman, or employee had an economic value that was considered property. Clearly related to this circumstance was the absence of a denunciation of slavery and bondage in the Declaration of Independence, the Articles of Confederation, and other documents. Under present U.S. law, specific performance of personal services is held as involuntary servitude, and it violates a fundamental commitment to personal freedom. Nonetheless, the contract holder may sue for damages either in money or in equity if the contract is unfulfilled.

ANOTHER STATE OF SOCIETY

Many among the most radical Anglo-Americans of the 18th century were almost indistinguishable from the old school *Levelers* (a.k.a. Levellers) of the previous century who were among the first to believe in a classless social order. These were America's first socialists since the Puritans had abandoned their plans for communal ownership and utopian sharing in Massachusetts in the 1620s. Some Levelers went so far as to declare that any deference given to the rich and socially elite, even in terms of positions in the colonial legislatures, was demeaning to the mass of the people and dangerous to American liberties in general. The radical movement in America initially had little to do with attempts to deconstruct the social hierarchy or to replace mercantilism with socialism, but some radicals with Leveler leanings ministered to the urban poor in the streets and expressed Leveler rhetoric when trying to garner support for the Patriot cause.

The term *leveler* had its origin in England in the Midland Riots of 1607 when those who opposed land enclosure had cut down or leveled the offending hedges that served as boundaries to open fields for communal farming and public grazing. Enclosure again swept Britain during the mid-19th century to greater effect, but on-and-off attempts to enclose common lands for the exclusive use of the upper classes had begun as early as the 12th century. English landlords had slowly destroyed the free-grazing cattle subcultures of the Scots and the Irish and replaced them with a sheep-based husbandry of enclosed pastures and the wool production so critical to English textile mill owners. During the English Civil Wars of the 1640s, the grassroots Leveler movement had undertaken a generally nebulous and unfocused program of reforms directed at the Parliament, the king, the Established Church, the law courts, and other government institutions. Just like the present-day Occupy Wall Street protestors, the lack of specific goals was somewhat debilitating to the momentum of the movement. Once their support was no longer needed, Oliver Cromwell turned against them, cruelly suppressing their movement. Thereafter, Levelers were considered political extremists, virtual anarchists, and social pariahs.[29] The return of the monarchy in 1660 found that Leveler activism had been largely abandoned, but some of its ideals remained in the undercurrents of English (and Anglo-American) society, especially with regard to the American distrust of standing forces. The Leveler appeals to reason rather than to scriptural references as the foundations of government served as a milestone in the development of English political thought. Ironically, the entrepreneurial Society of Friends (a socio-religious group known as Quakers) was formed during the same period of political unrest and adopted many Leveler ideas.

PATRIOTS

Like the present (2012) conflict over state and federal mandates and regulations, the political dispute in America between local or monarchial control was an old one. In 1688, the Crown (King James II), in the person of Governor Sir Edmund Andros, had briefly attempted to establish arbitrary royal rule over the so-called Dominion of New England (including the colonies of New York and New Jersey) in which the powers of the colonial legislatures were limited, the towns restricted to a single annual meeting, and the establishment of Anglicanism enforced. Colonial charters were confiscated—all but that of Connecticut, which was hidden in the hollow of an oak tree. From hence comes the phrase *charter oak*, which is common in Connecticut. The attempt to bring the northern colonies under royal rule failed due to the Glorious Revolution that overthrew James II. The new king, William III, reissued the colonial charters with additional guarantees of local sovereignty.[30]

The tea protestors of 1773, as well as the stamp tax protestors and others before them who were unhappy with the policies of the government in London, looked back to these circumstances and chose the term *Patriot Party* for its historical connections with like-thinking Whigs in Britain. This fact requires some further elaboration.

The Patriot Whig Party in Britain was a conservative group formed within the English Whig Party in 1725 in opposition to the administration of Prime Minister Robert Walpole (1721–1742). The monarch at the time was George II (reigned 1727–1760) who was not an influential monarch. He had publicly fought with his father, King George I, and had running disputes with his own children. During his reign, George II fought three wars in Europe (which spilled over into the colonies), and his son, the Duke of Cumberland, suppressed a rebellion in Scotland in 1745. In 1743, at Dettingen in Bavaria, George II became the last British monarch to lead an army in person on the battlefield. The king disliked Walpole, but could not dismiss him because of the minister's majority in Parliament. Consequently, George II was more of a figurehead than a monarch and the government came under the control of Parliament.

A half century before the American Revolution, the Patriot Whigs in Britain—rallying behind traditional and constitutional limits on government—were already claiming that the ministry had grown too powerful, too partisan, and too exclusive of more modest social-class representation. This included the exclusion from the ranks of Parliament of many newly rich merchants and their offspring. The Patriot Whigs, while numerous and effective in Britain, never achieved majority power while Walpole remained in charge of the House of Commons. Nonetheless, it would be the unofficial party of both William Pitt the Elder (1766–1768) and William Pitt the Younger (1783–1801), unfortunately bracketing the crisis years of revolution in America.

The elder Pitt, as secretary of state for the Southern Department and leader of the House of Commons in coalition with the Earl of Newcastle as prime minister from 1757 to 1760, ruled Britain like a king without a formal crown. He gained a reputation among the colonials as a great military strategist because he had helped to formulate the ultimate defeat of the French in the Ohio country and Canada in the French and Indian War. Many place names—towns, cities, and counties—continue to honor him in the United States today.

The Patriot Whig faction in Britain was loosely tied to the radical Whigs who were also active during the reign of George II, but the radicals would not prove politically effective until the 19th century. The radical Whig movement drew heavily on the discredited Leveler tradition that demanded improved parliamentary representation for all Englishmen—a key demand echoed by many radicals among American Patriots.

FREEDOM OF THE PRESS

The newspapers of the time differed greatly from the daily papers of today. Most were published weekly. Subscriptions were costly. Exclusive of postage or carrier fees, weekly papers averaged 8s. a year. Readers of one publication often exchanged their paper with subscribers of another, or they resorted to reading the variety of papers available in coffeehouses and taverns. Particularly important articles were often read aloud by one person to a group.

To fill space, newspapers relied on prose and poetry heavy with sentimentalism, reflection, and affectation of virtue, often copied from London magazines and newssheets in order to give the local publication an air of sophistication. Colonial papers not only carried local news but also copied articles that appeared in other publications in other cities, which may have been weeks old. A first report of an important battle or a measure passed in Parliament was more likely to have arrived by a mounted courier, a personal letter, or a traveler than by newspaper.

The news was anything but "late breaking" and the 18th-century news cycle encompassed days or weeks rather than hours. Throughout American history, the free press has been no less unrestrained and partisan than at present (2012). Press reports today generally travel faster than official reports, yet they are filled today with no fewer inaccuracies, anecdotal details, and unsubstantiated opinions than in the past.

Aspects of freedom of the press (truth is an absolute defense against libel) had been established in 1735 during the trial of New York publisher John Peter Zenger.[31] Absolute freedom of the press was not established by this case. Although a Member of Parliament, John Wilkes was imprisoned in London in 1768 for publishing a satirical poem populated with government officials, which was considered obscene and seditious libel. His readers appeared before the King's Bench Prison in his support, and the troops there opened fire on the unarmed men, killing seven and wounding 15, an incident that came to be known as the St. George's Fields Massacre and chillingly similar to the Boston Massacre of 1770.

Although the Patriot radicals advocated freedom from arbitrary rule, they engaged in their own forms of unjust suppression of the media, often blaming the messenger for the message. James Rivington, a New York publisher, for example, argued for neutrality in the press despite his own Tory convictions. This attempt at objectivity failed when a mob of Patriots, spurred on by Isaac Sears who disliked the editor intensely, destroyed his press because they thought him helpful to the Loyalist cause. After the battles of Lexington and Concord, Rivington felt obliged to place a public notice proclaiming that nothing he had ever done had proceeded from any sentiments in the least unfriendly to the liberties of America but only from the liberty of the press.

As the editor of the *New York Gazetteer*, sometimes called *Rivington's Gazetteer*, Rivington "at various times seemed to be the friend of both Whig and Tory—or neither." He was a friend and correspondent of Boston bookseller and Patriot Henry Knox before the war, but as the crisis progressed, his natural conservative leanings brought him and his newspaper firmly into the Loyalist camp. His printing office was twice destroyed by the New York mob. However, there is documentary evidence that Rivington may have been a paid double agent working for George Washington while "at the same time acting his role as Tory." Although he never openly admitted his activities as a spy, he enjoyed a good deal of prominence in New York after the war.[32]

Newspapers commonly accepted the contributions of patrons who fancied themselves writers. As political tensions heightened, flowery verses were replaced by Whig rhetoric or Tory recriminations. Local political and religious leaders took up the pen in order to rouse public opinion to one cause or the other. Using classical pseudonyms such as Lucius and Brutus, young men, often collegians, were welcome contributors who passionately spread patriotic fervor. Publications, such as *Rivington's Gazetteer*, became vehicles for Loyalist propaganda, while others, such as *Boston's New England Chronicle*, promptly changed its name to the *Independent Chronicle* and—so that there would be no question of its partisanship—added to its banner head "An Appeal to Heaven" with the figure of a Continental soldier on one side and a scroll "Independence" on the other.

Newspaper editors controlled the tenor of their publications, and those who supported positions unpopular in the region they served, suffered harsh consequences that ranged from lost revenue to broken presses or personal threats. Under pressure from street protestors, some Tory papers folded. In Boston, the Tory editor of the *Chronicle* closed his doors and fled to England. After 72 years of publication, the colonies' oldest paper, the *News-Letter*, printed its last issue in 1776. Some newspapers with a divided readership sought to maintain their income by trying to be objective and neutral, but impartiality was often viewed as a lack of patriotic spirit. Many truly objective publications suffered as much as those blatantly pro-British. The *Boston Evening Post* prided itself on presenting both sides of controversial issues, but following the events at Lexington and Concord, it suspended publication rather than be forced to take sides.

Some newspaper editors changed their politics completely depending on local conditions. The *Massachusetts Spy*, printed by Isaiah Thomas, initially took a bipartisan position, but shifted support to the Patriot Party after the fighting at Lexington. When the British occupied New York, John Gaine initially moved the *New York Mercury* to Newark, New Jersey, to avoid persecution by the regulars. When he returned to the British-occupied city, he renamed the publication the *Gazette and Weekly Mercury* and gave it a decidedly Tory slant.

THE PROTEST LEADERS

Among the leaders of the protest movement were men who were remarkably different in many ways, but dedicated to seemingly similar goals. Some were Anglicans, others Congregationalist, Huguenot, deists, and even Roman Catholics. They were financiers, planters, merchants, shippers, tradesmen, mechanics, artisans, lawyers, politicians, and ministers of the gospel. Some were wellborn and conscious of their wealth. Others were of more common origins and were conscious of the precarious nature of American success. Yet each wished to maintain or better his social position. All were active in mobilizing the resistance, but each did so in distinctive ways.

With respect to any dichotomy to be detected among these radical protest leaders, historian Gordon S. Wood has noted, "American revolutionaries seem [in hindsight] to belong in drawing rooms or legislative halls, not in cellars or in the streets. They made speeches, not bombs; they wrote learned pamphlets, not manifestos. They were not abstract theorists, and they were not social levelers. They did not kill one another; they did not devour themselves."[33]

These leaders often spoke or wrote employing the same words and phrases—in many cases repeating or directly quoting the political economists and theorists of an earlier century. They did not necessarily all attach the same unambiguous meanings to the words they used. Even the term *revolution* began as one that suggested a return to a previous state or position, as in the revolution of a waterwheel or of the earth about the sun, rather than the transformation of the monarchy to a democratic state. In declaring an end to arbitrary rule by a hereditary elite and pursuing the formation of a more responsive republic, they opened a new era in the history of government. Revolution thereafter implied an upheaval, a new order of things, a transforming occurrence or series of events after which the structure of government and society was fundamentally changed.

Yet many among the leaders of the protest attempted to cling to a precarious continuity of monarchy because no living person could clearly see the consequences of a people's democracy. Thomas Chandler, who ultimately remained a Loyalist, foresaw a distinctly democratic government as devolving into a Cromwell-like military dictatorship supported by a Congregationalist-led religious bigotry or a socialist-style meritocracy where all private property would be threatened by attempts to equalize wealth. There were protest leaders like Alexander McDougall and Isaac Sears, who themselves came from undistinguished families, who were courting the lower orders of society with just such notions. Chandler warned, "No denomination of men will enjoy liberty and security if subjected to the fiery genius of a New England Republican Government."[34]

The colonies of New England with their traditions of town meetings and councils of selectmen had some basis for a faith in the egalitarian concept, but the middle and southern colonies had little experience with the republican model. The leaders outside New England had long distrusted the people more than those who had inherited their power and influence. They had invested their faith in aristocracy and hierarchy. They offered alternatives to the New England model and viewed a government based on a pure democracy with suspicion and the rule of the mob as a prescription for disaster. The shift from speaking and writing about democratic reforms and fundamental rights to shouting, shoving, and burning to attain them was "a startling violation of decorum in an age when body language spoke volumes about authority and its vulnerability." Nonetheless, by going beyond humble supplication, the insurgents gave an effective spur to the American cause by evoking a cry of anguish from their intended targets that was heard all the way to London.[35]

TO WHERE FROM HERE

The initial encounters with the British had affected the independence of the colonies over two long and troubled decades (1764–1783), but many commentators fail to emphasize the duration of the revolutionary movement. The quest for independence was no sudden and short-lived malady that affected the body politic of the American people to be forgotten when the patient recovered. Yet, this independence would not be fully realized, in fact, until Americans faced Britain again as a cohesive nation instead of a loose group of states. Even in the early days of the American Republic, there were grave doubts about the ability of the central government to discipline itself with regard to the exercise of its own powers.

Among the first historians of the revolution was David Ramsay of South Carolina. In his history, he noted that the right of the people to resist their rulers when their liberties were threatened forms the cornerstone of the American republic. In an era when distance created a real separation in time from government and isolated the consensus of opinion among the people, the bond between Americans and their representatives always had been strongest on the local level. Voters could expect regular contact and interaction with their elected officials (much greater and more direct than today) and an interchange of ideas and opinions among themselves at town meetings and church services and in the markets and taverns. Delegates to the federal government spent the majority of their time in their home districts, not in the nation's capitol. The issue of creating a more responsive government—one of the first decisive questions faced by American lawmakers—was fundamental to the question of state versus federal sovereignty, and it had a direct impact on every citizen and their civil liberties.

It has been noted that when people govern themselves, they have self-government. But when they govern themselves *and others*, it is more than self-government, it borders on despotism.[36] James Wilson, one of America's first great political theorists and later an associate justice of the Supreme Court, believed that the popular election of governors, representatives, judges, magistrates, and other government officials effectively extended the influence of the people over government. The Senate was then filled through appointment by the state legislatures rather than through direct election, and the delegates to the Electoral College, then and now, determine the presidency. Wilson did not fear the executive branch: "They who execute and they who administer the laws, are as much the servants, and therefore as much the friends of the people, as those who make them."[37]

THE MODERN T.E.A. PARTY

This chapter has been largely about ideas and ideals. The great thinking of 17th- and 18th- century philosophers and observers was remarkable and enduring. During the Constitutional Convention, virtually every conceivable principle, device, or structural form of government in effect at the time or conceived in the pen of political theorists up to that time was discussed. Locke, Swift, Hobbs, Voltaire, Montesquieu, and others were quoted, dissected, debated, applied, discarded, and re-applied. Districting schemes, election laws, rotation in office, popular representation, executive prerogatives, voter manipulation, checks on the popular will, the rights of states and individuals, and other facets of governance were all considered. Much of the debate between the parties focused on whether the Constitution should be strictly or loosely interpreted, and many of the positions taken by the delegates on any one issue smelled of political expediency. Loose interpretation, favored by the nationalists, would allow for the expansion of federal powers into areas not specified in the founding document. If strictly interpreted as the anti-nationalists wanted, the federal government would have only the powers specifically given to it in the final document.

Some modern media critics opine that the concepts forwarded by the modern-day T.E.A. Party movement are based on an anti-history of America, a mere theatrical reenactment of former times or a naive illusion that is outdated and no longer applicable to American life. Harvard history professor Jill Lepore disagrees with this view. "Every generation tells its own story about what the Revolution was about . . . since no one is alive who remembers it anymore. . . . Either we're there, two hundred years ago," writes Lepore of the modern T.E.A. Party, "or they're [the founders of America] here, among us."[38]

Adherents of different forms of government today and of the dynamic forces of social change at work in the modern world carry with them different logics, different priorities, and different frames of reference from our revolutionary forbearers. The founders were mortal men, but they wrote immortal documents and created immutable ideals. To those who wish to question this assertion, let them first determine at what point fundamental truths of equality, democracy, consent, justice, security, privacy, individuality, or any other closely cherished humanitarian ideal becomes outdated. When did *self-evident truths*, or *human equality*, or the *laws of nature and of nature's God* begin their descent from fundamental precepts to inconvenient pieces of arcane phraseology? Was it on July 5, 1776, or on July 6, or on the centennial or bicentennial of their inclusion in the founding documents of America? Just how recent must a governing fundamental truth of human relationships be—or how old can it become—and still retain its validity?

The proposition that the foundational principles underpinning the expression of American exceptionalism are part of some other generation's history is intellectually dishonest. It smacks of an underlying partisanship that finds such foundational precepts inconvenient to the prosecution of some other political economy, social system, or utopian plan. Most Americans, rightly or wrongly, have considered such ideas in the last 200-plus years and found them antithetical to their traditional constitutional principles and personal liberties.

Some historians tend to discount the records of events that happened in the not-so-recent past as having gone through too many revisions with the addition of possibly spurious details and motives. Yet, as researchers widen the scope of their studies, they often find a more accurate record of what happened in the past than would be expected. It has also been a recurrent theme of American history that some among those who write about the revolution today tend to disparage the *abiding value* of its ideals for their own partisan purposes. In many cases, this has set academia and some civil groups against the common sense of a large portion of the American people.

Among the institutions in America targeted by these partisans were the dominant religions, the work ethic, the long-established forms of education, hierarchical authority, the nuclear family, and the Constitution. These important and historical characteristics of American life were thought to isolate the United States from the more enlightened industrial nations of Europe that had adopted a number of socialist doctrines as part of their government-dominated institutional structure. In this regard, strict construction of the Constitution was viewed as a particular obstacle to their plans to overturn American exceptionalism. The most fundamental challenge to their own more-than-a-century-old Marxist-Leninist fundamentals was their intention to "transform America's core ideals and governing consciousness."[39]

Even generally unbiased academic observers have agonized over the failure of these novel socio-political paradigms to deliver on their promises, and they have been unwilling to admit that the populace has garnered some obvious benefits under a better-regulated form of free market capitalism than that which existed at the beginning of the 20th century. American trade unions, in particular, have found that they can be more effective negotiating with employers as individual entities rather than as part of a nationalized collective labor movement. Many of the most egregious violations of worker and human rights were addressed through the use of legislation without overturning the free market system or the Constitution, thereby taking much of the vitality from the social justice progressive argument for more drastic changes. It seems rather that the dominant spirit underlying American electorate owes more to its "neighbor helping neighbor" or "leave me alone" sense of self-reliance and its dedication to small government libertarianism.

CHAPTER 6

Taxation without Representation

Confident of their God-given rights, driven by anger against an imperial government that treated them like second-class subjects, American insurgents resisted parliamentary rule, first spontaneously, as loosely organized militants who purged the countryside of Crown officials, and then . . . as members of local committees of safety that became schools for revolution.

—*T. H. Breen*, American Insurgents[1]

The colonists are the subjects of this kingdom, equally entitled with yourselves to all the natural rights of mankind and the peculiar privileges of Englishmen. . . . Americans are the sons, not the bastards, of England.

—*William Pitt, the Elder, 1766*[2]

AUTHORITY, NOT REPRESENTATION

The rhythmic cadence of the phrase *taxation without representation* oversimplifies a seriously complex and ongoing debate. Most colonials were perfectly serious in their belief that taxation without their consent was a violation of their constitutional rights as Englishmen. During the stamp crisis of 1766, Prime Minister William Pitt agreed that the Parliament had no right to lay a tax on America. All taxes submitted to the Crown "being free gifts of the people," it was thought inconsistent with the principles of liberty and the spirit of the British constitutional monarchy for the representatives of the people living in Great Britain to give away the property of the colonists in America who had no representation.[3]

With the repeal of the Stamp Act in 1767 and the offensive Townshend Acts in 1773, only the tea tax remained, and this had been cut in half from recent previous levels. Therefore, it can be argued that the colonials had won their argument with the Crown concerning taxation without representation over the preceding decade. Consequently, the question is asked, Was taxation without representation really the primary cause of the American Revolution?

The people of the British North American colonies manifest their indignation toward the Crown not only in terms of ideological concepts concerning taxation, but also with regard to the attempt by Parliament to radically transform the political and economic relationships among the Crown, the colonies, and themselves. Although the tax on tea was certainly the proximate cause of the tea parties, taxation alone was not the direct cause of the revolution as some contemporaries claimed and other traditional authorities have written.[4] Yet it is just barely possible to blame the outbreak of the revolution on tea or even on taxation without representation.

The lack of equal representation was a long-standing problem in the Empire. In 1689, during their revolt against the imposition of the Dominion of New England, Reverend Cotton Mather drafted a declaration that was read from the balcony of Boston's Town House. It accused Governor Edmund Andros of contradicting the Magna Carta, "the rights of which we laid claim unto." It also made reference to protests about taxation without representation, saying, "Persons who did but peaceably object against raising of taxes without an Assembly, have been for it fined, some twenty, some thirty, and others fifty Pounds."[5] This sounded more like a plea for freedom of speech rather than for better representation, and the crisis of government that it exposed ended not in lower taxes and more colonial representation but in an English Bill of Rights (1689) that had more to do with the prerogatives of Parliament, restrictions on standing armies, jury trials by ones' peers, the availability of bail, and the keeping of private arms than being properly represented. Yet, the protests surrounding the imposition of the Dominion—some of them armed—were only quelled through a reaffirmation of the former colonial charters and local forms of governance.

As with the present-day T.E.A. Party movement, taxation served only as a rallying point for deeper grievances regarding an unresponsive, over-regulating, and bloated government bureaucracy. The Patriots initially used taxation as a virtual cudgel with which to browbeat the representatives of the Crown while not directly challenging the concept of monarchy or the integrity of empire. In order to better understand the true nature of the prerevolutionary period, it may be necessary to decouple the historical anger over taxation and the grievances concerning colonial governance in British North America.

In the 18th century, many classes of people in the British Empire lacked direct representation in Parliament, including most of the population of Britain's largest cities, and many taxes were commonly imposed without direct representation even in the colonies. There was an idea circulated in England that the colonies had virtual representation in the House of Commons in the person of the proponents of the American cause, but these representatives were ones who the colonials never elected, never saw, and had no power to recall. William Pitt, the elder called this form of representation the rotten part of the British Constitution. The House of Commons was supposed originally to be no part of the standing government of Britain. It was to be called into and out of session by the king for the purpose of granting revenue to the Crown, but after 1688 it became a virtual means of control, issuing immediately from the consent of the people, not to be a brake on themselves but to provide a restraint for them on the governance of the king. Edmund Burke, although a supporter of the colonies, noted:

> For it is not the derivation of the power of that House from the people, which makes it in a distinct sense their representative. The king is the representative of the people; so are the lords; so are the judges. They all are trustees for the people, as well as the Commons; because no power is given for the sole sake of the holder; and although government certainly is an institution of Divine authority, yet its forms, and the persons who administer it, all originate from the people. A popular origin cannot therefore be the characteristic distinction of a popular representative. This belongs equally to all parts of government, and in all forms. . . . As a fundamental principle . . . in all monarchies the people must in effect themselves possess the power of granting their own money [taxation], or no shadow of liberty could subsist.[6]

Anglo-Americans, nonetheless, had been otherwise successful in governing and taxing themselves for many generations under the present system. They generally considered their representation within their own colonial assemblies fair by the standards of the day, but they also distrusted those elected officials furthest from them both geographically and socially. Boston, the eye of the prerevolutionary storm, was a city governed by the archetype New England town meeting. The colonies all had active, if sometimes headstrong, representative assemblies that shared power with an appointed governor who directed an unelected council or upper chamber of some sort. Burke noted of the American colonies: "Their governments are popular in a high degree . . . and this share of the people in their ordinary government never fails to inspire them with lofty sentiments, and with a strong aversion from whatever tends to deprive them of their chief importance."[7]

Early in 1764, Patriot radical James Otis had publicly launched for the first time the idea that Parliament had *no authority* to legislate for the colonies without their consent, a fundamental concept advanced by John Locke and other political theorists a century earlier and a favorite talking point of the Patriot Whig faction in Parliament. Otis suggested that the colonies be given their own representatives in Parliament in order to resolve the impasse. Otis' plan—echoed by moderates like Joseph Galloway of Pennsylvania—appeared to be a reasonable compromise between the legitimate needs of the British Empire to regulate its various parts and the rights of Anglo-Americans living in the colonies, but the distance in both time and space made such representation impractical and potentially too impersonal. Sam Adams, who took up the *no taxation without representation* mantra, was particularly adamant that no compromise along these lines be reached because his underlying objective had always been independence. When the unfortunate Otis began to show signs of mental instability—actual insanity that passed from bouts of unreasoned temper to delusions that called for physical restraint—his reputation faltered and his following dissolved to support other leaders, such as John Adams and Joseph Warren. Consequently, all such plans for the extension of representation were rejected either by the Crown or by many of the Patriot leaders.

The young King George III (only 22 years) had allied himself to political forces in Parliament who were openly hostile to the colonial governments in America. Parliament, through the Board of Trade, seemed willing to sacrifice the rights, the property, and the liberties of the colonials for the profits enjoyed by its friends among the London investors in the EIC and the Bank of England. The excesses of the Company eventually caused a monumental crash of EIC stock in 1769 and 1770, with many investors losing up to 25 percent of their equity. It was this that caused Parliament to require more revenue from America, not Britain's expenses in governing the colonies. The hypocrisy of the parliamentary program for America astounded political observers on both sides of the Atlantic.[8]

The June 9, 1755, *Boston Gazette* complained about an increase in the local tax burden. "The business of the Town is still decaying, the taxes are not at all lessened, but continue very high—A great many of our industrious inhabitants are gone into the country [the frontier], the burden now falls on a small number; and they less able to bear it."[9] Public debt in Massachusetts had skyrocketed between 1739 and 1763, and local taxes had almost doubled to pay for three major military campaigns in as many decades. Pacifist Pennsylvania alone had resisted expending any funds for defense before 1755, and Benjamin Franklin thought it a great accomplishment when the colonial assembly finally appropriated funds for a string of frontier refuge forts. Other colonies—New York, Connecticut, and Virginia, in particular—had also responded to these crises, and one in seven of the colonial men deployed to fight the French had died in service, the greatest number from Massachusetts.[10]

UNSTABLE LEADERSHIP

Robert Walpole is usually designated as the first de facto prime minister of Britain, and he served for 15 years from 1727 to 1742. There were six prime ministers in the next 20 years, but only Henry Pelham with a decade's tenure (1743–1754) served for more than a few years at a time. Every one of the prime ministers under George I and George II were Whigs. Under George III from 1760 to 1782, the British government went through seven prime ministers—six in the first decade. The almost constant change in leadership disappointed and polarized Parliament, and the apparent weakness of each prime minister left them subject to political challenge. The Earl of Bute (1762–1763) was the only formal Tory, and although he was a friend of the king, he remained in office less than two years. His immediate successors, George Grenville and the Marquis of Rockingham, did not have the king's confidence, and they supported the colonies as part of their platform to unseat the king's friends. In their failure to displace those who had influence over the king, they strengthened them.

In 1770, the opposition prime minister, the Duke of Grafton, was replaced by Lord North, finally giving the king a solid phalanx of friends in control of the ministries of government. For the next 12 years, George III and his minions would have a degree of influence over the implementation of policy rarely seen in British politics. Lord North, nominally a Whig, but with Tory sympathies and support, was prime minister longer than his six predecessors combined, and he inherited all the problems created during the previous decade of confused leadership in Parliament. Yet, he was so little troubled by the events taking place in America that only the destruction of £18,000 worth of tea belonging to the most powerful corporation operating in the British Empire moved him to action.

Moreover, King George III, a young man with little experience of government when he gained the throne in 1760, was surrounded by a coterie of corrupt, willful, and sometimes violent men—advisers who would prove generally unfit for the grave responsibilities they had assumed. Among these was Wills Hill, Lord (Earl of) Hillsborough, who was simultaneously secretary of state for the colonies and chairman of the Board of Trade from 1768 to 1772, and then secretary of state for the Southern Department from 1779 to 1782. This made him doubly influential, and in and out of office he opposed all concessions to the American colonists. Hillsborough applied his influence most directly in the colonies through his in-law William Tryon—governor of North Carolina (1765–1771) and then of New York (1771–1780). Even though Hillsborough left office temporarily in 1772, Tryon remained influential, becoming the leading instigator of Loyalist opposition during the revolution.

During the transition from Hillsborough to Lord Dartmouth as head of the colonial department in 1772, Dartmouth relied heavily on the counsel of one of his undersecretaries, John Pownall, the younger brother of the one-time governor of Massachusetts. Pownall was influential to the point that, although a subminister, he was writing Crown policy for the American colonies almost without supervision. Although Pownall seemingly understood the political culture of America better than many of his superiors, he repeatedly failed to anticipate policy implications and their unintended consequences. With Pownall's advice, Dartmouth responded to the Boston Tea Party by demanding the full and absolute submission of the town, the payment of all damages, and the transportation of those ringleaders responsible for the destruction of the tea to England for trial—as clear a violation of the English Bill of Rights as acquittal in Boston and conviction in Britain were equally certain.

MAKING IT PAY

The EIC was not only central to the tea crisis in America, but it was a major factor in transforming a generally well-run imperial system into a tax-and-spend governmental monster. Many of the same men and their friends that advised the king and informed government colonial policy were numbered among the directors of the EIC, who stood to gain a share in the immediate profit of £600,000 from the establishment of tea trading privileges in Anglo-America for the first time. These profits were also to be distributed among those merchants and dealers friendly to the administration.[11]

The EIC was the most successful business enterprise of the 17th and 18th centuries. Between 1709 and 1749, the total value of trade between Britain and Asia averaged more than £1 million a year. During these same years, the Company failed to pay yearly dividends to its stockholders only on two occasions, making EIC bonds the most secure investment of the first half of the century.[12] However, since the founding of the Company, the business model of the EIC had become increasingly reliant on foreign labor, restricted competition, exclusive markets, and risky forms of speculation. In 1773, the most egregious year for EIC excess, the Company inadvertently precipitated a financial crisis that threatened to bring the British Empire and the Bank of England crashing down on everyone's heads, including those in America. That year, there were two major and several minor hearings in Parliament into corruption in the EIC. Evidence showed that from 1757 to 1772 more than £2 million in presents (bribes) had been distributed to lubricate the gears of EIC trade, but little came of the evidence beyond a show trial of EIC administrator and military hero Robert Clive, of whom more will be said presently.

Before the revolution, Americans had been absolutely prohibited from trading in places like China, India, and many of the islands of the East and West Indies. Any trading that they did, they did as smugglers or interlopers—sometimes posing as Dutchmen, Swedes, or Austrians in the remote island ports of the East Indies where a want of an identifying language was no impediment to trade. The British trading empire was a closed and highly profitable economic system that reached halfway round the earth, and if not highly efficient in modern terms at least its lawful side seemed so at the time.

The merchant servants of the Company, leaning among the bolts of gingham, taffeta, and silk, and surrounded by the fragrance of cloves, tea, and sandalwood in Oriental lands, found that their environment quickly diverged from that of the investors in London.[13] An opposition politician investigating EIC corruption in India noted during a hearing in Parliament:

The history of the East India Company's servants was . . . for some years past, invariably the same. They went out to India; acquired great fortunes; returned home; aspired to seats in Parliament. . . . They contrived to get themselves decorated with titles and distinctive appellations. Whatever was the object they had in view, they never failed to show their attachment to Ministers [of government], by enlisting under their banners. . . . It was therefore to be feared, that in all enquiries . . . it [is] more the intention of the Ministers to screen [their] good friends, than to bring them to justice.[14]

The resident employees of the trading factories "in country" numbered from less than a half dozen to 50 or more. The latter number was very rare, being the case in only a handful of the most active trading ports. Lowest on the company ladder was the youthful *apprentice*, followed in ascending order by the *writer*, the *factor*, the *junior merchant*, the *senior merchant* (or chief agent), the *councilor*, and the *president* (or governor) of the factory council. Within each rank were numerous job assignments and a good deal of overlapping responsibilities. Positions on the presidency council were reserved for those who held the rank of senior merchants. The highest position was that of governor, also called president.

Some of the factors were very young men from good families in their late teens or early 20s, and within a decade they could become very wealthy in their own right. Employees invested in numerous commodities, such as rice, ivory, and raw silk, purchased in one port and sold in another. Gems, in particular semi-precious stones and corals, traded well within Asia and had the advantage of being easily transported back to England. Europeans participated with relative freedom in the Asian emporium trade from India and Malaysia to China, or from coastal Africa to the Persian Gulf and Red Sea.

The scheme for overall remuneration of EIC employees was parsimonious even by 18th-century standards for wages, but the rules governing private internal trade varied at different periods and were seldom strictly enforced. A full-time literate clerk in London could expect to earn £50 per annum and a manual laborer between £25 and £40. With a salary as low as £5 annually, however, EIC apprentices generally worked for the privileges of entering the factory proper and pursuing their fortunes through private trading on their own time. Although potentially lucrative, a career in trade in Asia was not considered a highly prized ambition for European youths because of the sometimes primitive living conditions, the incredibly high death rate "in country," and the very minimal annual wage. Mortality could reach 75 percent during the first five-year minimum term contract. The death rate fell off exponentially, thereafter, as the men became acclimatized, but a high mortality generally speeded up any timetable of promotion.

Company employees were expected to trade on behalf of the directors in London, but they were also allowed to trade on their own account. As the sailing season, both incoming and outgoing to India, was practical only in the three or four months between monsoons, there was plenty of time to do private trading. This provided high-powered incentives for employees at low cost to the Company even when their wages were flat. The synergies between corporate and private trade arose mostly from the private use of Company assets, especially the Company's trading privileges and native contacts in foreign lands. Moreover, the unique comforts and luxuries of life in the Far East, including a different and less restrictive set of sexual mores, often made up for some of the restrictions and inconveniences of working for the Company.[15]

Open licentiousness, however, brought charges of immorality against any men who exhibited neither scruples nor moral concerns in their liaisons. India itself was cast as feminine, exotic, and vulnerable—portrayed as the object of Britain's protective and patriarchal benevolence. In hearings before the House of Lords in the 1770s, Edmund Burke used the scandal of interracial [sic] sex between English traders and the women of India to impugn Paul Benfield and Warren Hastings, EIC officials of which more will be said shortly, charging the violation of the special purity of Hindustani women.[16] Salacious sexual scandals in exotic locales attracted attention, especially among English women living in London townhouses, who were becoming more actively interested in politics and business; yet, the reformers in Britain were much more concerned with the influence of patronage that, fueled by immense wealth, affected the body politic. Burke, who otherwise supported the American colonies in their protests, nonetheless, believed that unrestricted free trade led to demands for additional credit, credit led to greedy speculation, speculation to widespread corruption, and corruption to revolution.[17]

Corruption of the EIC system had actually peaked during the administration in India of Robert Clive from the 1750s to the 1770s, ending in a financial crisis and an attempt at stricter regulation in 1773 that directly affected America. The regulatory crackdown, characteristic of the North administration, was largely ineffective in changing the activities of the EIC. "The scandals of Clive, Hastings, and Benfield were both parables of the larger structure of imperial greed and exploitation, and only the most extreme examples of imperial business as usual."[18]

The isolated nature of the trading establishments fostered a social system among the employees that encouraged solidarity and loyalty. A good deal of minor corruption could go on without arousing the hounds. Nonetheless, when agents violated specific orders against private trade or did not fulfill their performance expectations, the directors took the matter seriously. Agents of the Company, including councilors and governors, were dismissed, rotated, and their bonds and property were subject to forfeit. Although the relationships between the Company and its employees were subject to severe constraints, the overall organization was successful in its main intent—the acquisition of Asian commodities through the agency of trade.

It was common practice among upper-class families to send out to the Far East otherwise healthy pubescent young men, who showed no sign of bettering themselves or their unsatisfactory behaviors at home. These were often second or third sons shipped off either to "reform or be rid of them." Many a lad who had an unfortunate tryst with a young lady of good family or had fallen afoul of the law through some thoughtless misdemeanor was shipped off to America, India, or China. Among many sounder heads it was thought that "the greater the scoundrel, the more likelihood there was of his returning with a fortune."[19]

OPULENT NABOBS

Paul Benfield, an example of a Company employee that made good in India, had entered the EIC in 1764 as a civil engineer and contractor earning his initial fortune from a building boom in Madras. He came to represent a group of creditors who had initially dealt with the Raja of Tanjore, but gradually shifted their loyalties to the Nawab or provincial governor of Arcot. Benfield soon realized that loaning money to the Nawab had great potential as a profit-producing investment for his syndicate since the governor offered 20 percent interest for some very large loans. By 1766, almost every Englishman in India was involved in the debts of the Nawab, either as creditors or agents for creditors. Benfield, a schemer whose self-interest was always several steps ahead of his ethics, soon became the Nawab's chief confidant. He ultimately influenced the Nawab to attack Tanjore, receiving half that region's revenue (taxes) in lieu of the Nawab's indebtedness, which debt was reportedly between £500,000 and £800,000. These revenue claims (known as a *jagir* or *jaghire*) were said to have brought Benfield £150,000 annually, making him the most nefarious of the *nabobs* (persons of wealth largely earned in India) to return to England.[20]

The *jagir* allowed the owner during his lifetime to collect a substantial income in taxes, goods, or produce from a region in lieu of its native government. The *jagirdar* system was a product of Mogul rule from the 13th century. It was a feudal system, but it may be considered a variant of the modern-day kickbacks that accompany defense deals and commercial government contracts. In the early days of the EIC, it was thought of more as the equivalent of a quitrent. Most EIC employees who held a *jagir* took their spoils in coin rather than in kind. From these, they were supposed to pay the expenses of governing their region, which they often failed to do in order to increase their income at the expense of the welfare of its inhabitants.[21]

The first man identified as a Bengal nabob, Edward Stephenson, used his wealth to purchase a baronial estate after his retirement from India in 1730, and he set a standard for the future conduct of nabobs by entering the House of Commons. The wealth of Asia was not unlimited, however. In 1763, after serving as governor of Madras for a decade, George Pigot (brother of Admiral Sir Hugh Pigot) returned from India with a stash of £300,000 and a diamond that he presented to the king worth £50,000. Amazingly George Pigot's lavish lifestyle in England outlived his money in just a decade, and in 1775 he returned to India to recoup his fortune. Such levels of personal spending boggle the mind.

The trick to maintaining one's India wealth was to translate it into political influence in Britain. Between 1763 and 1783, at least a dozen nabobs sat in seats in Parliament purchased with India money. While still in India, Benfield used his wealth to buy up a series of rotten boroughs in Britain, thereby securing for himself an absentee place in

Parliament. Benfield had not only purchased his own seat, but he also had used his wealth for his associates and allies funding the acquisition of eight other seats through similar means. He finally undertook the seat in person after being expelled for corruption from India in 1786 by Governor-General Lord Charles Cornwallis, but he remained influential in the operations of the EIC. Benfield was never subjected to a vilifying hearing before Parliament, as were Clive or Hastings.[22]

The EIC had long held a privileged position in relation to the government with many department ministers and members of Parliament being investors or even serving simultaneously as directors of the Company. Largely due to the influence of those most closely associated with the Company, the EIC was frequently granted special rights and privileges, including trade monopolies and exemptions from law, including an exemption from taxation under the Townshend Acts. These caused resentment among the Company's competitors, who correctly assumed that Parliament and the ministry were favoring their friends among the Company's investors. Charges of corruption and actual cases of massive fraud haunted the Company throughout its history.

THE YALE-EIC CONNECTION

It is certain that Americans were aware of these circumstances either through their personal knowledge as traders and merchants or through their agents and family in Britain. During the early years of the EICs advance, for example, Elihu Yale (of Welsh ancestry, but born in Connecticut and educated in England) went to work for the EIC. It is suggested by some that his elder brother, Thomas Yale (also of Connecticut) was among the first to negotiate trade contracts for the EIC with the Chinese.[23] In a 20-year career beginning in 1672, Elihu became the Company's second governor of the Madras presidency in India, where he built a fine hospital at Fort St. George and made a huge fortune for himself and the Company. During this time, Elihu was involved in a large number of private dealings, not all of which were permitted under Company policy, especially the purchase of land in India from native rulers using Company funds on his private account, essentially a *jagir*. Charges of corruption were brought against Elihu Yale in the last year of his governorship. He was recalled to Britain, but maintained the income from his several *jagirs*. In 1692, the fabulously wealthy Elihu returned to Britain where he installed himself in the family's hereditary manor house in Wexham, Wales.[24]

In 1711, the Reverend Jeremiah Dummer, the first American-born colonial to receive a doctoral degree from a European university (University of Utrecht, 1703), wrote from London to Governor John Pierpont, then a trustee of the Collegiate School of Connecticut: "Here is Mr. Yale, formerly governor of Fort George in [India], who has got a prodigious estate, and, having no son [his only son died of disease in Madras], now sends for a relation of his from Connecticut to make him his heir." Dummer was at the time an agent for the colony of Massachusetts living in London, though he later also served in that capacity for colonial Connecticut (1712–1730).[25] At the behest of Reverend Cotton Mather some years later, Elihu Yale made a large grant to the Collegiate School, which, in appreciation, renamed itself Yale College in 1718. Besides the profits from nine lots of India goods, Elihu Yale donated more than 400 books and a portrait of King George I to the school.[26]

By these means, the intellectual center of resistance to the British government in New England in the 18th century can be shown to have been connected to far away India. Moreover, many of the seemingly political appointees from Britain to America were first and foremost employees of the EIC, or of the Board of Trade, or of both. Because they were political operatives, most of these, but not all, remain unknown to modern readers. A few are outstanding from the historic record, including Ben Franklin who served as an agent in London representing the proprietors of Pennsylvania to the Board of Trade.

THE OHIO-EIC CONNECTION

To some extent, the organization and operation of the EIC has come to dominate the picture of Far East trading, yet until a young colonial began a shooting war in 1754 in the wilderness region of America known as the Ohio Country, its dominance in India remained in question. The Seven Years War (French and Indian War in America), arguably begun by George Washington's bumbling forest diplomacy, inadvertently brought India under the control of Britain and the EIC.

Before 1763, the French Compaigne des Indies Orientales had constantly challenged the British at almost every turn in India. In addition, the Dutch, the Spanish, and the Portuguese were still dominant in areas of the East outside India. The private army and navy of the British EIC were many times larger than the irregular forces of the local native rulers and comparable in force and discipline to those of several

European nations. Before 1764, however, the fate of the EIC with respect to its dominance in India was still in question.

Americans, specifically George Washington acting for the colony of Virginia, had started a frontier war with the French in 1754 over the rights of Englishmen to establish trading posts in the Ohio Country. The frontier encounter over trading posts and access to the Native American markets and resources mirrored developments in other parts of the globe and quickly got out of hand. The Seven Years War that resulted from this frontier conflict is often considered the first worldwide war with battles fought in Europe, the Americas, the islands of both the East and West Indies, and India itself.

At the outbreak of the Seven Years War, in June 1756, the Nawab of Bengal, Siraj ud-Daulah, siding with the French Company in Calcutta, imprisoned 146 British traders and EIC employees in a tiny dungeon, causing more than half of them to die in a single night, primarily of heat stroke, trampling, and lack of water. The so-called Black Hole of Calcutta incident led an EIC military employee, Colonel Clive to undertake to capture the city with the help of a detachment of EIC Sepoys (native soldiers in the employ of the Company). A short time later, at Plassey (1757), Clive defeated the forces of the Nawab, who had been reinforced by a small contingent from the French. This is considered one of about a dozen decisive battles in world history on a level with the consequences of a Saratoga or a Quebec. Clive's army of 3,000 men had defeated a force of 50,000 Bengals and Frenchmen, thereby securing southern India. This victory foreshadowed British ascendency through all South Asia.[27]

In 1760, the French Company, supported by Hyder Ali (ruler of Mysore and implacable foe of British rule in India until his death in 1782), was again defeated by a British EIC army under Sir Eyre Coote at Wandiwash. The main French post at Pondicherry was besieged and taken in 1761. The French Company never regained its former stature in India. Americans were fully aware of the resistance to British rule posed by Hyder Ali, and during the revolution a number of American privateers were named in his honor. By these means, the wars in Ohio and India and the revolution in Boston come full circle, but the story is not finished.

TAXES FOR THE COMMERCIAL STATE

For his victories, Clive (also known as Clive of India and Clive of Plassey) was raised to a Baronet in the Irish peerage and given lands in counties Limerick and Clare. He later assumed a seat in Parliament. In his career, which began in 1744 as a Company *writer* at age 18, he made three distinct voyages to India, each followed by an extended stay—the last as governor and commander-in-chief. His desire for personal gain and influence directed many of his actions and policies. In 1767, he returned to England from his second stay with a fortune of £300,000, besides his annual quit rents from his India *jagirs* worth £27,000. The prize value awarded to him for capturing the city of Calcutta alone was £140,000. Clive seems to have harbored a sincere desire to establish a just and efficient government in British India, but he simply could not curtail the rampant corruption, especially the acceptance of gifts by civil servants. The *jagirs*, in particular, had become a system of tax farming for the benefit of individuals rather than a system of revenue collection to benefit the people. Considered a natural-born general, Clive's military reforms of the army in India were much more effective than his administrative efforts, and he left behind in 1767 an EIC sepoy army larger and more effective than that of any native ruler.

Clive was primarily responsible for establishing EIC influence throughout India, and Warren Hastings, first governor general of Bengal (1773–1785), of whom more will be said later, determined its future dominance. Nonetheless, as the 1770s dawned, the EIC was on the verge of financial collapse. Its stock value tumbled 15 percent in a single month due to unwise speculation in the market. A catastrophic famine of four years duration (1769–1773) affected the EIC holdings in Bengal on the lower plain of the Ganges River. Ten million persons were thought to have died due to the long neglect imposed on them by greedy EIC agents who raised their tax demands in 1770 and 1771 in the teeth of the famine. They were also accused of forcing arable land out of food production and into the cultivation of opium poppies for export to China and cotton for the textile mills of Manchester.

When word of the ongoing disaster in India reached Britain, some of the Company's officers then residing in England were accused of inefficiency and self-aggrandizement, particularly Clive, the epitome of EIC success, who was living like a so-called opulent nabob in London. Tales of widespread corruption, extortion, and plundering in India were rife. Worse yet, they were largely true. In 1772, Clive's numerous and vocal critics, suspicious of the vast wealth he had accumulated, forced an examination of him in Parliament. Herein, Clive told of walking among the vaults of the rulers of India filled with gold on one hand and gems and pearls on the other, and he brazenly expressed astonishment at his own moderation in taking such a small portion of it. Although he was vindicated of criminal charges, Clive committed suicide in 1774, possibly due to severe depression and his addiction to opium, which he had taken for many years for chronic pain.

Ironically, the success of the EIC in assuming the governance of India led to its bankruptcy and the need to tax America in order to bail out its corporate finances and save the economy of the Empire. In 1772, the EIC began to take over the revenue collection in India. The *diwani* or right to collect taxes was first granted in Bengal in 1765, but in 1772, the Company set up government offices in Calcutta and under Hastings actively undertook the better governance of the region. Under the EIC, land taxes doubled in the first five years of the *diwani*.

In one of his first legal actions, Hastings had been forced to issue paper currency valued in rupees through the newly organized and British-owned Bank of Hindustan in order to save the economy of EIC-controlled India from a cash crisis. The attempt failed as paper rupees quickly depreciated in the absence of coin, leaving the natives impoverished and the Company in debt. Although EIC revenues in India increased from 15 million silver rupees to 30 million paper rupees on the account books, there was no actual increase in revenue in real terms. The demonetization of Indian coinage had slowly driven the silver rupee from the marketplace, as it was hoarded and melted down into bullion—a circumstance paralleled in Anglo-America and made worse through the imposition of poorly thought out monetary policy in London.

Initially, native district collectors were made responsible for the revenue generated in a region, but under the East India Company Act of 1773 the ultimate goal of British sovereignty over all India had been clearly stated, and British judicial personnel were deployed to India to administer Crown justice and to collect revenue. This soon became a system of predatory tax exploitation, with the Company using a large portion of the land revenue to fight its private wars on the Indian subcontinent.

EAST INDIA COMPANY ACT

With an abysmal sense of timing, Parliament chose to pass the East India Company Act and the Tea Act in the mist of its corruption hearings. With respect to the tea crisis in America, the EIC formerly had been required by law to sell its teas in England at public auction to merchant-shippers (including to Americans) for exportation to the colonies. In 1773, the radical innovations proposed by Parliament were the provisions that empowered the EIC to export tea to America directly. The Company was authorized to become its own exporter and shipper and to establish for the first time branch houses (trading factories) in America. This arrangement threatened to sweep away the English merchant who purchased the tea at the Company's auction in London, the Anglo-American merchant who bought it from the English merchant, and the American shipper who brought it across the Atlantic. American frontier traders also feared the competition of EIC agents trading among America's native tribes.

Moreover, in India, Hastings in his position as governor general had been given extraordinary powers under the Act to make not only administrative policy, but also to make both war and peace in India as he saw fit. These were powers frighteningly similar to those endowed on Sir Edmund Andros in America in 1688 that had spawned a crisis in colonial governance, a change in monarch, and a need for the English Bill of Rights. Had Americans driven their French competitors from the western lands only to replace them with EIC factors and nabobs for rulers?

Throughout its history, the directors of the EIC followed a deliberate course of deception, claiming a disinterest in expansion, but constantly working to increase their power and area of influence in India, China, Africa, and America. A few thousand Britons thereby ruled a large fraction of the world's population without their consent. Only in America was an effective resistance put up. If the right to collect taxes gave the Crown (in its own undisputed judgment) a claim of sovereignty over kingdoms and states that were hundreds of years old, thousands of miles away, and unrelated to Britain in language, custom, religion, or in any way other than through the trade of one of its corporations, imagine what consequences Anglo-America would have faced had the Boston Tea Party not resisted a 3d. tax in 1773.[28]

The Tea Act of 1773 involved no obvious infringement of the constitutional or natural rights of Americans as Englishmen, so far as the taxation principle was concerned. However, the EIC, by dealing directly with the American retailer, eliminated all the profits that ordinarily accumulated in the passage of the tea through the hands of these middlemen, who were often, as has been shown, members of the same Anglo-American firm or family. Most Americans agreed with legislation that protected the economy of the empire from foreign intruders, but they were not foreigners, they were Englishmen who supposedly believed in free trade.

In their domestic business activities, however, American merchants had shown a capacity that revealed their kinship with the men who had built up the great East India Company. The colonial merchant-aristocracy ruled their cities with an iron hand equal to that of the EIC, and their methods of harrying the price cutters among their own number and of discouraging country peddling were similar to those that modern businessmen and corporations use today. The New York Company (a fishermen's consortium established in 1675), the Free Society of Traders, (a Pennsylvania corporation founded in 1682), the New London Society United for Trade and Commerce (formed in 1732), the Spermaceti Candle Combine (of 1761), and the Philadelphia Contributionship [*sic*] for the Insuring of Houses from Loss by Fire (an insurance corporation organized under the leadership of Benjamin Franklin in 1752) were a few instances of their aptitude for business organization.

TOO BIG TO FAIL

In 1773, Americans were being asked to shoulder an unfair, if not excessive, additional tax burden proposed as an attempt to save the economy of the kingdom. At the same time, Britain's largest corporation, recipient of the government's largess and America's taxes, was undertaking a massive program of land acquisition in India from which the EIC stockholders hoped ultimately to realize millions in tax revenues under the *jagirdar* system. Anglo-Americans were rightfully suspicious that they were being asked to underwrite a virtual fraud, and they could not see how they were to benefit from it. Their concern was completely self-serving. They seemingly had few scruples concerning the dispossession of the natives of India from their land and were actively in favor of similarly dispossessing their own Native Americans.

Although the details of the tax scheme are almost impossible for modern readers to follow in any logical sequence (too many strands of history come to a nexus at this point), let it be understood from what follows that the Company stood to gain more than £1.4 million in revenues at the current price of tea in America passed from the people of the colonies to the investors in the Company through the British government. *The American colonies would experience an immense transfer of private wealth from themselves to the corporate coffers of the EIC by means of government legislation in London with none of it rebounding to themselves in terms of services or security.* [Emphasis added]. American merchants would become so cash-strapped by this transfer of coin as to be left in a state of permanent and unremitting debt. This is very similar to the modern equivalent of sending local tax dollars to Washington, D.C., in order to bailout Wall Street firms and American auto manufacturers at the expense of Main Street businesses and taxpayers.

As a major source of government tax revenue and private dividend income, the EIC stood second only to the Bank of England as a financial institution. Yet, in 1773, it owed more than its projected annual income. An over-investment in future cargoes, unexpected expenditures, and a loss of real tax revenue to the Company government due to the famine in India followed. The Company thereafter failed to meet some of its loan obligations to the Bank of England, and an unremitting depression followed in the wake of the stagnation in business and banking that the failure of the EIC to pay its bills had caused. Parliament stepped in to investigate the situation and selected a committee of its members to sit on the Board of Directors and better set the course of future EIC business decisions. The ministers to the king considered the Company too big to fail.

Just how the world's largest corporation declined into the red is complicated. After gaining the right to collect revenue in the subcontinent, the EIC had largely ceased importing specie (gold and silver) into the subcontinent to pay its bills, but still required the population of India to pay its taxes in coin, thereby impoverishing the people of India in a manner similar to that feared by Anglo-American colonials, who were laboring under similar requirements. As in America at the same time, India slowly changed from being an exporter of goods, for which it had formerly received payments in gold or silver, to being an exporter of raw materials, a re-exporter of China goods and a market for British manufactures, especially wool broadcloth. Lacking coin, many Indians subsequently lost their land or their small businesses to their creditors and reverted to tenancy or wage employment to make a living. This circumstance drove the total revenue collections down in real terms. Raw cotton, salt, indigo, saltpetre, and opium thereafter accounted for most of India's exports—the last item being used in lieu of bullion to pay for the growing list of goods, including but not limited to silk and tea, which had to be purchased from China for re-export.

Unbalanced Company books in India had led to a stock sell-off in London, and many thousands of pounds were lost by EIC investors and others as a downward trend affected other stocks. A 2.5 percent duty was placed on most exports from India, and salt and opium were included for the first time under this tax in 1773. The export of opium to China was a humanitarian disgrace for Britain and would lead to a war between the empires in 1842. Evasion of the salt tax would become for India what evasion of the tea tax was for America, with smugglers and customs agents constantly matching wits. The EIC conceived of an Inland Customs Line that incorporated natural features of the terrain with a great living hedge of thorns across the interior of India to prevent the smuggling of salt. The so-called Great Salt Hedge was begun in 1780 to fill the gaps between customs houses running 2,500 miles from Punjab in the Northwest to Bengal in the Southeast. It was completed in 1843, but was largely ineffective.[29]

GENESIS OF THE TEA TAX

Although in fierce competition with the Dutch tea traders on the Continent, as much as 90 percent of EIC tea profits had come from the sale of tea in Europe. The government, therefore, began a legislative program directed at reviving the Company's prospects at the expense of its competitors, often restricting smaller British companies with connections in America. Among the restrictions was the Indemnity Act, which disabused only the EIC among all British tea traders from tea duties in order to better protect the Company from competition.[30]

Robert Herries—whether the father or the son of the same name is uncertain, both being simultaneously major stockholders in the EIC—suggested a plan to the directors (*The Present State of the East India Company*) that would transform almost 17 million pounds (by weight) of surplus tea in the Company warehouses into much needed coin. Rather than converting all this product by attempting to sell it on the European market where the EIC faced a possible price war with the Dutch Tea traders, Herries suggested that the Company sell its tea directly on the American market free of all British export duties on the EIC. The Company was required to make good any deficiency in the revenues that might result from discontinuing certain other duties. This would drive the price of tea so low that even the Dutch smugglers would be incapable of making a profit in America, thereby creating an EIC monopoly. Although Herries' plan was not adopted in its entirety as first proposed, the directors of the Company found the prospect of capturing virtually the entire colonial market in tea most appealing.[31]

The ministry offered up this bailout, but in so doing it also disenfranchised any EIC stockholder with an investment of less than £1,000 from voting on Company business.[32] If this sounds like the General Motors bail out of 2009 in which the autoworkers union and the federal government were given an investor's portion of the company (50 percent each) and a significant loan of taxpayer money, while the legitimate stockholders of GM were given nothing, not even the justice of a bankruptcy court, so be it.

In the colonies, the local merchants were the ultimate beneficiaries of smuggling having inexpensive goods to sell and absorbing hard currency that was unavailable to them through legitimate means—primarily in the form of silver coins that circulated freely in the Mediterranean nations and the islands of the West Indies. If the legal markets were also to be closed to competition, American dealers would be forced to buy from the EIC and pay the customary tax in coin through the government and into the hands of the Company. Under this plan, the tea wholesalers in London would for the first time become the end-user retailers and the already scant supply of silver coin in the colonies would be drawn down at an alarming rate.[33]

Parliament renewed the Tea Act in 1773, which maintained the tax on every pound that had been in effect for almost six years, but cut it in half. The duties reportedly had reached levels as high as 25 percent of the import value of the tea cargo in London in 1764, averaging for all grades about 10d. per pound. This rate of taxation alone had fueled the illicit traffic in tea. Although the government had rescinded all Townshend duties except the tax on tea, it now gave the EIC a virtual monopoly on its sale and allowed it to draw back any duties. In other words, the EIC got to pocket the taxes at 3d. per pound of tea sold in America. Before the Act, colonial smugglers imported an estimated 900,000 pounds of inexpensive foreign tea each year. The quality of the smuggled tea did not match the quality of some of the dutiable Hyson Tea of which the Americans bought about 562,000 pounds per year. So low was the price of Bohea tea resulting from the Tea Act of 1773 that even smugglers could not sell it as cheaply as the Company. By this ruse, the Crown hoped to reaffirm the right of Parliament to tax the colonies as Americans submitted to the payment of the duty on the tea for the sake of their pocket books.

The colonials had seen this ploy play out before. The tax on tea under the Townshend Act of 1767, dropped from 10d. to 6d., was so contrived as to have the immediate effect of lowering the accustomed price of tea in America below that of any that could be smuggled from

Holland or elsewhere. The retail price in Boston immediately fell by several pence per pound. In the place of tea at that time, it would appear that the chief concern of the smugglers had turned to running illegal wines from the Canaries and the Azores and to the importation of Dutch, French, and German manufactures without stoppage at Great Britain—an illegal traffic vastly stimulated by the high duties demanded for their legal importation. This condition lasted less than two years when in 1769 the EIC once again advanced the price of tea in Great Britain in order to recoup some of its recent losses. This caused the exporting merchants in London to raise the price to the colonial retailers so that the consumer once again found it advantageous to drink smuggled tea.

Parliament authorized the shipment of half a million pounds of tea to the colonies in 1773 and demanded that the tax be paid in coin by the consignees in America when the cargo was landed. As has been shown, the main object of colonial anger in the case of the Boston Tea Party were the shipments belonging to the EIC sitting aboard three ships at the wharf in Boston. Additional ships loaded with tea were turned away in other colonies, but the cargoes arriving in Boston were allowed to dock. They were not allowed to unload, however. They were destroyed.

As with the destruction of the revenue cutter *Gaspée* in 1772, London was again outraged by the Tea Party and rewards were posted. The actors necessarily preserved silence in this daring exploit, respecting their connection with it. Their secrets were remarkably well kept, and but for the family traditions which survive, historians should know very little of the men who comprised the famous Boston Tea Party. This time, however, the ministry responded with a series of retaliatory bills, among which was a bill that required Massachusetts to reimburse the EIC for the loss of the tea and the exchequer for the lost tax revenues. One supporter of the Tea Party ridiculed the idea of paying for the lost tea. "If a man draws a sword on me to deprive me of life or liberty, and I break his sword, ought I to pay for the sword?"[34] The Boston Port Act officially closed the harbor to shipping, including food and fuel, and denied Massachusetts fishermen access to the Grand Banks—potentially a £300,000 annual loss.

The once busy harbor was turned into a virtual backwater. From town meetings and provincial congresses throughout America came word of support for the actions of the Bostonians. If Parliament was permitted do this to Boston, it could do it to any Anglo-American community. "Future ages will hardly believe that we were descended from the British, when they read of our having borne so long and resented so feebly these outrages," wrote one radical. From every quarter came resolves to scorn the British claims. Besides moral support, aid in the form of money and food flooded into Boston, and a call went out for a great Congress of colonial representatives to be held. Many colonists loyal to the Crown declared the country to be in a state of open rebellion from this time.[35]

THE COERCIVE ACTS

The closing of the port of Boston was followed by a series of acts known in Britain as the Coercive Acts of 1774. The Americans called these the Intolerable Acts. The Massachusetts Regulating Act put the colony under martial law. The Government Act and the Administration of Justice Act virtually ended colonial self-government in the province and freed the army and naval commanders from being sued in colonial courts. Lieutenant General Thomas Gage, a soldier, replaced Governor Hutchinson as the chief administrative officer of the colony. Under these acts, the most highly specialized colonial tradesmen and artisans suffered the most, and they tended to unite in open opposition to the actions of London.

Among the Coercive Acts were two, which tended to unite all the colonies. The first was a renewed Quartering Act that flew in the face of continuing legislative opposition in almost every colony. The second was the Quebec Act, which placed the trans-Appalachian lands under the administration of the province of Quebec and which "from political considerations" recognized throughout Canada and the French communities to the west "the free exercise of the religion of the Church of Rome." This raised renewed fears of a Catholic conspiracy against the Protestant population of New England and threatened to further deny the Atlantic-facing colonies the right to expand to the west. The First Continental Congress formally protested against it, and "in New York and New England still greater hostility to the measure was shown."[36]

THE CONTINENTAL ASSOCIATION

Ordinary men and women seemingly had little chance of transforming a political power of such global dimensions as the British Empire, and these were real people making individual choices about the politics of an empire against incredible opposition. A strategy of political resistance based on consumer choices, however, quickly transformed formerly private acts into a movement—the first of its kind in history. In September 1774, a meeting was held in Philadelphia that was attended by representatives of every colony save Georgia, which was dealing with a serious Native American uprising at the time. This First Continental Congress adopted a formal agreement known as the Continental Association. The chief provisions of the Association revolved about a renewed boycott of British goods, but it also established permanent committees to report on violations of the boycott. The non-consumption agreement would leave any merchant ill-disposed to the American cause with no market for the proscribed wares. The Association also promoted the expansion of local militia units and the stockpiling of arms and gunpowder. It quickly evolved into a structure for armed resistance that would ultimately provide a nucleus for the Continental Army.

Among other English items, such as finished cloth and metal goods, no tea was to be used, and Americans, who supported the Association, again made a great show of serving alternative beverages, such as rose hips, herb teas, and drinks made from the roots of sassafras and chicory. However, many colonials found it more difficult to forego the consumption of imported wine, and the enjoyment of horseracing, theatrical plays, and "other expensive diversions and entertainments" enumerated by the Association. The latter sacrifices, born of traditional Puritan ethics and parsimony and included at the insistence of the New England delegates, were intended to help prepare the people for the impending civil crisis through the fortification of their moral bastions.[37]

The enforcement of the non-importation and non-consumption provisions of this last iteration of the boycott was nothing other than ruthless. Those who violated the spirit of the association were accused of disaffection and betrayal of the liberties of America. The names of those reported to be in violation of the association were printed in newspapers, and merchants who refused to take the associator's oath were threatened with tar and feathers. Associators pledged to break off all dealings with offenders, and so-called Committees of Safety often ordered otherwise uncommitted persons to join the boycott or be proclaimed enemies of the people. It was from this point that many of the political lines of irreparable separation between the Patriots (Whigs) and Loyalists (Tories) were drawn.[38]

It was believed that if the association were more strictly enforced, it might bring Parliament to its knees by threatening a British economy that needed the cooperation of its colonies to function. "We want nothing but self-denial, to triumph," opined a writer to the colonial press. Thus, without firing a shot, America hoped to bring Britain to recognize the futility of contending with a people so dedicated to its economic ruin. Nonetheless, as the situation in Boston worsened, many colonials took the stance that open warfare was necessary and that conciliation was impossible.[39]

CHAPTER 7
Colonial Agitators

Will you suffer your liberties to be torn from you by your own representatives?

—*Alexander McDougall*

We need not spill the blood even of our misguided enemies, if we can otherwise reduce them to reason, and make them our friends.

—*Dr. Thomas Young*

WRITERS AND ACTORS

The celebratory euphoria surrounding the Treaty of Paris of 1763 and the end of the French threat quickly gave way to a number of new concerns especially the need to address the imperial debt. Consequently, the year saw the introduction of a number of parliamentary laws that raised the ire of America and turned the normal background mumbling against government into active protests. Given the level of protest seen against the Stamp Act alone, it is remarkable that it took a decade for the revolution to begin in earnest. It is especially remarkable given the number of persons agitating for trouble.

The most influential agitators in America were those whose activities led directly to the revolution, and although there was some overlap they can be divided into two relatively distinct groups—one in the political arena and the other physically active in the streets. The first group attempted to radicalize the political process in the colonies by launching opposition campaigns in the legislatures and by influencing that fraction of the press that was friendly to the American cause. These men manipulated provincial legislation or cast votes meant to confound the ministry in London. Their stock in trade was logical arguments, dignified resolutions, pious sermons, and politely worded petitions. They attacked George III by disparaging his ministers in

Those identified as enemies of American Liberty were often treated to less-than-careful rousting, as shown in this British illustration from the period. Note the prominent place of the sailor in his petticoat-breeches, known as slops, and round hat in the forefront of the mob. (Library of Congress)

their speeches and pamphlets, a "time-honored way of making the Crown reverse course while still preserving intact the dignity and independence of its sovereignty."[1]

Other radicals took a more physically active roll in the conflict by inciting street demonstrations among the working classes or taking to the streets themselves at the head of groups of ruffians known as the mob. They attempted to hijack the political dispute between the colonies and the parent state for their own ideological or social purposes. Their usual stock in trade was the rabble and ruffians of the streets, a liberal coat of tar and feathers, and the threat of the torch or the rope. The active arm of their efforts was the Sons of Liberty. Notable among the radical agitators were Samuel Adams, John Hancock, and James Otis in Boston, and Isaac Sears, Alexander McDougall, and John Lamb in New York City.

THE MOB

Respectable people considered all those who swelled the ranks of the poor as part of the mob, and it was past all bearing for many of the better sort that the tradesmen, mechanics, and storekeepers that led the mobs should presume to involve themselves in public affairs in such a manner. John Adams, a lawyer who was anything but a poor people's democrat, believed that certain portions of the mob were unthinking and easily manipulated. The poor were a natural source for antigovernment sentiment. It was they who the sheriffs of the courts, the city constables, and other administrators of the law threw into jail. It was their property—if they had ever owned any—that the officers of the courts and deputies had seized in lieu of unpaid debts and taxes. Many persons had been thrown into jail for no other reason than a crushing mountain of debt, and they had languished there under the insane concept of a debtors' prison while their friends and relations desperately scrounged about for cash that wasn't there.

Moreover, urban development and the growth of a commercial economy in the 18th century paralleled an increase in the number of sick, homeless, abandoned, and poor in the colonies. This was partially because a growing manufacturing economy could better support such persons on the margins of productivity than could one based on subsistence farming. Yet, there were other factors. The French and Indian War, in particular, had driven countless settlers from the frontiers and into the cities as homeless refugees. Many of these blamed the British army for not better supporting them in their time of crisis. In 1757, a report to the Boston Town Meeting noted that more than 1,000 persons were dependent on the charity of the city. In 1763, Boston spent almost £2,000 on poor relief—a quarter of its annual budget. New York's budget for the poor rose four-fold during the French war to almost £3,000. Similar numbers and public expenditures could be found in Philadelphia, Charleston, and Savannah—the natural refuges of many frontier communities. The reader will note the unfavorable disparity between the level of public charity in the colonies and the level of spending among London nabobs from the previous discussion.

When war refugees flooded the city of Philadelphia, moreover, a number of private charitable associations came to their aid directing funds largely to those of their own religion or common national origin. Among these were the St. Andrew's Society in Philadelphia, which served those of Scottish origin; Deutsche Gesellschaft su Philadelphia, established by the German speakers; the Society of the Friendly Sons of St. Patrick set up by the Irish; and the Corporation for the Relief of Presbyterian Ministers, Their Widows, and Children. Other cities had similar organizations for refugees.

Critics excluded from the ranks of those deserving charity all Quakers and antiwar sectarian groups because of their supposed spineless pacifist attitudes. Meanwhile, a virtual army of armchair hardliners, who could indulge vicariously in anti-Native American hatred from the safety of their city dwellings, was growing. These shared the sharp partisanship of the frontier settlers without having experienced the actual terror of Native warfare, and they became pivotal in forming the character of an anti-Quaker and anti-Pietist sentiment throughout the frontier region. High emotions and growing anti–Native American sentiment led provincial observers, editors, and journalists to sweep away any attempt to discover the causes of Native American unrest and correct them. Writers produced themes, pamphlets, verses, and plays based on the fundamental concepts of dehumanizing and demonizing the tribes of America, and many cartoons, including some by Ben Franklin, attacked the so-called flat-hat Quaker Party and their German-speaking sectarian allies for coddling the Native American enemies as the life-blood of their victims flowed into the rich Pennsylvania soil and turned its streams and creeks red. According to their detractors, Quaker-dictated toleration of non-English and tribal cultures had left the colonies prey to foreign agents and savage invaders, respectively. Many of these writers saw themselves as the guardians of Anglo-American liberty and security, and they hoped to reshape the politics of America through the weight of a frightened public eager to see something definite done against the Native attackers and their pacifist supporters.

The final defeat of the French in America, after four wars and more than 70 years of struggle, was widely seen as the removal of a great burden on the colonies. Generations of grandfathers, fathers, and sons had fought the French and their Indian allies on the frontiers. However, the thrill of victory was as short-lived as the echo of the final musket fired on the Plains of Abraham at Quebec. The end of the French and Indian War initiated a severe and unexpected economic crisis, and the attitude of the ministry in London to victory in America seemed incomprehensible. Settlers who had abandoned their frontier farms in panic were explicitly prohibited from returning to them by the Proclamation of 1763; conciliatory policies with the tribes, arranged by Quaker ambassadors, were announced; and ultimately, Parliament would pass the Quebec Act (1774) establishing an absolutist royal government in Canada and the Ohio Country, and fostering the toleration of the hated Roman Catholic religion whose Native American adherents still threatened "the westerly and northerly boundaries of the free protestant English settlements."[2] It was widely believed by the frontier settlers—and not without supporting evidence—that the Jesuits were actively inciting the Catholic Indians against the Protestant English settlements.[3]

"Settlers living on the frontier during the tumultuous times of 1765 saw and experienced things differently than the gentry living in Philadelphia or Boston, or even those learning and writing about it today," wrote John W. Thompson, historian of the frontier settlements as they were at the time. "Reading about the Indian atrocities in a Philadelphia tea shop is a stark contrast to the real life and death struggle on the frontier."[4] The anti-Catholic, anti-Native American undercurrent of colonial demonstrations should not be disregarded amid the more acceptable and idealistic protests against tea and taxes.

ALLEGHENY UPRISING— CLINGING TO THEIR GUNS

In May 1763, a serious Native American uprising in the Great Lakes interior was undertaken by a coalition of tribal nations under the leadership of the Ottawa warrior Pontiac. The negative effects of this uprising on colonial relations with London can not be underestimated, as it precipitated the first major armed insurrection by colonials against British authority since 1688 and underpinned the American belief in their right to keep and bear arms. This was the armed protest of the Conococheague Valley settlements in the Allegheny region of Pennsylvania.

At the end of the French war, the Grenville ministry had assured the colonials that the regulars in garrison on the frontier would be "a thin red line between kidnap, scalping, and massacre" and security for the white settlements now that the French were gone. The local militias and provincial regiments that had supported frontier expansion and protected the settlements for decades could retire their arms and live in peace with the tribes reassured by the intervening presence of the redcoats.

However, Pontiac's uprising in 1764 seemed to validate many of the negative convictions held by the colonials with regard to the regulars. Every British garrison in the Great Lakes region was taken by the Native warriors save two, Fort Pitt and Fort Detroit. Although the back of the uprising was broken by the regulars of the Black Watch (42nd Highlanders) under Colonel Henry Bouquet at the battle of Bushy Run (25 miles east of Fort Pitt), the British army seems to have been unable to fully secure the frontiers for more than two years. General Jeffery Amherst, in charge of the region, was recalled by the Board of Trade and replaced with Major General Thomas Gage. The formal treaty between the tribes and Sir William Johnson in July 1764 had hardly been a peace, much less a surrender. No lands changed hands, no hostages were taken, and no white captives were returned—all characteristics of previous agreements—and raids by disparate groups of recalcitrant warriors continued. Colonial confidence in British arms was severely shaken. The British regulars were humiliated and the bureaucracy in London was embarrassed by the effectiveness of the Native American attacks.[5]

Colonial sensitivities were further assaulted when the line of frontier settlement proposed by the Proclamation of 1763 was "deliberately distorted" by Parliament into a permanent barrier to settlement in 1764. The "undeniable primary principle" of this line was to foster a market for British manufactures along the coastline and to prevent the development of any colonial industry in the interior. Americans soon began to realize that their own best interests were not always those of the Crown. James Otis, writing from the perspective of the seaboard colonials, noted: "The late acquisitions in America, as glorious as they have been, and as beneficial as they are to Great Britain, are only a security to these colonies against the ravages of the French and Indians. Our trade upon the whole is not, I believe, benefited by them one groat."[6]

Imagine the surprise on the frontiers when, no sooner than the French war had ceased and Pontiac's rebellion had ended, the settlers witnessed a paradox—English merchants' wagons and pack trains under British licenses carrying arms and ammunition westward for sale to the same tribes who had destroyed their homes.[7] Matthew Smith and James Gibson responded to this circumstance for the frontiersmen in an open letter to Parliament. Called *A Remonstrance from the Pennsylvania Frontiersmen* (1764), the letter was published and widely read in the colonies. It stated in part,

> It grieves us to the very heart to see such of our frontier inhabitants as have escaped savage fury with the loss of their parents, their children, their wives or relatives, left destitute by the public, and exposed to the most cruel poverty and wretchedness [by the government]. . . . We humbly conceive that it is contrary to the maxims of good policy, and extremely dangerous to our frontiers, to suffer any Indians, of what tribe so ever, to live within the inhabited parts of this province while we are engaged in an Indian war, as experience has taught us that they are all perfidious, and their claim to freedom and independency puts it in their power to act as spies, to entertain and give intelligence to our enemies, and to furnish them with provisions and warlike stores. To this fatal intercourse between our pretended friends and open enemies, we must ascribe the greatest of the ravages and murders that have been committed in the course of this and the last Indian war. . . . We, therefore, pray that public rewards may be proposed for Indian scalps, which may be adequate to the dangers attending enterprises of this nature.[8]

The stark reality of scalping for money evidences the level of cruelty to which frontier warfare had risen on both sides. The tactics employed by Native American warriors were simple and effective, but barbaric and cruel by European standards. They generally struck first without a formal declaration of war, using the basic offensive tactic of surprise. It was not unusual for an abandoned cart or riderless horse to serve as the first sign of a larger problem. Most attacks, however, took the form of ambushes made in forested regions. These were especially effective against nonmilitary targets, such as small parties of settlers or fur traders, who slashed their way through the wilderness as if it had been granted to them personally by heaven, violating tribal rights and indiscriminately killing any Natives that they feared.

The most effective means of preventing such savagery was thought to be the forced separation of the Natives from the settlers with a line of outposts manned by trained soldiers standing to enforce it. This had been the rationale behind the Proclamation of 1763. Reality showed, however, that it was all but impossible for the Crown to regulate its relations with Native America and to maintain its political alliances among the tribes through trade without some military authority, whether imperial or local, appearing to impinge on the perceived rights of the white frontier population.

The first armed uprising of Americans against British governance in the colonies proceeded from this reality. It took place among the Conococheague Valley settlements on the Allegheny frontier along the Pennsylvania-Maryland border in the spring of 1765. The first rebel blood was shed there, and the first American victory over British arms was won there, 10 years before the fights at Lexington and Concord. A British fort was besieged; its commanding officer and part of its garrison were captured; veteran highlanders of the famous Black Watch fired on the settlers, were fired on in turn, and were defeated. The British regulars holding the stockaded post of Fort Loudon—built with colonial funds—raised the white flag surrendering and marching out under the muzzles of the long rifles of the Pennsylvania frontiersmen. Four years later, in 1769, a band of these same borderers stormed Fort Bedford and took it from the soldiers of another British regiment. The leader of these all-but-forgotten victories was a former Indian captive and militiaman named James Smith.[9]

When confronted with Indian attacks, the settlers in the West Conococheague settlements had either fled their homes for the safety of forts back east or took matters into their own hands in order to survive. Among those settlers that stayed to defend their homes were William Smith and James Smith of the so-called Black Boys, a core group of about 50 men who styled themselves as Rangers. They not only stayed on the frontier, but they banded together to protect their homes and families by taking the fight to the enemy. They were not then considered lawless men or disloyal agitators, but they had ceased waiting for the pacifist provincial government of Pennsylvania or the red-coated battalions ensconced in their forts to come to their aid. These realities showed the impracticality of British plans for the growth of the colonies, and disillusionment continued to build with each Indian raid that the regulars failed to prevent.

Almost all the colonies used rangers. Only Pennsylvania and New York seem to have neglected the establishment of a formal corps of these paid frontiersmen to watch their outlying borders in the colonial period. Of course, New York relied on their friends among the ubiquitous Iroquois, especially the reliable Mohawk, but the pacifists in Pennsylvania absolutely refused to take any steps toward creating military units, even defensive ones. Ben Franklin thought it a great accomplishment, in the heat of an active war with cabins in flames and mutilated corpses decorating the steps of the State House in 1755, to get even a grudging approval for the establishment of a string of frontier refuge forts from the colonial assembly. Ultimately the non-Quaker settlers of Pennsylvania paid the price of pacifism with their blood on the western frontiers.

Frontier settlers in many colonies resorted to the expedient of "forting up" during times of unrest, and chains of impromptu log forts and garrison houses were established along the colonial frontiers. The need to link these outposts led to the development of rangers, who scouted the gaps between forts looking for signs of unrest. The best-known group of rangers was that raised by Robert Rogers from among the tough woodsmen of the New Hampshire frontier. The rangers so captured the imagination of Americans that their name was given to the special striking forces of World War II (1941–1945), and Captain Rogers' detailed instructions for his volunteer rangers, written in 1758, still serve as the basis for the irregular tactics used by the Special Forces of the U.S. Army today.

Recently, historians have focused on the negative social attributes that supported these early frontier rebellions, like those of John Elder and his Paxton Boys or of the more notorious Nathaniel Bacon who led a rebellion in 1675 in Virginia, which were certainly based on pure racial hatred and intolerance of Native Americans. However, John W. Thompson notes:

> The 1765 Black Boys Rebellion that started in March and lasted through November of 1765 had the backing of most of the local settlers and the colonial justices that represented the Provincial government on the frontier. Although James Smith and his followers did pursue Indians who committed murders on the frontier [more than 100 whites had been killed], they did not murder innocent Indians like the Paxton Boys. Their actions were not the lawless actions of an unruly racist mob, as some have suggested. Rather, their actions reflected a strong desire to uphold laws designed to keep the settlers from being killed on the frontier.[10]

Believing strongly that the British were allowing unscrupulous traders to supply the Indians with weapons and ammunition, Smith's men
set an ambush on Sidelong Hill on the Forbes Road and stopped the
pack trains and burned the supplies belonging to one Robert Callendar,
who had obtained a license from Bouquet through the influence of
George Croghan, the Royal Indian Agent. Croghan seems to have
been less than innocent in this affair, even drawing the rebuke of Sir
William Johnson for misrepresenting the nature and destination of
the goods.

Three hundred armed men under James Smith then marched to
Fort Loudon where the traders had fled, demanding that they be given
up to the local justices of the peace for prosecution as violators of the
Indian trade laws. Lieutenant Charles Grant of the 42nd Highland
regiment commanded Fort Loudon. Grant was an officious man, and
he believed every distortion the traders told him concerning the confrontation over the goods. The permit the traders presented as a defense was from the commanding office at Fort Pitt for the carrying of
goods for the support of the troops.

Three local magistrates were present led by William Smith. Justice
Smith answered the permit by noting that no military officer's pass
would do without a local magistrate's pass also. Grant acted arrogantly,
dismissing the power of the civil authority in military matters. He neither accepted nor read the magistrates' legal warrants. They reminded
Grant that there was a civil government in Pennsylvania, not a military one; that the road over which the traders traveled was a provincial road not a king's highway; and that the fort was a provincial fort
not a royal one, built and paid for by themselves. They would not
have these used against them. The ultimatum of the magistrates might
have sounded ridiculous to the commander of British regulars, but the
presence of 300 armed and grim-faced frontiersmen outside the fort
caused Grant concern. However, it did not immediately convince him
to turn over the traders to the magistrates for trial.

Restraint was not high of the list of frontier qualities, and the Black
Boys thereafter opened fire on the fort. Smith's rangers kept it up for
two days and nights, so closely marking their targets that no one was
permitted to go in or out or even show his head above the parapet.
Firing was kept up on all parts of the fort, rifle and musket balls sending splinters of wood everywhere so that the sentries could not stand
upright in the bastions. Amazingly no one was hurt save James Smith,
who took a slight wound from the return fire early in the siege, but
Grant was forced ultimately to abandon the post, marching out with
military honors under arms with flags flying.[11]

The battlefield courage of its civilian leaders, and their unapologetic ruthlessness during the Allegheny Uprising, would become a role model for others who aspired to independence. (Author's collection)

A few days later, some of the valley men had their muskets and rifles confiscated by roaming British patrols. Some local men had a serious firefight with one of these patrols, which was forced to take refuge in a settler's cabin. Sergeant Leonard McGlashan of the 42nd was wounded, as was one of the locals, John Brown. McGlashan later related in a legal deposition that he was astounded at the time of the incident that these backwoodsmen actually meant to kill him. Grant was ultimately forced to surrender the firearms to Justice William McDowell who, though neutral, returned them to their owners as illegal seizures. The National Rifle Association considers these incidents in May 1765 involving the citizens of the Conococheague Valley the first fight for the right to keep and bear arms in America.

The people's right to have their own personal arms for their defense is related in the second of 10 amendments, suggesting by its position in the Bill of Rights its importance to the founders. It is also described in the English Bill of Rights (1689) and in the philosophical and political writings of Aristotle, Cicero, Machiavelli, Locke, the Patriot Whigs, and others. It was even upheld by the U.S. Courts for the defeated soldiers and citizens of the Confederate South in the aftermath of the Civil War. Nonetheless, the concept is constantly under attack by social reformers and the progressive movement. The individual right to defend oneself with firearms (shotguns) remains a basic common law prerogative even in the gun-phobic United Kingdom, and a wider understanding of the individual right to own guns is presently enshrined in U.S. statute law with respect to decisions of the U.S. Supreme Court in *District of Columbia v. Heller* (2008) and *MacDonald v. Chicago* (2010).

REGULATOR REBELLION— CLINGING TO THEIR BIBLES

Other rebellious groups that formed in 1764, such as North Carolina's Regulators, revolted against corrupt colonial officials who took advantage of the local farmers and their lack of knowledge of property law when they became debt-ridden due to famine and other unfortunate circumstances. The rebellion of the Regulators was no short outburst of colonial piqué, and some historians list it as a cause of the revolution. It lasted not months, but years, generally from 1764 to 1771, when it was brutally suppressed by the royal governor. Yet, the so-called War of Regulation—intended to regulate and reform government abuse— was waged against local authorities, not the Crown, and evidence suggests that many of these authorities later became Loyalist leaders during the revolution. The term Regulator went back to 17th-century England when local farmers attempted to put a stop to the extortion practices of local officials and particularly of the sheriffs of the courts under the fading Protectorate of Oliver Cromwell.

In 1764, the people from the western (Piedmont) counties of North Carolina were extremely dissatisfied with the governance of wealthy local officials, whom they considered cruel, arbitrary, and corrupt. The sheriffs of the courts had sole control over their local regions. Taxes were collected by these local sheriffs, many of whom were deemed to be greedy and acting for their own personal gain. The entire system, which depended on the integrity of local officials, was endorsed by the colonial governor, Arthur Dobbs, who feared losing their support. A small group of public officials and merchants—chief among them Dobbs' successor, William Tryon, and Edmund Fanning, a wealthy lawyer and town commissioner of Hillsborough—formed the Regulators main antagonists.

The core of the Regulator organization consisted of a number of radical Protestants, among them Scots-Irish Presbyterians and many Quakers and Pietists, led by Herman (a.k.a. Harmon) Husband, a prosperous farmer originally from Maryland. Husband quickly became one of the main spokesmen for the farmers' movement, as well as its chief chronicler and ideologue. His powerful ideas about social justice and moral virtue were tremendously influential among these farmers. One of the many to be inspired by the religious revival after hearing Reverend George Whitefield preach, Husband became disenchanted with his original faith and became first a "New Light" Presbyterian and then a Quaker. Husband always denied he was a Regulator, and indeed, as a pacifist he wouldn't take part in violence or threats of violence.

Historian of the Regulator movement Marjoleine Kars noted how social and religious undercurrents affected the rise of this political revolution:

> The voices . . . were not those of the learned ministers so ably captured by previous historians of religion. Instead, church minutes and the conversations among lay people recorded in the diaries of local Piedmont ministers revealed a world where farming men and women were deeply influenced by revivalist Protestantism and wrestled actively with crucial moral and political questions in their local communities. It seemed it could not be an accident that the Regulator Rebellion happened in the midst of this creative and subversive religious climate . . . the writings of Regulator spokesman Herman Husband suggests that the insurgent

climate created by the Great Awakening helped Piedmont farmers gain the individual and collective self-confidence to attempt to reform their government and rid it of corruption.[12]

The farmers repeatedly petitioned the governor and the assembly over their grievances, tried to set up meetings with local officials, and brought suits against the dishonest sheriffs. When such legal measures had little effect, they refused to pay their taxes, repossessed property seized for public sale to satisfy debts, disrupted court proceedings, and finally resorted to arms.

Governor Arthur Dobbs was an associate of the Ohio Company in Britain that sought to speculate in land in the Alleghenies. In 1762, Dobbs purchased two 100,000-acre tracts in the counties that were to become the focus of Regulator activity. Some of the early settlers contested Dobbs' right to the land based on their being first to clear and plant it. Instead of paying modest fees to the colonial government for claiming vacant land, farmers were being required to buy the farms they and their families had already created from the speculation company. They resisted Dobbs' efforts to survey his claims and blocked his attempts to eject them from their farms. They so scared county officials that none dared come to their neighborhoods to serve legal papers. Although Husband and about 20 families were dedicated to pacifism, the majority of these farmers were fierce Scotch-Irish Presbyterians with no such restrictions.[13] Historian James Webb, presently U.S. Senator from Virginia, himself an offshoot of Scots-Irish frontier ancestors, has noted that the "values-based combativeness, insistent egalitarianism, and . . . refusal to be dominated" were shared characteristics of these American frontiersmen.[14]

Upon the death of Dobbs in 1765, Governor William Tryon had come to the province, helped into office by Lord Hillsborough, an influential in-law who was a member of the Board of Trade and later secretary for the colonies. Tryon's out-of-hand dismissal of the farmers' grievances did much to escalate the conflict, and several demonstrations and mass meetings over the intervening years ended in counterproductive standoffs.

In 1770, a large group of irate Regulators disrupted the superior court in Hillsborough, beat up a number of lawyers, merchants, and officials, and destroyed the home of Edmund Fanning. The era obviously lacked even a modicum of decorum. The authorities retaliated forcefully. Husband had written to the proprietors of the colony warning that the greed for profits of the Ohio Company and its minions among the local officials threatened the liberty of the people. Almost as soon as the assembly opened, Husband, who had been elected a legislator for the second time in 1769, was accused of libel. Expelled from the assembly so that he could no longer claim legislative immunity, he was jailed and held in New Bern to prevent him from returning to the region. Popular sympathy for his plight grew the longer he remained incarcerated without a trial. Early in 1771, in the dead of winter, several hundred armed Regulators set out on a 200-mile march to rescue Husband, but they called off their march halfway through upon learning that the fearful authorities had set him free.

The assembly next passed a sweeping Riot Act that gave Tryon the authority and funds he needed to raise a military force and march against the Regulators. On May 16, 1771, about 1,100 provincial troops confronted more than of 2,000 farmers on a field near Alamance Creek about 20 miles west of Hillsborough. Seeking to bring about an

Tryon arrived with an army of reluctant militia and gentlemen volunteers (not Grenadiers as shown). The subsequent engagement near Alamance Creek is sometimes hailed as the first battle of the American Revolution (1771), and its repressive aftermath decisively ended the collective struggle of the Regulators. (Author's collection)

understanding, Husband accompanied the Regulators to the field, but seeing this was impossible he mounted his horse and rode away. His Quaker principles prompted him to avoid participation in a fight. A pitched battle ensued for more than two hours, thereafter leaving two-dozen farmers dead, along with 9 colonial troops. More than 150 men on both sides were wounded. One Regulator (James Few) was hanged on the spot without benefit of trial, one (Robert Thompson) was supposedly shot within the provincial camp by Tryon in a fit of rage. Six more farmers were hastily tried and hanged in Hillsborough. For the Scotsmen among the Regulators, the executions brought to mind the brutal aftermath of the Battle of Culloden in 1746. The brutality worked. At least 6,000 Regulators and sympathizers were forced to take an oath of allegiance as the victorious troops undertook a punitive march through the backcountry settlements. Some of the most dedicated Regulator leaders, including Husband, fled the province; other individual farmers remained defiant right up to the revolution.

One historian has called William Tryon "the evil genius of the royal cause in America" because of his many successes in prosecuting Loyalist raids on Patriot strongholds. He stood out early, however, in both North Carolina and New York as the most principled political architect of royal resistance to protest, as well as one of its most aggressive military leaders. During the revolution, Tryon operated with a force composed of more than 2,000 Loyalist militiamen encamped on Long Island near Flushing, Queens, in New York. He organized a stronghold on the north shore near Glen Cove and from here launched amphibious raids across the Long Island Sound into Connecticut.[15] During the 1779 raid on Norwalk, Connecticut, 88 homes, dozens of barns, and a church were burned, and a group of Patriot militiamen with a few small canon positioned on a local outcrop held off hundreds of Loyalist troops at the Battle of the Rocks.

1764: A YEAR OF DISAFFECTION

In 1764, with the French war finished, provincial soldiers and sailors suddenly released from their enlistments in wartime regiments or from extended cruises flooded the employment market just as the government officials cracked down on colonial maritime and commercial activity. These restrictions on business and the lack of coin and credit made the expansion of the work-for-wage labor force nearly impossible and an economic downturn ensued. As has been noted, 1764 was not a good year in America.

A fundamental tenet of British mercantilism was the belief that wages be kept as low as possible in order to foster the expansion of both commerce and employment. Government often made legislative concessions to business in order to insure a cheap labor market, and it was thought better to have a fully employed but underpaid work force than to have vagrants and homeless persons in the streets. It was the standing policy of colonial governments, however, to drive any unproductive stragglers out of their jurisdictions to lower the cost to local governments for poor relief. In 1764, for example, the Common Council of Philadelphia—ironically the City of Brotherly Love—banished from the city precincts thousands of unfortunates as idlers and dissolute persons sending them into the hinterland to find some friendlier town or to fend for themselves in the wilderness.

Swarms of constables were dispatched to the waterfronts and slums of other American cities to hunt out vagrants and loiterers so that they could keep down the cost of public charity. Orphans, abandoned children, and the capable infirmed were sent to the workhouse, if there was room in one, or bound out as indentures for a term of some years. The reader should note that only fortunate children in good health with parents or relations of means were offered apprenticeships or a place on a merchant vessel. Apprenticeships were a form of private education and often went to the highest bidder. Consequently, lacking well-meaning relations, a sea of unconstrained children and disenchanted teens were added to the mobs of former soldiers and sailors—made strong and tough in service—to give added voice to the political protests led by the radicals. Many of the young men from the disbanded provincial units of 1764 later joined the revolution serving as battle-tested officers and NCOs in the Continental Army.

The emerging middle classes in America were also sorely pressed in the postwar decade. Seizures of property and judgments for indebtedness skyrocketed after 1764. In the city of New York, they rose 500 percent in just two years, and in Philadelphia 625 percent in the same period. The average indebtedness in hundreds of cases was under £50. This was no meager sum, but it emphasizes that the middle class was feeling the pain of the postwar economic downturn.[16]

There were, moreover, several significant postwar financial panics and economic collapses. These involved the failure of large colonial partnerships or family owned concerns. As 1763 ended, the firm of Scott and MacMichael folded leaving an unindemnified debt of £50,000, followed in less than two years by the collapse of Nathaniel Wheelwright's business concerns valued at £170,000. These reversals, worth hundreds of millions of dollars in modern money and made worse by the cash restrictions of the Currency Act of 1764, "touched off an unprecedented financial panic and an epidemic of bankruptcies" that affected numerous colonial merchants up and down the line and stopped almost all the extension of credit to even long-established businesses. Ironically, this circumstance kept a number of small debtors out of prison as creditors accepted assignment of assets in lieu of coin in the bad economy.[17]

In each commercial center, a few wealthy merchant families had emerged, and several were later deeply involved in the tea crisis either as tea consignees or as tea protestors. Many of these took steps during the panic of 1764 to protect their wealth, canceling major purchases from tradesmen, deferring cash payments to creditors, withdrawing vessels from trade, calling in debts and commercial paper, and further deepening the colonial malaise.

The chief cause of these hard times in New England was attributed to the restrictive trade and currency regulations of 1764. The *Boston Post Boy* (June 5, 1765) reported that the number of trading vessels clearing for the West Indies was cut to one-fifth those employed before the legislation took effect. Coins had virtually disappeared from circulation, and John Hancock, whose own trading connections were endangered, noted that "times are very bad . . . in short such is the situation of things here that we do not know who is and who is not safe."[18] The Hancock family's commercial correspondence of this period contained a genuine sentiment bordering on economic despair, and the Philadelphia merchant, Stephen Collins, repeated the plaintive outlook in many letters to his London creditors, alleging that the wave of colonial bankruptcies were owing to the stagnation of trade brought on by the policies of the government.[19]

In many jurisdictions, unemployment was virtually made a criminal offense, and begging and loitering were discouraged. Further laws were passed in the 1770s to protect the cities from increasing numbers of undesirables, but the sparsely filled ranks of colonial law enforcement proved ineffective in keeping them outside the bounds of the cities. They had nowhere to go except as squatters on tribal lands, which were legally and practically closed to them because they generally lacked the means to purchase land, tools, oxen, or carts in any case.

Still, a cadre of capable but underemployed day workers was needed to fill the ranks of the military and navy at short notice, and in the interim to do the temporary or disagreeable jobs that ordinary Anglo-Americans did not want to do: cleaning public privies, shifting cargoes, digging ditches, sweeping streets of manure, or stacking firewood—the last being a backbreaking and continuous task in a region where wood supplied all the daily heating, laundering, and cooking needs of every household.

The daily supply of wood needed in a colonial household had to be cut and stacked for seasoning and then shifted to cover periodically so that it was kept dry year round before burning. Slaves were used for the onerous task of shifting stacks like these in the South, and a farmer blessed with many children assigned the task to them as part of their chores. It was important elsewhere, even in the cities, to support a surplus of young men at subsistence levels to do these tasks. Consequently, by the time of the Boston Tea Party, it had become the function of urban government only to keep the mob in check, not to eliminate it completely.[20]

The efforts of the ministry to restrict trade and shipping, and frankly to limit out-of-control smuggling after the French War, threatened the livelihood of a whole segment of the waterfront population. Forty-five thousand tons of shipping and upwards of 3,000 men were employed in the fisheries in 1764 alone.[21] The common talk among the merchants of Boston was that legitimate trade in New England was at an end, and unemployed maritime workers of all types were added to the mobs of displaced and disaffected landsmen that made the earliest calls for liberty in America.[22] The merchant shippers could not remain idle while their profits evaporated, their vessels rotted at anchor, and their harbor fees and other debts accumulated. Many turned to illegal expedients. The so-called Smuggling Interest thereby became a factor of great potential strength in public affairs in all the seaports.[23]

It has been noted that the people of the colonial waterfronts took an active role in the increasing public disorder. Before there were Sons of Liberty and Liberty trees in Boston, there were the Sons of Neptune— as the sailors, mariners, and former privateers called themselves—who rioted in the streets of New York for the rights of Englishmen.[24] The natural rowdiness of the waterfront denizens ranged from mere mischief, such as tavern brawls, to sometimes bruising battles between large groups of men. Flowing rum, loose women, and pent-up frustrations of being marooned ashore for long periods with no hope of profit made seamen prime candidates for inclusion in any public demonstration.

Although the mobs of Boston and New York stand out in the historical record, the populations of the smaller port cities of Connecticut and Rhode Island were particularly notorious for their resistance to the government. During the three winters on station in New London aboard HMS *Cygnet*, British naval officers Charles Leslie and Philip

Durell found the citizens of the town disrespectful of their office, disobedient to the law, and discourteous to their persons. Most of the respectable population refused to be seen in public with Royal Navy officers or to attend private functions where they were openly received. Townsmen initiated brawls wherever the British Jack Tars settled down to drink or eat while on shore leave, and many sailors were waylaid and beaten after trying to spark the young ladies of the town.

Spontaneous demonstrations erupted at the sight of a revenue cutter, and Royal Navy press gangs looking to man a shorthanded vessel met with unprecedented levels of non-cooperation and even violence among the people. In 1764, Rhode Islanders fired on a Royal Navy cutter *St. John* that was engaged in the suppression of smuggling, and in 1769 the people of Newport seized and burned a revenue service sloop ironically named *Liberty*. It must also be remembered that it was the mariners of Providence, Rhode Island, who attacked and burned the Royal Navy cutter *Gaspée* for no reason other than a virulent response to the arrogance of its commander in 1772.

Also, for no apparent reason and without warning, the seafaring population of Machias, Maine, attempted to seize the youthful commander of the Royal Navy cutter *Margaretta* while he sat at Sunday services ashore in 1775. Midshipman James Moore barely escaped by jumping into a waiting boat and pulling for his vessel. On the next morning the Americans in a lumber transport closed with *Margaretta* and the cutter was taken with heavy losses on both sides. In this first naval battle of the revolution, Moore was mortally wounded with a ball to the chest and another to the stomach. The youth died after two agonizing days ashore. Of the British compliment of approximately 30, eight marines and sailors were killed. Among the two dozen Americans involved in the actual combat, three died and a dozen were wounded.

THE SONS OF LIBERTY

Called "Sons of Liberty" by British Colonel Isaac Barre in a speech before Parliament, like-minded groups of street protestors belonging to this organization could be found almost everywhere in the colonies. The Sons of Liberty had been founded in Boston with the announcement of the passage of the Stamp Act in 1764 and officially formed as a network in 1766. Physical resistance to the Stamp Act and the stamp agents had begun in a small counting room above the Chase and Speakman distillery, where the cofounders of the group met with Sam Adams (the ostensible instigator of the idea) and others from the town government to form the so-called Loyal Nine. These were not the leaders of Boston society, but rather its workers, business owners, and tradesmen working in concert with its like-minded lawyers, local magistrates, and judges.

More than nine persons seem to have been part of this leadership group at one time or another, between its founding and the outbreak of the revolution. Among those active in the group in Boston were Benjamin Edes (an Adams friend) and his partner John Gill, publishers; Chase Avery, John Avery, and Gabriel Johonnot, distillers; Joseph Field, sea captain and mariner; John Smith and Stephen Cleverly, brass founders; Thomas Crafts, painter and Japanner (decorator in the Oriental style); Henry Bass (an Adams cousin) and George Trott, jewelers; Thomas Young, Joseph Warren, and Benjamin Church, medical doctors; William Phillips, James Otis, and John Adams, lawyers; William Cooper, the town clerk; John Scollay, selectman and chairperson of the town council; Paul Revere, silversmith and engraver; and John Mackay, John Hancock, Henry Welles, John Rowe, William Molineaux, and Solomon Davis, all various merchants and shippers.[25]

Although tradesmen and professionals seemed to direct the majority of the protests, the workingmen of Boston performed the actual activities and fomented violence in the streets. They often gathered by torchlight under the elm tree in Hanover Square near the Chase and Speakman distillery, which became known as the Liberty Tree. A shoemaker by the name of Ebenezer Mackintosh (a.k.a. McIntosh)— a leader of the attack on the Hutchinson house—was styled captain and had charge of the illuminations, the posting of signs, and the hanging of effigies.[26]

Some unaffiliated groups of persons also used the names Sons of Liberty or Liberty Boys to carry out acts of revenge and other violence not related to the cause, and the genuine organization(s) was forced to carefully police itself of pretenders, opportunists, and opponents, whose strategy was to degrade the reputation of the genuine organization, a tactic used against the T.E.A. Party in 2010 and 2011. There was some difficulty in doing this. The organization was necessarily secret with private passwords to protect the members from Tory spies. Rowe, Molineaux, and Davis often acted as spokesmen before the Town Meeting; and Thomas Hutchinson called these men to the particular attention of London as heading the Patriot committee of merchants. Governor Sir Francis Bernard complained that some of the ringleaders walked the streets with impunity, and he abandoned all hope of restoring order. Though he dared not do so, Bernard threatened to send Sam Adams, John Hancock, and others thought to be leaders to England for trial as agitators of the mob.

In Boston, the Sons of Liberty may have numbered about 300 persons. On public occasions, each member wore an identifying medal suspended from his neck with the figure of an upraised arm grasping in its hand a pole surmounted with a liberty cap and surrounded by the words "Sons of Liberty." On the reverse was a representation of the Liberty Tree standing in an empty Hanover Square provocatively marked "Liberty Hall."

The Sons of Liberty was a self-governing authority—almost a shadow government within each city where it was established—issuing warrants for the arrest of suspect disaffected persons and often arranging beforehand the outcome of local elections and town meetings to its own advantage.[27] Hutchinson noted his own analysis of the situation in Boston:

> When there is occasion to . . . hang effigies or pull down houses, [the mob] are employed; but since [order] has been brought to the system, [the Sons of Liberty] are somewhat controlled by a superior set consisting of the master-masons, and carpenters, [and merchants] of the town. . . . When anything of more importance is to be determined . . . a general meeting of the inhabitants of Boston [is called], where Otis, with his mob-high eloquence, prevails in every motion, and the town first determine[s] what is necessary to be done, and then apply either to the Governor or Council, or resolve that it is necessary that the General Court correct it; and it would be a very extraordinary resolve indeed that is not carried into execution.[28]

The first widely known acts attributed to the Sons of Liberty took place in Boston when an effigy of Andrew Oliver (the distributor of stamps for Massachusetts) was found hanging in a tree on Newbury Street. Led by Mackintosh, the Sons of Liberty secured a promise of resignation from Oliver, despoiled the Hutchinson home, toppled the cupola from his roof, and burned his furnishings in a pile in the street. They also attacked the houses of the comptroller of the customs and the registrar of the admiralty—destroying the legal records and sworn depositions against smugglers in the hated admiralty court in the process.[29]

In Connecticut, more than 500 angry demonstrators surrounded Distributor of Stamps Jared Ingersoll. In response to one of the least violent demonstrations in New England, Ingersoll instantly resigned his post, threw his hat in the air, and cheered for liberty. The protests against the stamps and the agents of the Crown in Rhode Island quickly turned violent, however. At that time, HMS *Cygnet* (commanded by Charles Leslie) was the largest warship in the harbor at Newport. The local stamp agent, Augustus Johnston, the chief customs agent, John Robinson, and several of their friends retreated to the warship in fright when riots broke out. Leslie ran out *Cygnet's* guns and made a great show of clearing the ship for action and preparing to repel boarders by raising the nettings and distributing cutlasses and pikes to the crew. This ploy kept the rioters at a distance. The siege of the vessel lasted several weeks after forcing the resignation of Johnston. The governor of the colony, Samuel Ward, was fully in sympathy with the protestors.

Although the details differ, circumstances in the other colonies were not greatly different from those in New England. In New York, violence broke out when a mob gathered to burn the lieutenant governor in effigy and harassed the troops with a surprising lack of regard for their own safety in the face of fixed bayonets. Several homes were invaded and looted. Windows were broken and fires set in the streets. Only the restraint practiced by the soldiers and their officers prevented an exchange of gunfire. In New York, an indiscriminate group of lawyers, merchants, and printers was thought by the Crown to be at the bottom of the protests, but the overt street activists like mariners Isaac Sears and Alexander McDougall, vintner John Lamb, and cabinetmaker Marinus Willett made a much more lasting presence as street brawlers and rabble-rousers. Even the colonial legislature was split between the powerful Delancey (a.k.a. DeLancey) and Livingston families.[30]

Factions in the New York assembly were initially more interested in winning legislative power from the royal governor in the short term than in maintaining the rights of the people. Some among the socially superior upper classes in the city of New York, including those in both the Delancey and Livingston factions, were openly friendly to the local Sons of Liberty. While the Delanceys used the uproar to better consolidate their own power in the assembly, their political rivals, the Livingston's, won the true support of the mob.

Alexander McDougall, for instance, was initially an undistinguished figure on the New York waterfront, but during the controversy the former privateer emerged as a first-rate agitator. He published an anonymous pamphlet titled *To the Betrayed Inhabitants of the City and*

Colony of New York (1769), in which he blasted the New York Assembly for violating the trust of the people. Lieutenant Governor Colden offered a reward of £100 for the name of the author, and James Parker, the printer, was forced under close questioning to disclose that the pamphlet came from his shop in New Jersey. Parker was charged with libel and sedition, but he died in 1770 while the case was pending. Parker is best known, however, for founding the first newspaper in New Jersey, the *Constitutional Courant.* The paper bore the tongue-in-cheek imprint "Printed by Andrew Marvel, at the Sign of the Bribe refused, on Constitution-Hill, North America." Parker's one-room press building from 1765 still stands in a small local park in downtown Woodbridge, New Jersey.[31]

Fearing that McDougall might bring down the New York Assembly, partisan members led by James Delancey accused him of sedition, and had him arrested and indicted. The Assembly was ultimately dissolved in any case. While imprisoned to await trial, McDougall announced from jail, "I rejoice. . . . The cause for which I suffer is capable of converting chains into laurels and a gaol [jail] into a paradise." While spending three months under arrest, McDougall received delegations of radicals who showered him with donations of food and furniture that made his cell more comfortable. He commonly entertained large parties therein, including many women. His persecution by the Delancey family turned the mob against them. The members of the Livingston family, always opposed to the designs of the Delanceys, took up McDougall's cause, and the radical population of the city embraced them. Fearful that McDougall and his followers posed a clear danger to their businesses, the merchants of the city affected his release on bail. He was never brought to trial.[32]

Other than Governor William Tryon, James Delancey of New York was probably the best-known American Tory. The grandson of the judge of the same name, who had presided over the freedom of the press trial of John Peter Zenger, Delancey was the county sheriff of Westchester under the British regime. Driven from the city in 1776, he formed a group of like-minded Loyalists known as Delancey's Refugee Corps. These men formed one of the most effective Loyalist militia units to serve during the rebellion, and Delancey was made a lieutenant colonel in the British army hierarchy. The unit was headquartered at Morrisannia, a section of the Bronx (ironically owned by Patriot leader Gouverneur Morris) where many displaced Loyalist families subsisted in makeshift shacks surrounding the Morris mansion on the spoils of raids undertaken by the Refugee Corps. Delancey increased the size of his corps until it reached 450 men by recruiting among the refugee families. They became the British scourge of the "neutral ground" surrounding the city in present-day Westchester County, where both armies attempted to patrol in order to use its resources as an open larder for provisions.

New York was always a hotbed of antigovernment protest. The struggle for political dominance in New York, however, was no unevenly matched contest between mobs of like-minded citizens and a few customs officials as it was in Boston or Newport. No general population in America was so evenly split in its loyalties or so evenly distributed. From first to last, rebel sympathizers and government Loyalists were in constant conflict and turmoil.[33]

The New York stamp agent, James McEvers, had immediately resigned in 1764 leaving the colonial lieutenant governor, Cadwallader Colden, responsible for the stamps until the newly appointed governor, Sir Henry Moore, should arrive. Unlike many colonial officials, Colden was openly dedicated to implementing the Stamp Act, and the stamps were moved to Fort George at the tip of Manhattan where they were secured. Colden was sure that the Sons of Liberty intended to seize the stamps as a propaganda victory. The Sons of Liberty then staged a particularly effective demonstration, massing several thousand protestors in a candle and torchlight procession down Broadway. The demonstrators finally penetrated the outer defenses of the fort and threatened the watch.

In a letter, later found among Colden's effects, written on November 2, 1765, the writer (whose scribbled signature is generally recorded as E. Carther) gives a picturesque and detailed account of the so-called Stamp Act Riot perpetrated by the Sons of Liberty in New York the previous evening, part of which is reproduced below:

> In the evening the citizens began to muster about the streets. About 7 in the evening I heard a great huzzaring [cheering] near the Broadway. I ran that way with a number of others where the mob just began. They had an effigy of the Governor [actually Colden, Gov. Henry Moore being en route to the colony] made of paper, which sat on an old chair, which a seaman carried on his head. The mob went from the Fields [a park] down the Fly [Beekman Street] huzzaring at every corner. . . . The mob went from thence to Mr. Mc Evers who was appointed for stamp master [by] London. Since he did not accept it [the position of stamp agent] they honored him with 3 huzzars. From thence they went

to the fort that the governor might see his effigy. . . . The merchants were exceedingly pleased, and the mob still increasing from thence with about 5 or 600 candles to alight them. . . . I ran down to the fort to hear what they said. As the mob came down it made a beautiful appearance. . . . They placed the gallows against the fort gate and took clubs and beat against it. And there gave three huzzars in defiance. They then concluded to burn their effigies and the governor's coach . . . before [Colden's] eyes.[34]

Ten packages of the stamps were ultimately turned over to the Sons of Liberty by order of a very frightened city council and burned. These were the only stamps or stamped paper to fall into the hands of the protestors anywhere in America. This incident was a major blow to royal prestige in New York and elsewhere in the colonies.

Sir Henry Moore missed almost all this activity. As the new governor of New York, arriving in late 1765, he calmed the protests by meeting directly with Sears and other leaders of the Sons of Liberty. Moore agreed with them and the colony's assembly to ignore the Stamp Act, and he gained additional goodwill by reducing military deployments within the city. His openness and courtesy earned him tributes, whereas other colonial governors were being burned in effigy. He died suddenly in 1769 generally respected by all in the colony. William Tryon was appointed to replace him.

The protests in Pennsylvania and Delaware were less well defined, mirroring to some extent the lack of support for either the position of the Crown or that of the protestors in those places. Philadelphia was a city noted for its moderation and southeastern Pennsylvania for its pacifism. Tiny Delaware was considered at the time all but an appendage of its larger neighbor—a circumstance that continues to irk its residents to this day. The Sons of Liberty having an undue influence in a largely loyal colony of Delaware, some consideration must be given here to its antecedents.

Due largely to ambiguities in the royal land grants made to Thomas West (Lord De la Warre) and William Penn, the so-called Three Lower Counties that made up Delaware (New Castle, Kent, and Sussex) had undergone "a long series of wrangles and dissentions" that led to "unpleasant relationships" with other parts of the Pennsylvania colony. In 1701, Penn had recognized the eventual separation of the Lower Counties, and in 1704, he granted them their own separate assembly.[35] The situation was further complicated by the long-standing local controversy over the desirability of continuing Pennsylvania's proprietary government.[36]

In 1763, Charles Mason and Jeremiah Dixon fixed the boundaries in the region in the form of the Mason-Dixon Line, and in 1765 Caesar Rodney, Thomas McKean, and George Read were appointed to represent the Lower Counties at the Stamp Act Congress. The people of Delaware were not particularly hard pressed by the taxes imposed by the Townshend Acts—their lifestyles being described as "simple and plain." Nonetheless, they seemingly took offense at the invasion of their rights as Englishmen. Immediately after the Boston Tea Party, mass meetings were held at New Castle, Dover, and Lewes, and the 18 members of the assembly were instructed to send a letter to the governor, John Penn, expressing loyalty to the king, but protesting the imposition of the Boston Port Act and the proposed taking of persons accused of treason, or any other felony, to London for trial.[37]

Having been granted virtual independence in 1704, the idea of the three counties of a separate colony of Delaware further distancing themselves from Britain was not widely accepted in the 1770s. There remained, moreover, strong support for Tory policies in largely Anglican Sussex County and in overwhelmingly pacifist Kent County. New Castle County, with its commercial ties with Baltimore and Philadelphia and its largely Presbyterian and Scotch-Irish population, was, on the other hand, a stronghold of Patriot power.[38]

There were in Delaware a great number of influential men who were fully aware of the need to resolve their grievances with the Crown, but who were unwilling to renounce their allegiance to the king. Holding a 7–3 majority in New Castle County (but being an overall minority in the rest of the colony), the Patriots worked hard to support the Sons of Liberty throughout Delaware. Among the leadership of the Sons were Dr. James Tilton, Judge Thomas Rodney, William Killen (once tutor to John Dickinson), and John Haslet (an experienced officer from the French wars). The Sons of Liberty in Delaware proved well organized, unified in their purpose, and unnervingly ruthless in the prosecution of their cause. They were capable of forcing the election of many like-minded men to positions of authority throughout the colony. Considering the political makeup of the population, some of these choices were of necessity lukewarm Patriots—among them John Evans, John McKinly, and even John Dickinson. Shortly after Caesar Rodney was elected president of the colony, the Patriots were able to break the morale of the Tories through the vigorous enforcement of the Test Oaths and the confiscation of their property and firearms. Haslet, in particular, pursued with great vigor the disarmament of all persons considered disaffected from the cause. Once disarmed and pushed from the political arena, the Tories proved incapable of competing with the superior organization of the Sons of Liberty.[39]

A serious Loyalist effort, known as the Black Camp Rebellion, was made in Delaware in 1780. About 400 Tories terrorized the Whig population of Sussex County by seizing their weapons, kidnapping their militia officers, and generally placing the countryside in an uproar. Patriot forces pursued these Tories into the swamps, and the local committee of safety arrested 37 men and tried the group for treason to America. Found guilty, they were sentenced by the court to the most hideous punishment of being hanged, drawn, and quartered. However, all the prisoners were later paroled by the General Assembly. The leader of the Delaware Loyalists, Cheney Clow, was apprehended in 1782 near the end of the war and executed.[40]

In Philadelphia, the movement toward cooperation with the protestors in Boston or New York was devoid of any real vitality, and influential citizens like Pennsylvania's Joseph Galloway doubted the efficacy of severing the city's commercial ties with Britain except in the case of dire emergency. The stamp collector in Pennsylvania initially blamed the outbreak of violent protests on the machinations of Presbyterian ministers, but a committee composed of five merchants and printers seems to have actually led the protestors.

Nearby New Jersey, on the other hand, was a patchwork of strongly held sentiments with neighboring townships, taking diametrically opposing views on almost any issue involving the Crown. During the revolution, New Jersey would rarely be under the total control of either party, and it would become the site of the greatest number of war atrocities enacted on the civilian population by its own residents.[41]

Governor William Franklin of New Jersey turned to Captain James Hawker of HMS *Sardoine*, who was on station in the Delaware River opposite Newcastle (Delaware) on the western border of the Jersey colony, for aid in the stamp crisis. Hawker accepted the task of securing New Jersey's stamps on his own responsibility, and he also accepted those of nearby Pennsylvania. When winter ice began to build in the river threatening his ship, Hawker took *Sardoine* from the water, placed it in a cradle above the normal high-tide mark, and made a fortress of it bristling with cannon and swivel guns. He let it be known that anyone attempting to take the stamps would be fired upon. No one tried.[42]

Hawker was gallant almost to the point of disbelief. He had once sent a boat from *Sardoine* to the wharf at Charleston, South Carolina, to inspect a schooner he suspected as a smuggler. He recorded that "a mob collected [that] immediately threw stones, logs of wood, staves, and any other thing they could lay hold of into the boat, wounded the officer and men and obliged two of them to jump overboard to prevent worse." Hawker had armed all his crew, save a skeleton watch, and made for the merchant schooner in several of the ship's boats standing "in the bow of the foremost myself, with the British flag in my hand." He was met by the Sons of Liberty, "armed with cutlasses, axes, stones, clubs, etc. to resist me forcibly." A violent clash worthy of a Hollywood motion picture was but a heartbeat away when the owner of the vessel, with a cooler head, brought forth the vessel's clearance papers and cargo manifest, which showed that it was legitimate, and ended the confrontation.[43]

The Committees of Correspondence in each colony were utilized as a means of coordinating the actions of the Sons of Liberty. Dr. Thomas Young, a protégé of Sam Adams and a radical frequently charged with being too impetuous in his speech, nonetheless urged others among the Sons of Liberty to be more circumspect in their activities. Young wrote to Adams that "patient endurance" was a characteristic of a good soldier, and Adams responded that patience was also a characteristic of a good patriot. Young later wrote to Hugh Hughes, a leader of the Sons of Liberty in New York, advising him that raising a great movement among that part of the population that was not yet aligned with the cause needed to be done slowly and in a determined manner: "We need not spill the blood even of mistaken [misguided] enemies . . . if we can otherwise reduce them to reason, and make them our friends. Should the conflict nonetheless end in blows, we can lose nothing by deferring the combat till our forces are well disciplined and all mankind possessed with the justice of our cause."[44]

Sons of Liberty protests were to be found in every colony, but activities in the plantation colonies were usually less violent and less dramatic than in the northeastern or middle colonies. Prominent among them was Patrick Henry, whose "Liberty or Death" slogan spoken in the Virginia House of Burgesses was widely adopted by Patriots throughout the colonies. The aristocratic planters were generally more favorable to dignified protests in writing by representative assemblies than they were of physically assembling in unseemly protest in the streets. There were, nonetheless, a number of momentous confrontations.

Moving geographically through the South in consideration of the protests waged in the 1760s, the people of Maryland immediately requested the resignation of their designated stamp agent, Zachariah

Hood. Fearing violence, Hood fled to New York where he demanded that Captain Kennedy order one of his ships to Annapolis as a floating stamp distribution station. Kennedy absolutely refused to sanction the idea, but he sent Captain John Brown of HM brig *Hawke* to Annapolis anyway, to insure the peace of the colony and to serve as a place of refuge for loyal colonial officials should they need it. The only violence seen in the colony was a tavern brawl involving a group of Jack Tars from HMS *Hornet* that resulted in the outnumbered sailors being thrown into the Chesapeake Bay after receiving a minor battering at the hands of some local toughs loosely regarded as Liberty Boys.

Nonetheless, an earlier case involving Brown, a Royal Navy officer and de facto customs agent, illustrates the lack of cooperation between the services, the hostility of the colonial courts, and the tactics used by American merchants, all of which plagued the enforcement of the Revenue Acts. Brown had been thrown into jail briefly in New York by Judge Richard Morris when he tried to libel a merchant ship as a smuggler, but could not post the outrageously large bond of £10,000 imposed by the judge for possible damages to the ship and cargo. Brown, a £30 per month captain—as the pro-Patriot judge was well aware—could not amass such a vast sum, nor would the local customs official, Charles Apthorp, aid him. This set of circumstances resulted in a five-month-long adjournment of the case, a suit for damages brought against Brown by the shipowners, and the ultimate release of the vessel without charges.[45]

Virginia customs agents avoided violence by immediately issuing unstamped papers. Nonetheless, in May 1765, seven anti-stamp tax resolutions were proposed in the Virginia House of Burgesses. The *Virginia Resolutions* claimed that only the colonial legislature had the right to tax Virginians. "Taxation of the people by themselves, or by persons chosen by themselves to represent them . . . is the only security against a burthensome taxation." The first reaction in the colonies to the unprecedented *Virginia Resolves* was one of shock, yet many Americans found themselves in accord with their primary thrust of no taxation without representation.[46]

In North Carolina, Lieutenant Constantine J. Phipps delivered the stamps to the colony in HM sloop *Diligence*. In compliance with his orders, Phipps placed the stamps into the hands of the governor, William Tryon. In the absence of a stamp agent, who had resigned, Tryon ordered that the stamps be transferred to HMS *Viper*, commanded by Jacob Lobb, who was on station at Wilmington. Lobb accepted the stamps and then unwisely attempted to enforce their use, seizing three vessels for having unstamped papers as they approached the mouth of the Cape Fear River. The Sons of Liberty, backed by the people of Wilmington, took their revenge by stopping all provisions and water to the Royal Navy ships in the harbor and by jailing a boat's crew from *Viper* that came ashore. In February 1765, one thousand protestors surrounded the customs house to demand the release of the seized merchant vessels. Three days later, boats from both *Viper* and *Diligence* combined in a nighttime amphibious operation to secretly infiltrate Fort Johnston that overlooked the harbor and to spike all the colonial cannon found there. With the ships' guns run out of their ports the next morning, Lobb and Phipps released the three merchant vessels, thereby diffusing further unrest in the colony. The stamps remained unused.

Captain Jeremiah Morgan of HM sloop-of-war *Hornet* caused the legislative assembly of North Carolina to vote that he be arrested if he again set foot in the colony. In February 1767, the *Virginia Gazette* noted of Morgan: "[He] is very assiduous, and lets nothing escape him . . . was he to stay, we should be ruined to all intents and purposes." In September 1767, the Liberty Boys of Norfolk, Virginia, led by the mayor of the town, physically attacked Morgan and his men when they came ashore looking for deserters. The Royal Navy men had to fight their way back to their boat. A warrant was later issued for Morgan's arrest by the local magistrate.[47]

The stamps for South Carolina and Georgia reposed for some time in the hold of HMS *Speedwell*, commanded by Robert Fanshawe. Thereafter, South Carolina's stamps were permanently deposited at Fort Johnson in Charleston, never to be used. Upon receipt of Georgia's stamps, however, Governor James Wright actually attempted to issue them and put the Stamp Act into practice. Wright was notable as the only governor to actually have issued documents with the stamps attached. Although Fanshawe supported the governor with a detachment of marines, Wright backed down as soon as a mob of protestors appeared before his home. The stamps were quickly returned to the hold of *Speedwell* for their protection.

In every colony, the stamps spent at least some time under the protection of the Royal Navy; and, with the exception of those few stamps burned in New York or issued in Georgia, none were destroyed or taken. The navy had done its part during the crisis, but the Stamp Act had been a total failure as a source of revenue and as a government policy. Although the act had failed miserably everywhere in the colonies, London considered what happened in New York the worst failure of the whole Stamp Act affair.

Whether openly brazen, like Morgan, or bravely romantic, like Hawker with flag in hand, these sea officers embodied both the best and worst features to be found among the men of the Royal Navy. Devoted to the best interests of their sovereign and their empire, most Royal Navy commanders stationed in America suffered from a common misconception of the colonials as crude, avaricious, and innately disloyal. In following their instructions concerning the customs in too literal a manner, these naval officers drove many otherwise loyal colonials from private grumbling to active resistance, if not open rebellion. Had every British officer and agent carried out the Crown's program to the letter, as did Morgan and Hawker, the American Revolution may have begun a decade earlier.[48]

CHAPTER 8

Frontier Economics

The wood was so thick, that for a mile at a time we could not find a place of the size of a hand, where the sunshine could penetrate, even in the clearest day.

—*Conrad Weiser, colonial Indian agent*

WILDERNESS EVERYWHERE

The Proclamation of 1763 was a largely unsung cause of colonial unrest on the frontiers, as has been suggested earlier. However, Anglo-Americans were not only dealing with the acts of Parliament; they were also wrestling with the laws of frontier economics. The frontier was virtually everywhere in America, and a day's ride into the interior from any settlement revealed an almost impenetrable forest broken only by the trails and fields of Native Americans and nature's waterways. For the Europeans, the thought that North America was a wilderness populated with wild men and savages was a great advantage to the newcomer who wished to establish his own claim to land in the New World. Land and its legal disposition were of no small regard to the first settlers in America, and they took the legalities of property transfer and tenure quite seriously.

The concepts of wilderness and civilization were at opposite ends of a spectrum with a scale in between suggesting thorough shading or blending of the two in the center, which was marked *the frontier*. The

frontier was possibly best described in European terms as "ploughed"—
a balance between man's needs and God's clockwork nature.[1] "The
frontier [was] the outer edge of the wave—the meeting point between
savagery and civilization."[2]

Just how wild a region had to be to qualify as a wilderness in the
minds of colonial settlers is not certain. Some small amount of previous settlement—such as well-established Native American villages and
burial grounds—seems to have been tolerated as a sign of previous
ownership. Any form of civilization that failed to demonstrate its influence in European terms such as cartways, buildings, barns, and
fenced fields seems to have been dismissed. The Dutch in Manhattan
and Long Island had purchased land from the tribes, and the Moravians of Pennsylvania had scrupulously acknowledged repeated Native
American land claims paying for the same parcels several times. In the
17th century, William Penn had made a large purchase in the Delaware Valley that was turned into a fraud (The Walking Purchase) by
the agents of his heirs, who manipulated the somewhat ambiguous
terms of the agreement in 1735 to dislocate virtually all its aboriginal
owners among the Delaware nation.

It is true, however, that many of the Native American tribes of New
England had been decimated by disease or intertribal warfare and had
seemingly abandoned their land even by their own standards of ownership. White relations with the Pocumtuck Nation can serve as an
example of how even legal land transfers could generate unwanted consequences. The Pocumtucks of Deerfield in the Connecticut River
Valley were so decimated by disease and intertribal warfare that whites
could have simply occupied the land without resistance, but the prospective settlers chose to do the right thing and purchase it from the
survivors of the tribe. The total cost to the Massachusetts government
was modest, and the land was transferred so that those white citizens
who chose to establish themselves at Deerfield might do so freely and
with a clear conscience. It seems in this case that the English were
trying to follow the law, and the sum offered was not unfair in
17th-century terms. Yet the problem was that the whites were following English law as it pertained to Native American land ownership and
sovereignty. The selling of land was made to imply an acceptance of
the English concepts of land ownership by the tribe that they had not
otherwise confirmed or understood. To the Pocumtucks, the transac-
tion had been a simple exchange of value for value; for the English, the
exchange was a form of submission. The English had simply ignored
the necessity of establishing this level of consensus by dictating their

own sovereignty over the Native American population—sovereignty that they loudly proclaimed on the international stage as proof of British dominion over the lands occupied by all their Native American allies. In this way, they claimed all of Iroquoia in central New York as land granted to the Iroquois through the sufferance of the Crown, although the tribe had possessed it for generations before any white had entered the region. Such arrogance could only come from a special sense of ethnocentricity that the British exhibited elsewhere in their empire, especially when they considered the original occupants of a region inferior—people of different races like Native Americans, Africans, Chinese, Hindus, and Indonesian islanders, as well as white Welshmen, Scots, Irishmen, Germans, Dutchmen, and ultimately colonial Americans.

WEALTH UNDER YOUR FEET

Privileged friends of the Crown and numerous charter companies were given grants of land in the colonies amounting to hundreds of thousands of acres. Land was a form of wealth, but if it could not be put into production, it was simply a liability for its proprietors. These men attempted to transform their land into cash by selling or renting it. Property agents and speculators attempted to make a profit through these land transactions, the way realty agents do today, but they could make no commissions unless the price of the land was within reach of those who were willing to occupy, clear, and plow it.

The first arrivals to New England in 1620 benefited from the abandoned fields of the Native Americans. Two years of poor production and rising discontent over the continuation of communal farming at Plymouth (the first failure of communal socialism in America) caused the Puritans to parcel out the land thereafter in lots of 20 acres. Each person in a family received an allotment with no family being given more than 100 acres. The parcels were randomly distributed among the existing fields in long strips much as yardlands had been assigned in Medieval English villages. Each allotted family tract was assured a frontage on the ocean or on a navigable stream so that small boats and barges could provide transportation. The community livestock (cattle, hogs, chickens, and goats) also was divided, but the pastureland and marshes were kept in common with sections allotted to individuals for the production of sweet and salt hay. Ultimately, the long discontinuous strips of farmland were sold, exchanged, and consolidated into family fields, and it was found that the new system of family farming caused overall productivity to increase.

As a result of these changes, a community that had lost half its members to starvation in 1621 had in 1625 a small amount of excess corn available for trade with the natives of Maine for furs. Soon, the colony was producing not only enough excess corn to trade with the tribes, but also enough to open trade with the Dutch in New Netherlands in return for manufactured goods. This marked the birth of commercial agriculture in New England as well as the initiation of an agricultural export trade from the region—New England's first significant violation of British mercantilism. By 1638, there were 356 separate family fields under cultivation in the Plymouth Colony covering five square miles. The division of land among families and the establishment of a feasible pattern of family farmsteads during the first decades of Puritan colonization set the standard for New England farming thereafter. Herein lay the seeds of wealth accumulation for future generations, but the farmers of New England generally failed to develop a commercial agriculture outside the need to feed the succeeding waves of incoming settlers, some 12,000 persons in the single decade of the 1630s.

Most Americans lived off the land divorced from the maritime trades and the details of commerce. The agricultural nature of the colonial economy and the subsistence farming of the frontiers were highly visible. (Author's collection)

Notwithstanding the commercial successes or failures experienced by disparate ethnic and national groups, agriculture generally remained the foundation of wealth everywhere in British North America. It came to be practiced across a wide spectrum, ranging from small subsistence farming in New England and on the frontiers to the well-ordered farms of Pennsylvania and the great commercial plantations of the South with their wealth-producing surplus of agricultural exports. Disentangling the farm labor system from this network of diverse agricultural establishments can be difficult. Some men in the Chesapeake, with superior resources or better connections, acquired substantial holdings spread over 1,000 acres, but New England maintained a more settled appearance, much like that of an English country village. In any case, the agricultural skills of colonials in all regions of British North America were not highly differentiated. Farm workers were often segregated from their landowning contemporaries only by their legal status as indentured workers, hirelings, or slaves.

As has been noted, the passion for land in New England had cooled within just a few generations of the first landing at Plymouth. The New England legislatures had allotted lands collectively to different church groups whose religious leaders partitioned the allotments among their congregations as they pleased. The succeeding generations of New England farmers found it difficult to add to their acreage, especially in the rocky coastal regions. This forced families to seek additional land to disperse to their children many days journey away from their initial holdings.

In New York, huge land grants were made to influential individuals instead of to disparate groups. The resulting *patroon* system, left over from the Dutch, was followed up and down the Hudson Valley, and powerful families like the Livingstons, the Phillipses, and the Warrens preempted individual ownership through an almost feudal system of tenancy and rents populated by German-speaking Europeans recruited for the purpose. A large number of Palatine Germans, who originally settled the Mohawk Valley and the Schoharie Lands of Central New York, came to America in 10 ships under contract as indentures in 1710 to Robert Livingston, who planned for them to establish a forest products industry along the rivers and streams of those regions. However, they quickly became disgruntled with being tenants and moved on to establish farms of their own. Many of these migrated down the Delaware and Susquehanna Rivers to Pennsylvania or west along the Mohawk River to form discreet German-language communities, like Palatine Bridge, Blenheim, Catskill, Bushkill, or simply Germantown. The family of Conrad Weiser, colonial Indian Agent in Pennsylvania in the 18th century, had been one of these, moving when he was an adolescent from Schoharie Creek near Schenectady to the Schuylkill River near Reading. By this means, many scattered German-speaking settlements were established on the frontier early in the 18th century. Where similar systems of tenancy were attempted in New Jersey, riots followed. Consequently, there developed in New Jersey a more evenly dispersed pattern of landholding.

In Pennsylvania—gateway to the frontier—land could be purchased from the proprietor through his agents. One hundred acres could be had for between £5 and £15 sterling, equivalent to from 1s. to 3s. per acre in coin, or approximately a day's wage for a craftsman for each unimproved acre. While a handful of Quaker and German (Pennsylvania Dutch is a misnomer) farms reached 1,000 acres, the majority was between 100 and 400 acres. A good 100-acre farmstead with dark rich soil could be had for £10 sterling in 1730, and it was worth approximately £120 in colonial currency three decades later when it had been cleared of trees.

The Germans among the immigrants to British North America were praised, in particular, by their 18th-century contemporaries for their "indomitable industry . . . earnestness . . . frugality and . . . consummate agricultural skill" in putting land into commercial production. These skills were attributed to a form of traditional inheritance "from thirty generations" of land cultivators in the Rhineland. In both New York and Pennsylvania, "the soil, though heavily timbered, was fertile and only needed the hand of the patient husbandman in order to bloom as the rose." The Germans certainly seem to have fulfilled this condition admirably. "While their English and Scotch-Irish neighbors usually followed the course of rivers and large streams, thus lessening the labor of clearing, the Germans . . . would plunge boldly into an unbroken wilderness, often fifty or sixty miles from the nearest habitation, knowing well that where the heaviest forest growth was, there the soil must be good."[3]

All deeds for land ownership were in the name of the male head of household. Most German fathers divested their land during their lifetimes on their children when they married or when they reached majority; but they tried to maintain a "home place" within the family by acquiring land for divestiture to their sons and daughters in the vicinity of their own farmsteads. Most men devolved the "home place" into the hands of a son, often the youngest son, on the event of their own death. This was a throwback to European inheritance practices that were especially common among those landholders emigrating from the margins of the Alpine foothills. The youngest son was expected to shelter and care for his mother, and being young he would likely outlive her—or at least that was the rationale. German fathers also partitioned land for their daughters (in their husbands' name) and sometimes for their male grandchildren, often under the condition that the children would also care for their parents or their grandparents in their old age. These arrangements provided a sort of family based social security for the aged and the widowed.

As one moved south, land became less expensive. In North Carolina, before the intrusion of the land speculation companies, it was almost free except for government fees if purchased from the proprietors. This attracted many cash-strapped Scots-Irish and other relatively poor immigrant groups. All seven of the Carolina proprietors save one (Sir George Carteret) sold their proprietary interests in 1729 to the Crown. North Carolina and South Carolina were virtually separated in 1710, and in 1729 each was made a royal colony falling under parliamentary regulation and governance.

Landowners in the southern colonies at the beginning of the 18th century made up only 11 percent of the population, the lower percentage revealing the large number of slaves, indentures, and hired farm workers. One-third of the landowners held more than 350 acres of land and a mere handful of great landowners controlled more than 1,000 acres each. Two-thirds of all farms were less than 350 acres before 1750. Thomas Jefferson complained, "The aim of the farmers of this country . . . is not to make the most they can from the land, which is, or has been cheap, but the most of [their] labor, which is dear, the consequence of which has been, much ground has been scratched over and none cultivated or improved as it ought to have been."[4]

Historians tend to speak of agriculture in the colonial period as being composed of a mass of subsistence farmers living hand to mouth from year to year. However, it is known from probate inventories that even subsistence farmers invested heavily in agricultural equipment. A number of factors influenced farmers with regard to their choice of what crops to grow or livestock to raise for commercial purposes. The food needs of the people in the community or nearby town were high among these, but the farmers' estimate of what might be exported was equally important. The agents of merchants at a coastal seaport, in the West Indies or even in Europe, could strongly affect the price paid for agricultural produce.

Evidence suggests that at least one quarter of the income of the average Anglo-American farmer was spent on goods and consumables manufactured elsewhere.[5] While a family might spin a few fathoms of woolen yarn and turn it into a still fewer yards of broadcloth, almost all the woolen broadcloth used by American colonists came from British mills. William Tryon flatly declared that "eleven twelfths of the population . . . are clothed in British manufactures."[6] Among the farming implements listed in a single family inventory from Pennsylvania in 1735 are: two wagons, a plow with two irons, two mauls, three iron splitting wedges, four hoes, a spade, a shovel, a mattock, three dung forks, two broad axes, a joiner's axe, a joiner's adze, an undisclosed number (sundry) of additional carpenter's and joiner's tools, seven scythes, five sickles, two cutting knives, three felling axes, and assorted chains, hooks, and harness. All these items were either brought to Pennsylvania from Europe or accumulated in the colonies in the course of just 25 years. This attests somewhat to the "rapidity with which the new settlers became prosperous" if they applied themselves.[7]

The stark reality of frontier economics for the early settler is captured in this print. (Author's collection)

Many of the Scots-Irish and German immigrants that arrived late in the process of land acquisition with little money moved through the settled areas to the frontier where they simply squatted on the land. It has been estimated that two of every three acres occupied on the frontiers were held with no legal rights other than the improvements made on them. Many families had a roof over their heads and were debt free, but they were also essentially penniless.[8]

Nonetheless, Durs Thommen, having immigrated to Pennsylvania in 1736, wrote home to those in his village at Niederdorf commending the abundant, affordable, and fertile land, praising the low taxes and rents, and generally describing how well Germans were doing in the colony. His description suggests why so many of his countrymen took the risk of coming to America: "I took a [farmstead] with about 435 acres, two houses and barns, and have, believe it or not, 6 horses, 2 colts, 15 cattle, and about 35 sacks of oats, 46 sacks of wheat, 25 sacks of rye, and 23 sacks of corn. For all this land I have to pay no more than 7 shillings . . . for tithes, quitrents, and other dues. In this country there are abundant liberties in just about all matters."[9]

FREE FOR A FEE

Even though the land granted in royal colonies was ostensibly free, the paperwork required by government was expensive. The whole granting process probably cost an average small farmer several months' net earnings in terms of fees, but in royal colonies it was not possible to obtain legal title to land simply by squatting on it. The cost of the land patent application alone was about £12 for any tract of less than one square mile (640 acres). The governor received 10s.; the governor's secretary got 5s.; the colonial secretary's office got 1s. 5d.; the clerk of the Court of Claims got 1s. for his trouble (equivalent to an open bribe for expediting the process) and another 7s. 6d. for the petition; the auditor was entitled to £3 for entering the patent in his records; the attorney general received £2 for examining the patent to be certain that the wording was correct and that the title was clearly and accurately conveyed; and the colonial secretary charged £5 for having written out the original patent and 10s. for his trouble (another bribe). The fees—all in coin—had to be paid in order to obtain clear title to vacant land. New owners could thereafter sell the land or devolve the land to their heirs absolutely at their pleasure and without consultation with government officials.[10]

SURVEYORS FOR THE KING

In the colonies, young gentlemen dominated the position of surveyor either as an occupation and a source of income or as a preoccupation and a productive hobby. There were no formal courses of study to become a surveyor, but from colonial times the College of William and Mary had set some loose performance standards for the profession in Virginia and Maryland. Young gentlemen could train themselves, however, through reading such books as Robert Gibson's *Treatise on Surveying* (1767) or John Love's *GEODESIA, The Art of Surveying and Measuring of Land Made Easie* (1720), but a foundation in mathematics, hands-on practice in the field, and influential connections within government were essential to pursuing a moneymaking career. The fundamental job of a surveyor was to help implement the transfer of land from the Crown to private ownership. The process started with the purchaser's selection of a tract. The county surveyor recorded it in an entry book and commonly charged the applicant at the rate of 5s. for every 50 acres surveyed. This was above and beyond the patent fees paid to the colonial officials.[11]

In the mid-18th century, many settlers, disgusted with the machinations of the various land companies, agents, and politicians, avoided the practice of surveying their land claims altogether and simply marked boundaries themselves by cutting notches in trees or making piles of stones at the corners of boundaries. Indian paths and streambeds continued to be used by the whites to define the boundaries of purchases and land grants, sometimes creating difficulties in future years when assessing the legitimate limits of ownership between those who had conflicting legal interests. This ad hoc system of land division was plagued by mistakes and conflicting claims that made proof of land ownership after the revolution difficult and costly.

Before 1729, when the proprietors of the Carolinas abandoned their land grants in the region to the Crown, a full survey of any patent at the buyer's expense was required to begin the process of getting title. This made securing such patents virtually impossible for small farmers because of the expense involved in doing the survey and drawing the plat map of the grant. When the elected assemblies of North and South Carolina took over control of the land patent system, changes were made to the procedures for surveying and distributing land that lowered costs substantially through the sale of previously surveyed parcels and tracts. Colonial officials created short cuts in order to move the process along, and it soon became easier for land speculators to amass huge amounts of acreage. Between 1731 and 1738, more than one million acres were added to the tax rolls in the Carolinas alone.

So-called Old Virginians from the tidewater area and investors in England dominated the Ohio Company, the largest colonial land speculation company of the period. However, a newly rich group of more aggressive colonial Virginians became the rivals of the Ohio Company. These colonial speculators formed new partnerships, like the Loyal Land Company and the Mississippi Company. The power of each group ultimately depended on its influence with the governor of Virginia. Under Sir William Gooch, acting governor in the 1740s, the Ohio Company was out of favor in Virginia. In fact, in order to receive its original grant, the shareholders had appealed to influential persons in London who put pressure on the Virginia governor to act— among them the Duke of Bedford, who received shares in the company as a reward. By this means, influence in Britain often translated into a mere fiction of self-government in the colonies.

The acquisition of a patent for the Ohio Company was the ostensible reason for Lawrence Washington's trip to England in 1749, as evidenced by his letters to the colonial governor and others. Lawrence Washington—eldest sibling of George Washington—also selected and promoted the site of the new town of Alexandria, Virginia, on the western banks of the Potomac near his own land holdings. He deemed this a suitable location because its deep water access allowed ships from London to sail directly to the wharf, where it was thought they could best serve the land development objectives of the Ohio Company for which he was an agent. The fortunes of the Ohio Company improved when Robert Dinwiddie, whose financial interest in the Ohio Company preceded his arrival in America, became governor of Virginia in 1751 and faded again when he resigned due to ill health in 1757 to be replaced by Francis Fauquier. The latter was essentially a powerless figurehead for a decade (1758–1768), friendly to the colonials but overshadowed and overwhelmed by British military commanders during the war with the French. The well-liked Norborne Berkeley, Baron Botecourt (1768–1770) and the much-hated John Murray, Lord Dunmore, the last British governor of Virginia, followed Fauquier in office after his death.[12]

Following the many years of war with the French that stifled development of their patents, the Ohio Company shareholders, who had spent more than £310,000 to advance the company before the French and Indian War, believed that with the final British victory in North America their land business would be renewed and a profit would finally be realized. The sudden change in British policy, culminating in the restrictive Proclamation of 1763, came as a tremendous blow to these aspirations and unrealized profits. Moreover, while the stockholders of the Ohio Company wrestled with the Proclamation as a Crown colony, the agents of other companies in proprietary Pennsylvania were negotiating large land grants. Historian David M. Friedenberg has noted: "The leading aristocrats of colonial Virginia had little influence on the lords controlling British policy in London. Benjamin Franklin and his colleague Samuel Wharton [agents for Pennsylvania], who were far more astute in such matters, knew where to apply pressure and whom to corrupt. The Virginia autocrats, in their private cocoon of black slaves and small white planters and mechanics, reacted with rage when they could not have their way: that rage transformed itself into a colony whose aristocrats were united in revolution a few short years later."[13]

A new company in competition with the Ohio Company was organized in Virginia in 1768 by a set of wholly colonial investors that included George Washington, John Augustine Washington (another brother), and several members of the extensive Lee and Fairfax families. The fact that no member of the company came from England is significant because it was the first such to do so, suggesting perhaps a new more independent attitude among Anglo-Americans. The purpose of the so-called Mississippi Company was to explore the possibility of a land grant farther west from western Pennsylvania into what is now Kentucky. Prior to the successful culmination of the French and Indian War, such a grant would have violated French claims in the region. Now, only the Proclamation of 1763 stood in the way, but the Crown could grant permission. The original petition was for several million acres with a western boundary at the Mississippi River. The group also requested that the king forego quitrents, fees, and taxes for 12 years, in return for which they would attempt to establish at least 200 families on the land. Arthur Lee, whose father had been an initial sponsor of the Ohio Company, was in London at the time and acted as agent for the new company.[14]

The British ministry rejected the petition of the Mississippi Company mainly because no English lords or merchants resident in England participated in it. However, to buy off pressure from the many colonials who were joint shareholders in both the Mississippi Company and the Ohio Company (and there was a good deal of overlap), the latter company having English participation, two shares in Vandalia (a.k.a. the Walpole Company), a powerful London-based syndicate with interests in Pennsylvania, were given only to the Ohio Company co-owners. George Mercer, the Ohio Company agent in London, got an extra share (a bribe) for his cooperation. The Mississippi Company thereby disappeared with several American families absorbing considerable loss. The Ohio Company was then quickly merged into the Walpole Company (Grand Ohio Company), in which Ben Franklin also had an interest. This company ultimately negotiated an even bigger grant known as the Indiana Grant that was never developed because of the interposition of the revolution. The involvement and interconnection of soon-to-be Patriot families in these financial machinations is commonly unreported in standard histories of the revolution, lost as they are among less seamy facts and more glorious concepts involving liberty and political rights.[15]

In 17th-century Virginia, King Charles II had granted the Northern Neck of Virginia between the Potomac and Rappahannock rivers to several of his supporters. Thomas Lord Fairfax, president of the Board of Trade and Plantations, acquired and combined these grants in the 18th century. It will be recalled that the Fairfax family was intimately attached through marriage to both the Washington and the Lee families, and it will be shown that they were involved also with the family of Thomas Jefferson.

Concerned by attacks on his claim (up to five million acres) by the Virginia House of Burgesses, Lord Fairfax appointed the colonial surveyors who were to sell his land in Virginia on his orders. The problem of knowing the extent of the tract of land, however, created complications because the patent was to begin at the headwater of the Rappahannock River, which was not known with precision at the time. Fairfax claimed that the headwater of the Rappahannock was the Rapidan River and that all of the lands within the forks of the Rappahannock were part of the so-called Fairfax Tract. A commission was formed in 1744 to resolve the question, and Joshua Fry was appointed to represent the interests of the king in the colony. Fry, in turn, recommended his associate, Peter Jefferson, father of Thomas Jefferson, to serve as the second of two surveyors acting for the Crown.

Among the young surveyors representing the interests of the colony were George William Fairfax (age 23), James Genn (age 30), and George Washington (who went forth with his mother's permission at age 16). Geen (a.k.a. Ginn) was Washington's first work supervisor and a veteran surveyor of Prince William County. Fairfax, the youthful master of Belvoir plantation and biracial first cousin of his Lordship, was Washington's brother-in-law through Lawrence's marriage with Anne Fairfax.

At a remarkably young age and largely through the influence of the Fairfax family, George Washington was thereafter appointed official surveyor for the frontier county of Culpepper. Nonetheless, the majority of his work as a surveyor was done in Hampshire and Frederick Counties. In 1748 and 1749, he made two remarkable maps of Alexandria for his brother, Lawrence, and in 1752 he purchased his first property of 1,500 acres along Bullskin Creek in Frederick County. In his career as surveyor, Washington platted more than 200 tracts of land, and ultimately acquired title to more than 65,000 acres in 36 different locations.

In 1745, the governor's Privy Council had accepted the land claims of Lord Fairfax with the stipulation that he recognize the grants within the tract previously made by the colonial government. The granting of the same land by various agencies was a major weakness of the royal patent system and a source of friction between the colonial governments and the imperial administration in London. Lord Fairfax moved his main residence from London to the Shenandoah Valley at White Post in Clarke County in 1752.

Having set the metes and bounds of the Fairfax Tract in 1745, Peter Jefferson, Joshua Fry, and Dr. Thomas Walker thereafter formed the Loyal Land Company and petitioned for 800,000 acres in a region that is now southeastern Kentucky. The Loyal Land Company had four years to present a qualifying survey of the land to the Crown, and the men often had to run survey lines straight through seemingly insurmountable obstacles. This meant clambering over rocks, crawling through brush, and wading through icy streams. Another surveyor, Thomas Lewis, described working with Fry and Jefferson: "It was with the greatest difficulty we could get along, the mountains being prodigiously full of fallen timber and ivy as thick as it could grow, so interwoven that horse or man could hardly force his way through it." The survey was completed in late 1749. Walker was named president of the company, and, as the visible head of a large landholding company, he was often chosen to serve as an ambassador to the Native American tribes frequenting the region. He represented Albemarle County in the Virginia legislature during the revolution.[16]

Fry and Jefferson were selected by the Crown in 1749 to extend the survey boundary between Virginia and North Carolina. Beginning where a 1728 survey by William Mayo had stopped, Fry and Jefferson carried the line 90 miles into the mountains to the west. In 1751, they collaborated on a map of Virginia that became the standard cartographic reference of the colony in the 18th century. Shortly thereafter, war broke out with France, and Fry was appointed military commander of the provincial forces. His second in command was George Washington. A few months later, Fry was thrown from his horse and killed in the fall. Washington succeeded him as commander of the Virginia militia, and Peter Jefferson assumed the post of county surveyor for Albemarle County. In 1754, Peter Jefferson became a member for the county in the House of Burgesses.[17]

In order to limit friction with the Native American nations, King George III had signed the Proclamation of 1763, which prohibited any white settlement west of the Appalachians and which required those already settled there to return to the east immediately. Yet, the line between the Indian lands and the colonies was "so hastily adopted" that it took no account of the settlements already made, of the royal lands granted by certain colonies, or of the investments assured to the land companies in their charters. Not a single shilling of indemnification was offered to the colonials in the proclamation for the losses they would sustain. Only land purchased from the tribes by the Crown would be recognized and trade over the line was restricted to licensed merchants. The settlers and companies that had taken the earliest steps on the frontiers and made the largest investments of labor and money were now those most disadvantaged. Following the dictum that possession was nine-tenths of the law, the governor of Virginia and several members of his privy council stressed that those who had abandoned their lands during the French war return to them immediately—even in violation of the Proclamation—or risk any hope of retaining them in the future.[18]

In a letter in 1767 to William Crawford, a Pennsylvania surveyor, George Washington wrote concerning his own interests in circumventing the restrictive frontier policy as expressed in the Proclamation of 1763. Crawford had just informed him concerning two desirable tracts near Fort Pitt—but within the restricted zone—in which purchase Washington might be interested:

I can never look upon the Proclamation in any other light . . . than as a temporary expedient to quiet the minds of the Indians. It must fall, of course, in a few years, especially when those Indians consent to our occupying those lands. Any person who neglects hunting out good lands, and in some measure marking and distinguishing them for his own, in order to keep others from settling them will never regain it. . . . Keep all this matter secret. . . . All of this can be carried on by silent management and can be carried out by you under the guise of hunting game, which you may, I presume, effectually do, at the same time you are in pursuit of land. When this is fully discovered advise me of it, and if there appears a possibility of succeeding, I will have the land surveyed to keep others off and leave the rest to time and my own assiduity.[19]

The charter of the Loyal Land Company had expired in 1757 and the French and Indian War had made its prosecution in wartime impractical. The petition for renewal of the charter was made as the war neared an end, but it was denied based on the forthcoming promulgation of the Proclamation of 1763. Nonetheless, the company continued its operations, with Walker (as Indian commissioner) carefully inserting into the Treaty of Fort Stanwix in 1768 wording favorable to the land company and to other traders (among them Samuel Wharton and William Trent) suffering under the Proclamation, and again into the Treaty of Lochaber in 1770 made with the Iroquois and Cherokee, respectively. Walker thereby protected his own investments and those of his friends and business partners.

The lands previously sold by the Loyal Land Company west of the Appalachians also came into conflict with patents granted by Governor Dinwiddie to Virginia militia officers to attract their service during the French war. George Washington represented the officers of the Virginia Regiment during the lengthy negotiations with the governor's Privy Council that eventually affirmed all the lands sold by the Loyal Land Company. To quiet the claims of the veterans, the men were assigned alternative acreage from a much larger and separate tract. Washington received 40,000 acres (20 percent of the total awarded to all the soldiers), but his loss in prospective shares in the various land company patents had been larger than his award under the veterans agreement. The resolution of these disputes would have been impossible had both Governor Dunmore in Virginia and the colonial secretary, William Legge, Earl of Dartmouth, in England not been personally involved in the land speculation.[20]

Washington also arranged to have his friend Crawford appointed Surveyor of Soldiers' Land, and their association would continue until Crawford's death in 1782. Washington's acreage map of the Soldiers' Land shows tracts surveyed and apportioned to other members of the Virginia Regiment close to him, including Colonel Adam Stephen, Dr. James Craik, George Mercer, George Muse, Colonel Andrew

Washington appeared at the negotiations in 1769 in his military uniform from 1763 just as he would in 1775, when stumping for appointment as commander and chief of the Continental Army at the Continental Congress in Philadelphia. (Library of Congress)

Lewis, Captain Peter Hog, Jacob Van Braam, John West, and the heirs of Colonel Fry. Several of these individuals were distinguished surveyors and mapmakers in their own right. Mercer was the agent of the Ohio Company; Dr. Craik was Washington's personal physician, life-long friend, and second in rank among army surgeons in the Continental Army; and Van Braam had been Washington's French to English interpreter at Fort Necessity in 1754.[21]

Through his position as negotiator with the tribes and agent for the Loyal Land Company, Dr. Walker had then succeeded in thwarting the restrictive land policy of the Crown due to his close contacts with the members of the Virginia legislature. Indeed, after the revocation of their patents in 1763, the sheriff was ordered to remove settlers unless they had purchased their land from the company. In effect, the settlers were forced to buy land they had already improved from a company whose charter had lapsed. This elicited a complaint to the Crown from George Mercer (a recipient of a Soldiers' grant) representing the rival Ohio Company in London. Listing the various land patents to the dominant political faction in the Virginia legislature, he wrote, "No less than 1,350,000 acres of land were granted by the governor and council to borrowed names and private land-mongers, which were incapable of making effectual settlements." By 1773, almost 1,000 surveys had been made in the area, on which basis more than 200,000 acres of land, slightly more than one-quarter of the original grant to the Loyal Land Company, were sold.[22]

Ironically, Mercer was a close associate of George Washington from their days in the French wars and an elected member of the House of Burgesses (1761–1764) for Frederick County. He was absent in London during 1763 and 1764 as an agent of the land company, and would be burned in effigy before the Westmoreland County Courthouse for accepting a commission as a stamp distributor for Virginia and Maryland during the Stamp Act crisis. Mercer surrendered his commission thereafter and returned to London where he convinced the Crown that the introduction of troops to America would be insufficient to quell the disturbances. His testimony as an influential and loyal eyewitness to the protests undoubtedly helped to facilitate the repeal of the Stamp Act. Although living in Paris during the revolution, he remained an unrepentant Loyalist receiving cash disbursements from the Crown for his support until his death in 1784.

In 1773, after a decade of dispute with the frontier settlers, rumors spread through the colonies that it was again the Crown's intention to secure an Act of Parliament that would vacate all American titles to land by annulling the former colonial patents, thereby causing all titles to land to revert to the Crown from which they would have to be repetitioned. These rumors were given increased credence when, by order of the king, Governor Josiah Martin closed the royal land office in North Carolina that April. Although the Court of Claims continued to sit, applications for new entries, warrants, and patents were denied. Governor Martin issued a formal statement of denial to suppress this rumor, but in February 1775, two months before Lexington and Concord, the royal land offices throughout the colonies closed forever.[23]

The United States today is carefully divided into townships, sections, and lots that Americans take for granted without a full understanding of the underlying system that is at work. Although implemented in the postrevolutionary period, the origin of the *rectangular section system* (1764) is credited to Captain Thomas Hutchins, a colonial engineering officer and surveyor serving on the Ohio frontier during the French and Indian War. Ironically, in an effort to raise tax money to pay down the debt accumulated in the revolution through the sale of public lands in the so-called Old Northwest Territory, the United States adopted a section system of land sales under the Land Ordinance of 1785 that made 40 acres the smallest unit of transfer.

SELF-SUFFICIENCY

Settlers in the backcountry added productive acreage to their farmsteads each year by clearing the land. "Sweat equity" allowed competent farmers to add about two acres of newly cleared land each year to their family estates. Those considered the most able farmers cleared the land by cutting down all the trees in early summer, hauling off the valuable logs, and leaving the least valuable wood and branches on the ground until the following spring. This was scavenged for firewood during the winter and the leavings were burned in early spring to complete the clearing. The burning left a layer of fine ash to fertilize and soften the ground between the remaining stumps. Thereafter, the stumps were usually allowed to rot of their own accord, but they could be pulled after a few years with the help of a team of oxen. Once the stumps were removed, the rocks and boulders could be dragged by oxen to the edges of the field on a sledge and dumped. In the winter, these stones were made up into walls topped with split rail fences for the enclosure of sheep or cattle.

Only on the oldest farms were stonewalls laid up in this manner, particularly in the more settled rocky regions of New England and New York. During the revolution, British officers, believing that real soldiers would confront their enemies in the open, were repeatedly outraged by the American tactic of firing from behind stonewalls—especially on the return march to Boston from Concord in 1775 and at the battle at Eastchester in the Bronx that allowed Washington to retreat unimpeded from Manhattan to White Plains in 1776. In this regard, American General Israel Putnam is reputed to have observed of the troops: "Americans are not at all afraid of the heads, though very much afraid of their legs; if you cover these, they will fight forever."[24]

On most frontier farms, hogs and chickens were simply set free to take advantage of the marginal forest overgrowth and multiply until rounded up. Early settlers often let loose their livestock to graze among the stumps in recently cleared fields, but the native grasses proved to provide less nutrition than European varieties that were purposely propagated. Moreover, the animals imported from Europe often brought with them as part of their manure common European grass seeds from their shipboard fodder. These grasses spread naturally in the older settlements and were obviously superior to native grasses. This led colonial farmers to import English grass seed stocks, such as bluegrass or white clover, and to actively seek their propagation.

During the first half of the 18th century, farming everywhere was a largely hit or miss proposition, based on generations of traditional practice, but this was slowly changing to a more science-based program of studied agriculture. Lands were often farmed on a three-fold rotation: one-third sown with summer crops, one-third with winter crops, and one-third left fallow each year to recover their potency. This was the system that the Pilgrims had initially attempted in 1621, but the chaos engendered in working within the climatic differences between England and New England led to widespread starvation. In Ireland, Scotland, and France, farmers within acceptable distance of the shore used seaweed or river mud as a fertilizer, and in many places legumes (beans, peas, chickpeas, lentils, and other nitrogen-fixing crops) were planted in an attempt to maintain fertility, although the mechanism was unknown.[25]

The improved plough of the 18th century automatically produced furrows separated by a distance as it lifted soil and filled it over. Commonly, field hands had carried bags of seeds from which they would grab a handful of seed and broadcast it with a sweep of the arm over the plowed field. Most of the seeds was blown away or eaten by birds before ever having a chance to take root. The new method using the seed drill (invented by Jethro Tull) was economical of seed and it made weeding easier, but the widely placed furrows were wasteful of acreage. These simple changes increased food production, however. It is estimated that the average productivity of wheat was about 19 bushels per acre in 1720. It increased to 22 bushels by the middle of the century and reached a peak of around 30 bushels per acre in the 1840s.[26]

Eventually, as the systematic study of agricultural improvement became fashionable, more interest began to focus on Tull's ideas. In 1731, he published his book, *The New Horse Hoeing Husbandry, or an Essay on the Principles of Tillage and Vegetation*, detailing his system and its machinery. Tull was widely travelled in his research, but his ideas were considered controversial until adopted by large English landowners. Some historians have called him "a crank whose hostility to crop rotation and manuring stand as a setback to the movement toward progressive farming in many parts of England and America."[27]

Tulle's horse-drawn plough led to an increased interest in breeding mules, a hobby shared by Thomas Jefferson, George Washington, and other scientific farmers, who began their experiments with male donkey stock from France and Spain mated to brawny and well-muscled female horses. Mules did 20 percent more work and ate 20 percent less than horses, and they required less grain as a portion of their feed. While mules were noted for their bouts with stubbornness, they were more sensible and less flighty than horses in harness. A mule proponent expressed the following sentiment on the subject: "It is a noble sight to see those small, tough, earnest, honest . . . mules, every nerve strained to the utmost, examples of obedience, and of duty performed under trying circumstances."[28]

Ben Franklin had a great respect for farming and the people who worked the land. He called agriculture the business of America. Following his retirement from the printing business in 1748, Franklin purchased a 300-acre farm in New Jersey, but politics got in the way of farming, and thereafter he spent more time in Europe than in America. While in London in the late 1750s, Franklin became a member of several societies interested in improving agriculture. Herein, he discussed the cultivation and production in America of safflower for dye, of hemp for textiles, and of olive oil for cooking. He also expressed a somewhat impractical interest in starting a silk industry in America to compete with that of China. Throughout his life, Franklin helped promote agricultural knowledge, and he may have introduced Scotch kale, Swiss barley, and Chinese rhubarb to the colonies from Europe. He also introduced to England from the colonies Timothy grass and Newtown Pippin apples, and a number of trees, nuts, and shrubs to France.[29]

The average subsistence farmer in Anglo-America in the 1760s tended about 18 acres of crops on a 100-acre farm. A man with grown sons could farm an additional amount of land in proportion to their number. Fertilization with manure was left as an accident of livestock grazing on fallow fields. Additionally, fruit tree orchards and small kitchen-garden plots of an acre or two that included a variety of herbs and greens surrounded the family home.[30]

Nonetheless, a better term than *subsistence farming* might be *self-sufficient farming*. Although survival was the initial goal of all colonial farmers, had it been their sole objective they could have stayed in Europe and dispensed with a dangerous and time-consuming ocean voyage, the threat of Indian attack, and dislocation from familiar surroundings, family, and friends. On the contrary, as the seasons and years passed, colonial farmers attempted to put more land under cultivation and to grow and dispose of at least some of their farm produce for cash. Nonetheless, the common residents of frontier communities, scraping a living from among the stumps of the newly cleared forests, would not realize a surplus of agricultural produce for decades.

In America, a mere handful of great landowners controlled more than 1,000 acres each. Two-thirds of all farms were less than 350 acres before 1750. These small landowners aspired to emulate their social betters by raising their standard of living at the expense of black labor, and all free white Americans were reared in an atmosphere that supported a reasonable expectation that they could themselves become slave owners or the employers of hired help. By draining swamps, clearing additional fields, and planting cash crops, they hoped to increase their incomes to the point that might afford the purchase of a slave or two. There was no greater social leveler among white men than that they could command the labor and obedience of another race. Thereafter, the yeoman farmer hoped to capitalize on his newfound status as part of the slaveholding gentry and stabilize his family's social position by marrying his daughters above their former social station.

CHAPTER 9
Summary: The Lessons of the Tea Party

The tyrant will always find a pretext for his tyranny.
—*Aesop, writer and fabulist, 6th century BC*

ORIGINS IN CONFLICT

The reader has been introduced to many possible causes of the American Revolution: unresponsive government, arrogant officials, religious hatreds, increasing taxation, ill-advised legislation, uninhibited corruption and cronyism, big business bailouts, and a cash-starved economy. However, without the people there would have been no tea crisis, no revolution, and no American nation. The people of America were the ultimate foundation of revolution. Although the ethnic composition of modern America has changed radically since colonial times, many of the distinctive "folkways" (customs) of the major immigrant groups coming to colonial America have persisted on a regional basis into the 21st century. Although few migrating groups shared all these folkways, a single feature stands out that binds them together. They all experienced significant cultural conflict before coming to America.[1]

The late professor of American history, Richard Hofstadler, warned those making only a cursory study of the early mix of cultures in the colonies that America may not have been as diverse as some data suggest.

When one counts the various peoples—the Scots, Welsh, and Irish, the Dutch, Swedes, and Finns, the French, Germans, Swiss, and Jews—the pluralism of white America even at the end of the seventeenth century seems impressive. But if one counts people rather than varieties and gives weight to numbers, the basically English character of the colonies emerges. . . . During the eighteenth century, however, the ethnic homogeneity was rudely and finally shattered . . . and peoples of other stocks migrated or were imported in such substantial numbers that by the time of the Revolution half the population south of New England was non-English.[2]

Historian James Webb has also noted of his own Scots-Irish immigrant ancestors: "A central government that wished to impose its will on the tough, weapons-wielding folks who dwelled in the hollows would be guaranteed a hostile reception unless it had the full cooperation of local leaders. . . . They fought the Indians and then they fought the British."[3]

In his study, *The Scandal of Empire, India and the Creation of Imperial Britain* (2006), historian Nicholas B. Dirks has also noted: "One of the many lessons of America for England was the need to control the circulation of its own people. Otherwise [the colonials] would first claim to be more English than the English [and] then they would siphon off the potential profits of empire, and finally they would declare independence."[4]

GIVING UP THE TEA

The Boston Tea Party is one of the most iconic symbols of the American Revolution, yet it was an episode of just a few hours duration. It may not have precisely mirrored the causes for which Americans went to war 16 months later. That December night in 1773, the tea was ignominiously deposited into Boston Harbor due to the tax imposed on it. Yet the question remains: Was taxation the primary cause of the revolution that followed, or was the Crown's arrogance in tampering with the long-established systems of local governance and commerce, absent even the issue of taxation, a more significant cause of the revolution?

As with the present-day T.E.A. Party movement, taxation served only as a rallying point for deeper grievances regarding an unresponsive, over-regulating, and bloated government bureaucracy. The so-called Patriot Party of the Revolutionary Era initially used taxation as a cudgel with which to browbeat Parliament while not directly challenging the sovereign rights of the monarchy. Those who allowed their protests to spill over into wider social issues are not commonly listed high among the founders of America. In order to better understand the true nature of the prerevolutionary period, it may be necessary to decouple the historical anger over taxation and the grievances concerning colonial governance in British North America.

The rhythmic cadence of the phrase *taxation without representation* makes it a favorite teaching device for middle school history instructors. As the reader has seen in the previous chapters, the people of Anglo-America manifest their indignation toward the Crown not only in terms of ideological concepts concerning taxation, but also and more importantly with regard to the attempt by Parliament to *fundamentally transform* the political and economic relationships among the Crown, the colonies, and the people themselves. As previously illustrated, this was an essentially *English* question of political sovereignty and with whom sovereignty ultimately resides that had been fought over many times and left largely unresolved in 17th-century Britain before it took on the mantle of a great trading empire.

In the 18th century, many classes of people in the British Empire lacked direct representation in Parliament, including most of the population of Britain's largest cities, and many taxes were commonly imposed on Americans without direct popular representation even in the colonies. Most Americans had no right to vote (even after the revolution was won), and they recognized the proper role of hierarchy in everyday life—in society, in the military, in the workplace, in politics, and in their houses of worship. They had been governed, led, employed, and taxed by the colonial upper classes without major complaint for many generations. Boston—the eye of the prerevolutionary storm—was a city governed by the archetype New England town meeting, and the colonies all had active, if sometimes headstrong, representative assemblies. Generally, there was a governor and council to represent the interests of the Crown and an assembly to represent the landowners and business interests—the delegates empowered by their consent to aid or restrict the royal prerogative as circumstances warranted. The common people relied on the latter group—aristocrats and gentlemen—to defend their rights. The first colonial Constitution guaranteeing representative government—the Fundamental Orders of Connecticut—was signed in Connecticut in 1639, and the last—the

Charter of Privileges—had created the representative assembly in Pennsylvania in 1701. The Fundamental Orders recognized no specific allegiance to the English Crown, while the Charter added to the royal patent the right to trial by jury, freedom of the press, and religious toleration.[5]

Increased taxation may have angered the American people, but it is just barely possible to blame the outbreak of the revolution on taxation alone.[6] Certainly, British propaganda attempted to paint the Patriot Party in America as petty, parsimonious, and unwilling to pay their fair share of the cost of running the empire. It must be acknowledged that a half-century of French wars had created a vast debt for Britain (£125 million) that had to be addressed. Twelve percent of the imperial debt, however, represented a cash bailout (estimated to total £15 million) given to an ailing EIC, and many Americans asked why they were being asked to pay the costs of a private corporation in its crisis when they had not shared the profits in its heyday.

As a major source of government and private income, the Company stood second only to the Bank of England as a financial institution, and the government considered it too big to fail. Public taxes in Massachusetts, on the other hand, had almost doubled to pay for three major military campaigns in as many decades. Although pacifist Pennsylvania alone had resisted expending any funds for defense before 1755, other colonies—Massachusetts, New York, Connecticut, and Virginia, in particular—had also responded to these crises, and one in seven of the colonial men deployed to fight the French had died in service.[7]

Before the accession of George III in 1760, the Crown had seemingly chosen to loosely govern its Atlantic colonies. Thereafter, the ministry exerted a degree of influence over colonial policy rarely seen in British politics. Parliament, through the Board of Trade, seemed willing to sacrifice the rights, the property, and the liberties of the colonials for the profits enjoyed by its friends among the London investors in the EIC. The hypocrisy of the parliamentary program for America astounded political observers on both sides of the Atlantic.[8]

Although the Stamp Act protests of 1764 are generally assigned as the beginning of active resistance to the Crown, weightier matters quickly overshadowed taxes. In 1768, Lord Hillsborough, the colonial secretary, dispatched four regiments of regulars to Boston. Their presence was clearly intended to intimidate the colonials and to suppress dissent. This was an error that fed into the abhorrence of standing armies, and of redcoats in particular, that had long affected Anglo-Americans. Few other courses of action could have more certainly assured the marshalling of the colonial militias and the consolidation of antigovernment sentiment.

The false Gunpowder Alarm of September 1774 in Massachusetts is often considered to be the end of effective British governance in the colonies outside the largest cities. Up to 10,000 armed colonials may have responded to the false alarm that the British were stealing their gunpowder in a propaganda spectacle of American resolve and the efficiency of its alarm rider system. These included as alarm riders a score of people like Paul Revere, William Dawes, Dr. Samuel Prescott, and 16-year-old Sibyl Ludington. Although in Philadelphia at the time, Sam Adams was probably behind the sounding of the false alarm.

When revolutionary hostilities finally began on April 19, 1775, the *proximate cause* of the fighting was an encounter over the confiscation of colonial gunpowder and weapons, not tea or taxes. Sam Adams wrote of the turnout of almost 30,000 militiamen besieging the redcoats on the heights above Boston: "There are some persons, who would, if possibly they could, persuade the people never to make use of their constitutional rights or terrify them from doing it. No wonder that a resolution of this town to keep arms for its own defense, should be represented as having at bottom a secret intention to oppose the landing of the King's troops."[9]

Yet, the right to keep arms is rarely, if ever, posited as a *primary cause* of the revolution. It appears nowhere in the Declaration of Independence, largely because it was taken for granted as a right shared by all Englishmen from the time of Magna Carta (1215) and specifically noted in the English Bill of Rights (1689). The Second Amendment to the United States Constitution was heavily influenced by the English Bill of Rights, which restricted the right of the monarch (at the time James II) to have a standing army or to interfere with the personal right to bear arms. Even Sir William Blackstone, a British jurist and Tory politician at the time of the American Revolution, assumed the legitimacy of the right of Englishmen to keep and bear arms as a consequence of the natural right of resistance and self-preservation (right to life) as expressed in the works of John Locke.

The elderly and respected Keeper of the King's Storehouse in Boston, General William Brattle had scrupulously delivered to the selectmen of all the surrounding towns those stocks of public powder and arms entrusted to his keeping, but he maintained those belonging to

the Crown with equal honesty and care. Had he abandoned his responsibilities to the Crown, he may have been chosen to lead the revolution instead of George Washington.

Among the first moves of the Patriots after the Powder Alarm was
to secure the gunpowder, canon, and muskets legally belonging to the
colonial assemblies, particularly in New Hampshire, New York, and
Virginia. The seizure of arms and powder at Fort William and Mary
in Portsmouth harbor in December 1774 was the first capture made
by the Americans in the war of the revolution. Similarly, a group of
Liberty Boys under Marinus Willett and Isaac Sears broke into the
provincial magazine in New York and made off with powder and
600 muskets in January 1775.

Finally, the so-called Gunpowder Incident involving Governor Lord
Dunmore (John Murray) of Virginia and the militia led by Patrick
Henry took place on April 20, 1775, one day after the Battles of Lexington and Concord, but well before news of these hostilities had
reached Virginia. Dunmore ordered the nighttime removal of colonial
gunpowder from the magazine in Williamsburg to a ship in the harbor,
causing a great deal of unrest among the militia. The confrontation
was resolved when Dunmore paid Henry £300 for the colonial powder
that was taken and retreated to a naval vessel for his own safety.

The colonials also had meaningful evidence that the Crown planned
to dissolve their local governments—at least in Virginia, Massachusetts,
and New York. In 1767, Parliament, under the leadership of Charles
Townshend, had suspended the legislative powers of New York as a
punishment for their disobedience under the Mutiny Act. This was a
warning, which could not be mistaken. In the other colonies, sympathy
with New York spread far and wide and carried with it deep disquiet
and indignation. Dunmore had declared the Virginia House of Burgesses dissolved in March 1773, nine months before the Tea Party, but
the delegates had refused to be disbanded, adjourning to the Raleigh
Tavern to reassemble within sight of the Virginia State House. There
was also evidence that a similar fate awaited the legislature of Massachusetts that had declared a day of prayer and fasting in support of
Virginia. Sam Adams released to the public a series of letters written
by Governor Thomas Hutchinson and Lieutenant Governor Thomas
Oliver to Ministers of Parliament in England in 1773.[10] These letters
seemed to indicate that there was a plan afoot to rescind the Constitution of the colony, dissolve its legislature, and impose direct ministe-
rial rule. The Hutchinson-Oliver letters were genuine and their most
damning implications were used successfully as Patriot propaganda.

Summoned to Castle William in Boston Harbor, Sam Adams confounded the denials of the governor with Hutchinson's own words. Historian Herbert H. Bankcroft described the scene: "In that moment Samuel Adams was pre-eminent, and all the greatness and force of his mind and character concentrated to raise him up as the great tribune of the people. The incarnation of right and justice, the true champion of the people, he stood before [Hutchinson] the fit representative of a weak, vacillating, proud, and stupid ministry, and made the [governor] quail before him."[11]

Like the present (2012) conflict over state and federal mandates and regulations, the political dispute between local or parliamentary control was an old one. In July 1676, Nathaniel Bacon and his army of Virginia citizens issued the "Declaration of the People of Virginia" criticizing and overturning Governor William Berkeley's administration. The rebellion collapsed when Bacon died of an illness, but Berkeley began a program of summary executions, dispatching royal troops into the hinterland to hunt down the rebels. King Charles II thought the reaction extreme and declared that Berkeley killed more Englishmen in Virginia than had he in retaliation for the beheading of his father (Charles I). In 1688, the Crown, under Governor Sir Edmund Andros, briefly attempted to establish arbitrary royal rule over the so-called Dominion of New England in which the power of the legislatures of New England, New York, and New Jersey were to be severely limited. At that time, two companies of red-coated British troops, a 74-gun ship of the line, and a contingent of Anglican clergymen had descended on America in an effort to suppress dissent with respect to the Glorious Revolution. The attempt failed. This was a time of civil war throughout the kingdom. King James II (Stuart) was deposed in England in 1688, and the individual colonies returned to their previous form of local governance in 1691 by decree of William III and Mary II (Stuart), James' daughter.

Decades later, in 1754, with the dilemma of local or imperial governance still unresolved, Benjamin Franklin addressed the ongoing problem by visualizing a better-defined relationship between the Crown and the colonies in his Albany Plan of Union, and Joseph Galloway (later a Loyalist) also suggested that the problem could be resolved by a federation of Anglo-American *states*—very much like the British Commonwealth accepted in the 19th century.

Early in 1764, however, Patriot radical James Otis had publicly gone a giant step further than either man, launching for the first time the idea that Parliament had *no authority* to legislate for the colonies without their consent—a fundamental concept advanced by John Locke and other political theorists a century earlier and a favorite talking point of the Patriot Whig faction in Parliament. Otis suggested that the colonies be given their own representatives in Parliament in order to resolve the impasse. Like Franklin's plan and Galloway's proposal, Otis' plan appeared to be a reasonable compromise between the legitimate needs of the British Empire to regulate its various parts and the rights of Anglo-Americans living in the colonies to a modicum of self-government. Yet, the Crown rejected all such plans, as did the majority of Patriots, who wished instead to maintain their cherished form of local governance.

Where among these weighty matters does a tax of a few pennies on tea reside? Oddly, the tea tax does not appear specifically among the more than two dozen complaints against the king listed in the Declaration of Independence nor do any of the multitudes of commodity taxes imposed by Parliament during the taxation crisis appear. Only one of these complaints stands to incriminate the dispute over *taxation* as a cause of the rebellion, and it is carefully coupled to the demand for consensual government. Moreover, half the complaints in the Declaration speak directly to the fundamental alteration of the role of royal government in America—a virtual disempowerment of the colonial legislatures, the desire by the Crown to extend an *unwarrantable jurisdiction over*, or to *dissolve* or *limit the authority of* its colonial assemblies.

Formerly, American colonists had generally accepted the doctrine that Parliament could pass acts regulating trade and imposing duties on imports. These were the building blocks of *mercantilism*, the economic foundation of the empire. Prohibitions, restrictions, duties, and the granting of monopolies were the common stuff of 18th-century economic policy.[12] Under mercantilism, the production of raw materials from the colonies was more important to Britain than the maturation of colonial commerce and industry. But the Americans had been quietly reversing the equation by manufacturing clandestinely and trading outside the empire for themselves. Within a generation, many formerly scarce goods had become items of ordinary everyday consumption in the colonies, and the influence of commercial contracts had quietly displaced that of royal prerogatives.[13]

However, beginning with the reorganization of the empire initiated by George III, there developed a decided change in attitude toward colonial trade, government regulation, and taxation by the British ministry and its officials. Several very unpopular pieces of legislation were passed through Parliament—the Proclamation of 1763; the Stamp Act, the Sugar Act, the Currency Act, and the Navigation Acts of 1764; the Townshend Acts of 1767 and 1769; the Tea Act of 1773; and the Quebec Act, Boston Port Act, and Coercive Acts of 1774, among them. Each restricted colonial commerce and further attempted to dismantle the authority of the colonial assemblies. Their totality caused the Americans to take up arms to defend their Rights.

It has also been argued that the initial confrontation between the people and Parliament occurred prior to any crisis over taxes. The Proclamation of 1763 closed off all the Native American lands west of the Appalachians to white settlement, and required those settlers already there to remove themselves to the east without any form of compensation from the Crown for their losses in labor, crops, buildings, cleared fields, fences, and other improvements. The colonial legislatures had also expected to redeem their own debts through the sale of recently acquired Indian lands, but now this plan had been thwarted. During the following winter, a sensational series of anti-Indian and antigovernment riots and rebellions broke out among a furious population of indignant backcountry settlers, who supported the revolution in remarkable numbers.[14]

On the coast, New England fishermen found that driving the French from Canada had brought them a new set of competitors for the output of the Atlantic fisheries. English firms, backed by London financiers and influential investors among the Members of Parliament, had moved into Atlantic Canada with large fleets of well-financed commercial fishing vessels working out of Nova Scotia and Newfoundland. The fishermen of New England, in particular, were left with shrinking output, legally restricted markets, and a prohibition from fishing among the richest parts of the ocean.[15] Outnumbered three to one, many New England vessels continued to go to sea, not to fish, but to confound the mercantile system. They carried maritime provisions, rum, wine, and a full line of replacement gear to their competitors— ropes, lines, nets, hooks, salt, barrels, sails, caulking, planking, and masts—each considered a form of smuggling under the law.[16]

In this regard, the "profoundly commercial character of American resistance" becomes evident.[17] It was the vigorous enforcement of the maritime regulations under the new administration that was the cause of much of the colonial alienation. Customs officials and the naval officers at ports of entry, in particular, seem to have become "tactless, arbitrary, and mercenary" in the performance of their duties.[18] Added to these was a new five-person American Board of Customs Commissioners located at Boston but appointed from London. The greatly

enlarged customs bureaucracy they represented annoyed the Bostonians, and when the Board arrived in late 1767 protests and jeering
crowds met them and redcoats formed cordons to protect them. Royal
Navy warships sitting in the harbor, formerly symbols of imperial
strength and security, were now viewed as threats to liberty and tools
of despotism.[19]

It would be an error to consider these attitudes concerning the customs and regulations a mere expression of colonial pique. Enforcement
had been extended beyond the purview of local magistrates to almost
all coastwise traders, including the smallest who might move cargoes
only a few miles along the shoreline in sailing skiffs or a few hundred
yards across a boundary river between colonies, like that of New York
and New Jersey. The controversial *writs of assistance*—unlimited search
warrants—allowed both the customs and all naval officers to search
anywhere for smuggled goods without having to obtain a specific au-
thorization from local justices.[20]

In fact, after 1764, violations of many regulations had been raised
for the first time to the status of major crimes and the penalties to
confiscatory levels. This followed a recent trend in British law that
expanded the definition of criminality to many behaviors (victimless
actions) formerly thought legal. Previously, prosecution of almost all
criminal offenses was private, usually paid for by the victim. Interme-
diate punishments for serious offenses were strikingly absent. Punishments for minor crimes were designed to shame the offender, such
as public whipping or exposure in the stocks. English courts imposed
only two sentences on convicted felons. Either they turned them loose
to labor in the colonies or they hanged them immediately. Transportation as an indenture, in lieu of death, was a form of pardon. [21]

Disgruntled skippers, shippers, and merchants now stood in long
lines to have their paperwork processed by petty bureaucrats or risk an
appearance before an Admiralty Court—somewhat akin to answering
a modern parking ticket before a military tribunal. It is significant that
many colonial assemblies supported their governors and justices of the
courts in hindering the prosecution of these violators. Colonial governors, like Thomas Fitch (CT) and Samuel Ward (RI), and sympathetic
judges, like Richard Morris (NY) and John Andrews (RI), regularly
erected legal impediments to the prosecution of smugglers and the
forfeiture of their vessels and cargoes. The governors and the judges
often accomplished this through the active contravention of the law,
purposely throwing vice-admiralty cases into the civil courts where
they could drag on for months.[22] The intransigence of the settlers of

the Conococheague Valley in 1764, who rejected all forms of governance other than that of their locally elected magistrates and justices, is
thereby brought into sharper focus as no isolated aberration, but rather
a theme within the broader resistance to the arrogance of power.

The whole of Anglo-America seemed to unite in opposition to
the attempt of Parliament to restrict the growth of colonial commerce. Charles Townshend, Lord of the Exchequer, was directly opposed to any policy of conciliation or moderation with respect to the
colonies. He supported the Declaratory Act that attempted to underpin the Crown's right to saddle the colonies with new tax legislation.
Townshend proposed a further series of measures in 1767 that regulated
almost all the yield of colonial production in North America.[23] The
repeal of most of these commercial regulations in 1773 was considered
a great victory for the colonies, thus relieving the issue of unrepresen-
tative taxation two years before the outbreak of war. Only the 3 penny
tea tax remained as a symbol of Parliament's right to tax America.

The importance of all the aforementioned measures to the revolution, however, was that they raised to prominence a group of extraordinary radical leaders from within the colonies. Many leaders among
the protestors made political and economic assumptions based on
their own experiences with the Crown, but also on what they saw hap-
pening in other parts of the empire. Like the Boston Massacre (1770),
previous violent British actions in Ireland, the West Indies, England,
and in Scotland contributed to the conclusion that Anglo-Americans
had a grim future as free and prosperous persons if they remained subject to the changes in policy established by Parliament.[24]

That the Americans instead became nationalists seeking an independent republic of their own was really a byproduct of their initial
success in forging a cohesive economic response among themselves
and in uncovering the staggeringly arrogant attitude of the government to their complaints at almost every phase of the dispute. Herein,
a wider consensus had been forged for more than a mere tax protest.
In 1774, Lord Dunmore wrote to the colonial secretary, reporting that
the Continental Association that sponsored the commercial protests
was acting as a newly formed governmental authority—an observation
shared by Governor Hutchinson concerning the Sons of Liberty.[25]
Thereafter, the cause of independence took on an emotional force and
a life of its own that was shared by a large enough segment of the
American population to come to fruition.

Prominent among the most influential agitators in America was
Patrick Henry whose "Liberty or Death" slogan spoken in the Virginia

House of Burgesses was widely adopted by Patriots throughout the colonies. Intellectuals, lawyers, and politicians among the Patriots often wrote or spoke of restoring their *political liberty* in terms of legislatures, rights, and privileges. Others argued with equal fervor for *economic liberty*.[26] They pointed to an annual imbalance of trade, a 450 percent increase from the year 1700 (£270,000) to 1750 (£1,260,000).[27] Some religious dissenters among the Patriots espoused *religious liberty* fearing enslavement to the Church of England.[28] Others, especially among the street mobs and wharf denizens, acted in terms of a pseudo-libertarian concept of *personal liberty*, which may in fact have been closer to the consensus among the people.

These were the foundations of revolution. Americans—Anglo-Americans no longer—wore liberty caps, gathered around liberty poles, designated liberty trees, and rang liberty bells. Yet, the shift from discussing, speaking, and writing about liberty in its many intellectual forms to shouting, shoving, burning, and shooting during a protest demanding it was startling.[29]

It can be argued that the colonials won their argument with the Crown concerning taxation with the repeal of the offending laws. By 1773, only the tea tax remained, and no right-thinking American Patriot was buying, selling, or using tea in any case.[30] As ordinary Americans affirmed their trust in one another and organized paramilitary organizations and local militias, they discovered that the language of rights and liberties was more than mere rhetoric and faded scratching on ancient velum. These protestors were no mere provincials attempting to save a few pennies tax on a pound of tea. Among them were those who were well read and politically sophisticated. An English king (Henry V) had once proclaimed the theory of *Divine Rights* for the Crown (*Dieu et mon droit*, [*by God and my right*], the royal motto), but a Congress of the people had declared the theory of *Unalienable Rights* for all Americans, including life, liberty, and the pursuit of happiness.[31]

Americans initially undertook to regain the former structure of British polity, not to discard it. Indeed, the cause for which they—and the T.E.A. Party 235 years later—acted was in their eyes "downright conservative."[32] Yet, in its consequences, the revolution that the Patriots undertook to avoid *fundamental change* imposed upon them from without was as radical as any that followed. Thereafter, America was *fundamentally transformed* from a dependency of people subject to the whims of the elite and the powerful to an independent nation subject to the rights and will of the people.

Notes

INTRODUCTION

1. Francis S. Drake, *Tea Leaves: Being a Collection of Documents and Letters Relating to the Shipment of Tea to the American Colonies in the Year 1773 by the East India Tea Company* (Boston: A.O. Crane, 1884, Kindle edition), loc. 1925.

2. T.H. Breen, *The Marketplace of Revolution: How Consumer Politics Shaped American Independence* (New York: Oxford University Press, 2004, Kindle edition), loc. 333–342.

3. Breen, *Marketplace*, loc. 495–503.

4. Breen, *Marketplace*, loc. 743–750.

5. The total loss was equivalent in 2011 to more than £1.4 million. See Drake, *Tea Leaves*, 871–878.

6. J.L. Bell, "Henry Bass Spills the Beans on a Political Protest," *Boston 1775*, http://boston1775.blogspot.com/search/label/Loyall%20Nine.

7. Colin G. Galloway, *The Shawnees and the War for America* (New York: Viking, 2007), 174.

8. T.E.A. Party, used hereafter to differentiate the modern political movement from the Boston Tea Party, which initially stood for "Taxed Enough Already."

9. Jill Lepore, *The Whites of Their Eyes: The Tea Party's Revolution and the Battle over American History* (Princeton, NJ: Princeton University Press, 2010, Kindle edition), 20–21.

10. Peter L. Bernstein, *The Power of Gold: The History of an Obsession* (New York: John Wiley & Son, 2000), 158.

11. See the Economic History Association, EH.net, http://eh.net/hmit/.

12. Nicholas B. Dirks, *The Scandal of Empire: India and the Creation of Imperial Britain* (London: Belknap Press, 2006), 13.

13. Charles Dickens, *Barnaby Rudge: A Tale of the Riots of 'Eighty* (Public Domain Books, Kindle edition), loc. 1070–1071.

14. Ira Stoll, *Samuel Adams: A Life* (New York: Free Press, 2008, Kindle edition), loc. 10.

15. J. Hector St. Jean de Crévecoeur, *Letters from an American Farmer*, (reprinted from the original 1782 edition with an introduction by Ludwig Lewisohn) (New York: Fox, Duffield & Co., 1904), 287–288.

16. Ralph Ketchum, ed., *The Anti-Federalist Papers and the Constitutional Convention Debates* (New York: New American Library, 1986), 1–2.

17. Edmund S. Morgan and Helen M. Morgan, *The Stamp Act Crisis: Prologue to Revolution* (Chapel Hill: University of North Carolina Press, 1995), 127.

18. Lawrence Sterne, *The Life and Opinions of Tristram Shandy, Gentleman*, 2 vols. (London: n.p., 1770, Kindle edition), 1:899. The novel was originally serialized in the London newspapers.

19. Sterne, *Tristam Shandy*, loc. 190.

20. Lester J. Cappon, ed., *The Adams-Jefferson Letters: The Complete Correspondence between Thomas Jefferson and John and Abigail Adams* (Chapel Hill: University of North Carolina Press, 1959), 2:451–452.

CHAPTER 1

1. "The Boston Tea Party," Old South Meeting House, http://www.old southmeetinghouse.org/osmh_123456789files/BostonTeaPartyBegan.aspx.

2. Drake, *Tea Leaves*, 341.

3. Drake, *Tea Leaves*, 920. The logo included a "Valentine" heart with an *X* through it. In each of the lower spaces made thereby the letters one by one *E, I, C*.

4. As told in Esther Forbes, *Paul Revere and the World He Lived In* (1942; Reprint, New York: Houghton Mifflin Company, 1999), 200.

5. Drake, *Tea Leaves*, 835–836.

6. Forbes, *Paul Revere and the World He Lived In*, 119–120.

7. Forbes, *Paul Revere and the World He Lived In*, 122.

8. Gordon S. Wood, *The Radicalism of the American Revolution* (New York: Vintage Books, 1993), 222–223.

9. Forbes, *Paul Revere and the World He Lived In*, 61.

10. Neil L. York, "Freemasonry and the American Revolution." *The Historian* 55, no. 2 (1993): 315–331.

11. S. Brant Morris, "The Eye in the Pyramid," *The Short Talk Bulletin of the Masonic Service Association of the United States,*http://www.howstuffworks.com/framed.htm?parent=question518.htm&url=http://web.mit.edu/afs/athena.mit.edu/user/d/r/dryfoo/www/Masonry/Essays/eyepyr.html.

12. Unattributed author, "Freemasonry and the American Revolution," Acadia Press, http://www.saintsalive.com/resourcelibrary/freemasonry/free masonry-and-the-american-revolution.

13. Drake, *Tea Leaves*, 746.

14. Brian Gardner, *The East India Company* (New York: Dorset Press, 1971), 48.

15. Forbes, *Paul Revere and the World He Lived In*, 200.

16. Drake, *Tea Leaves*, 1058.

17. Drake, *Tea Leaves*, 1067.

18. This incident is also reported to have taken place the previous night. See Robert D. Marcus and David Burner, eds., *America Firsthand, From Settlement to Reconstruction* (New York: St. Martin's Press, 1995), 96.

19. Lepore, *Whites of Their Eyes*, 187.

20. "New Hampshire Reaction to the Boston Tea Party in 1773," *New Hampshire State Sons of the American Revolution*, http://www.nhssar.org/essays/TeaParty.pdf.

21. Drake, *Tea Leaves*, 2230, 2403.

22. The following incidents have been placed here somewhat out of chronological order to facilitate the flow of the discussion.

23. "Domestic Intelligence," *Town & Country Magazine*, June 1774, from http://nobleharbor.com/tea/teaissues.html.

24. Drake, *Tea Leaves*, 212–213.

25. "The Annapolis Tea Party—the Burning of the *Peggy Stewart* and the Ruin of Anthony Stewart," *Sea Kayak*, http://www.seakayak.ws/kayak/kayak.nsf/0/1EFB85C4277832EB8525716F005EB3E2.

26. Breen, *Marketplace*, 4940.

27. John C. Miller, *Origins of the American Revolution* (Boston: Little, Brown and Company, 1943), 267.

28. Drake, *Tea Leaves*, 2230, 2403.

29. Arthur M. Schlesinger, "Colonial Merchants of the American Revolution, 1763–1776," 78, no. 182. (New York: Columbia University Press, 1918), 211.

30. Drake, *Tea Leaves*, 2038.

31. Schlesinger, "Colonial Merchants," 211.

32. Miller, 267.

33. Claude Halstead Van Tyne, *The Loyalists in the American Revolution* (Ganesvoort, NY: Corner House Historical Publications, 1999), 11–12

34. Drake, *Tea Leaves*, 2016–2020.

35. The writer is unidentified and was not the New York lawyer James Alexander who had used the same pseudonym during the John Peter Zenger case. The lawyer died in 1756. See Drake, *Tea Leaves*, 3708.

36. Stoll, *Samuel Adams*, 4, 7.

37. Eran Shalen, "'Written in the Style of Antiquity': Pseudo-Biblicism and the Early American Republic, 1770–1830," American Society of Church History, http://www.faqs.org/periodicals/201012/2223320001.html.

38. Gad Hitchcock, "An Election Sermon," Teaching American History, http://teachingamericanhistory.org/library/index.asp?document=2374.

39. Stoll, *Samuel Adams*, 126.

40. John Allen, "An Oration, Upon the Beauties of Liberty, or the Essential Rights of Americans" (Boston: 1773) in *Political Sermons of the American Foundig Era, 1730–1805*, ed. Ellis Sandoz (Indianapolis: The Liberty Fund, 1998), 315. Also available at Gaspee Virtual Archieve, http://www.gaspee.org/Allen.html#Top.

41. Allen, "An Oration," 321.

42. Bernard Bailyn, *The Ideological Origins of the American Revolution* (Cambridge, Belknap Press of Harvard University Press, 1967), 23.

43. Shalen, "Written in the Style of Antiquity."

44. Claude Halstead Van Tyne, *The Loyalists in the American Revolution* (Ganesvoort, NY: Corner House Historical Publications, 1999), 11–12.

45. The term *boycott* was named for Captain Charles C. Boycott who opposed the reforms of the Irish Land League. The word *boycott* was first used in the *Times* of London in November 1880.

46. Drake, *Tea Leaves*, 4547.

47. Drake, *Tea Leaves*, 1048–1055.

48. Stoll, *Samuel Adams*, 447.

49. Wood, *The Radicalism of the American Revolution*, 20–21.

50. Julie Flavell, *When London Was Capital of America* (New Haven: Yale University Press, 2010. Kindle Edition), loc. 1324–1325.

51. Wood, *The Radicalism of the American Revolution*, 26.

52. Flavell, *When London Was Capital of America*, 1341–1342.

53. Flavell, *When London Was Capital of America*, 1412–1425.

54. Flavell, *When London Was Capital of America*, 2542–2544.

55. Drake, *Tea Leaves*, 58.

56. Flavell, *When London Was Capital of America*, 1025.

57. Flavell, *When London Was Capital of America*, 1039–1040.

58. Flavell, *When London Was Capital of America*, 1065.

59. Flavell, *When London Was Capital of America*, 1039.

60. Flavell, *When London Was Capital of America*, 1680–1681.

61. Armand Francis Lucier, ed., *French and Indian War Notices Abstracted from Colonial Newspapers*, vol. 1 (Bowie, MD: Heritage Books, 1999), 7.

62. James M. Volo and Dorothy Denneen Volo, *Daily Life on the Colonial Frontier* (Westport: Greenwood Press, 2002. Kindle edition), loc. 2670.

63. "London Prints, Printmakers and Macaroni," *The 18th-Century American Women*, http://b-womeninamericanhistory18.blogspot.com/2009/06/about-london-printmakers.html.

64. Alexander Hamilton, "The Farmer Refuted," in *The Papers of Alexander Hamilton*, ed. Harold C. Syrett and Jacob E. Cooke, 27 volumes (New York: Columbia University Press, 1961–1987), 1:88.

65. Forbes, *Paul Revere and the World He Lived In*, 125.

66. Quoted in Neil R. Stout, *The Royal Navy in America, 1760–1775* (Annapolis, MD: United States Navy Institute, 1973), 82–83.

67. See Dorothy Denneen Volo and James M. Volo, *Daily Life in the Age of Sail* (Westport: Greenwood Press, 2001), 266–267.

68. Marblehead, Salem, and Nantucket were further seaward, and Beverly, Newburyport, and Portsmouth were under less official scrutiny.

69. Russell Bourne, *Cradle of Violence, How Boston's Waterfront Mobs Ignited the American Revolution* (Hoboken, NJ: John Wiley and Sons, 2006. Kindle edition), loc. 47.

70. Wood, *The Radicalism of the American Revolution*, 27–28.

71. Wood, *The Radicalism of the American Revolution*, 27–28.

72. Wood, *The Radicalism of the American Revolution*, 28.

73. Wood, *The Radicalism of the American Revolution*, 3.

74. See Eric Foner, *Tom Paine and Revolutionary America* (New York: Oxford University Press 1976), 75.

75. A Patriot Committee of Safety condemned dozens of Loyalists to be hung, drawn, and quartered—a gruesome and drawn-out execution. It is uncertain if the sentence was carried out, but the fact that the sentence was issued at all shows that such punishments were still to be considered.

76. Until his death in 1765, William Augustus ("Butcher" Cumberland) was the power behind the throne of George III, and in 2005 he was voted the *Worst Briton* of the 18th century by the BBC.

77. Benjamin Franklin, Quoteworld.org. Retrieved from http://www.quoteworld.org/quotes/4954

78. Voltaire made a similar argument concerning the diversity of religion in Britain in *Philosophical Letters* (Letter 6, "On the Church in England"). See Wood, *The Radicalism of the American Revolution*, 14.

79. These terms are not quite synonymous. The term *Tory* was a political one usually contrasted with *Whig*, whereas *Loyalist* was generally referred to those aligned with the Crown after the outbreak of the revolution.

80. Richard B Morris and James Woodress, eds., *Voices from America's Past: The Times That Tried Men's Souls, 1770–1783* (New York: McGraw-Hill, 1961), 31–32.

81. Claude Halstead Van Tyne, *Loyalists in the American Revolution* (Ganesvoort, NY: Corner House Historical Publications, 1999), 182.

CHAPTER 2

1. Breen, *The Marketplace*, 2430
2. Schlesinger, "Colonial Merchants," 107.
3. Tara Maginnis, "The Costumer's Manifesto," Costumes.org, http://www.costumes.org/HISTORY/100pages/BANYAN.HTM.
4. Maginnis, "The Costumer's Manifesto."
5. Maginnis, "The Costumer's Manifesto."

6. Steven E. Sidebotham, "The Berenike Project," The National Geographic Society, http://www.archbase.com/berenike/english5.html.

7. Drake, *Tea Leaves*, 216–217.

8. Benjamin Woods Labaree, *The Boston Tea Party* (New York: Oxford University Press, 1966), 144.

9. Carol Berkin, *First Generations: Women in Colonial America* (New York: Hill and Wang, 1996), 175.

10. Hammond Lamont, ed., *Burke's Speech on Conciliation with America* (Boston: Ginn, 1897), 39–40.

11. Drake, *Tea Leaves*, 247–251.

12. Labaree, *Boston Tea Party*, 91–92.

13. Thom Hartmann, "The Real Boston Tea Party Was against the Wal-Mart of the 1770s," *The Thom Hartmann Program*, http://www.thomhartmann.com/blog/2009/04/real-boston-tea-party-was-against-wal-mart-1770s.

14. Carroll Storrs Alden and Allan Westcott, *The United States Navy: A History* (New York: J. B. Lippincott Company, 1945), 5–6.

15. Breen, *The Marketplace*, 2430.

16. Alan MacFarlane and Iris MacFarlane, *The Empire of Tea: The Remarkable History of the Plant that Took over the World* (Woodstock, NY: Overlook Press, 2004), 32.

17. Simon Schama, *A History of Britain: The Wars of the British, 1603–1776*, vol. 2 (New York: Hyperion, 2001), 409.

18. Schama, *A History of Britain*, 39.

19. Schama, *A History of Britain*, 39.

20. Drake, *Tea Leaves*, 49–54.

21. Sophie D. Coe and Michael D. Coe, *The True History of Chocolate* (London: Thames & Hudson, 2007), 166.

22. MacFarlane and MacFarlane, *The Empire of Tea*, 66.

23. Marika Hansbury Tenison, *Book of Afternoon Tea* (Devon, UK: The National Trust, 1980), 10.

24. Roy Moxham, *Tea, Addiction, Exploitation, and Empire* (New York: Carroll & Graf Publishers, 2003), 21.

25. MacFarlane and MacFarlane, *The Empire of Tea*, 69–70.

26. Flavell, *When London Was Capital of America*, 4119.

27. Flavell, *When London Was Capital of America*, 2509.

28. Forbes, *Paul Revere and the World He Lived In*, 143–144.

29. Dorothy Denneen Volo and James M. Volo, *Daily Life during the American Revolution* (Westport: Greenwood Press, 2003, Kindle edition2), 260.

30. Richard Carney, "The Edenton Tea Party," *The North Carolina History Project*, http://www.northcarolinahistory.org/encyclopedia/50/entry.

31. Drake, *Tea Leaves*, 108–112.

32. Brian Gardner, *The East India Company* (New York: Dorset Press, 1971), 47.

33. James I was also James VI of Scotland in his own right, having inherited the throne through his mother, Queen Mary (Mary Queen of Scots), who had been beheaded by Elizabeth.

34. Alfred Thayer Mahan, *The Influence of Sea Power upon History, 1660–1783* (1890; Reprint, New York: Dover, 1987), 50–53.

35. Dorothy Denneen Volo and James M. Volo, *Daily Life in the Age of Sail* (Westport, CT: Greenwood Press, 2002, Kindle edition), loc. 2560–2565.

36. Volo and Volo, *Daily Life in the Age of Sail*, 2560–2565.

37. Nicholas B. Dirks, *The Scandal of Empire: India and the Creation of Imperial Britain* (London: Belknap Press, 2006), 8.

38. Fragments of patterned Chinese silk from ninth-century AD have been found at sites in Scandinavia.

39. Spain maintained a focus at Manila in the Philippines.

40. The fenced-in enclosure of iron replaced a wooden structure some time before 1822.

41. Paul A. Van Dyke, *The Canton Trade: Life and Enterprise on the China Coast, 1700–1845* (Hong Kong: Hong Kong University Press, 2005), 54–55.

42. Samuel Eliot Morison, *By Land and by Sea* (New York: Alfred A. Knopf, 1953), 130.

43. Breen, *The Marketplace*, 5264.

44. Gardner, *The East India Company*, 48.

CHAPTER 3

1. Richard Hofstadter, *America at 1750: A Social Portrait* (New York: Alfred A. Knopf, 1971), xv.

2. Hammond Lamont, ed., *Burke's Speech on Conciliation with America* (Boston: Ginn and Company, 1897), 5.

3. Dirks, *The Scandal of Empire*, 11.

4. Sterne, *Tristram Shandy*, 1317–1318.

5. Lucy M. Salmon, *The Dutch West India Company on the Hudson* (Poughkeepsie, NY: Published privately, 1915) 15–20.

6. Schama, *A History of Britain*, 409.

7. Bourne, *Cradle of Violence*, 77–78.

8. Samuel Eliot Morison, *Sources and Documents Illustrating the American Revolution 1764–1788 and the Formation of the Federal Constitution* (New York: Oxford University Press, 1965), 72.

9. Flavell, *When London Was Capital of America*, 170.

10. Flavell, *When London Was Capital of America*, 1412–1413.

11. Flavell, *When London Was Capital of America*, 559–560.

12. Volo and Volo, *Daily Life on the Old Colonial Frontier*, 98–99.

13. Beginning in the 1990s, the age of marriage increased slowly. In 2010, the age of first marriage for women moved from 21 to 26.

14. Jeanne A. Calhoun, "A Virginia Gentleman on the Eve of the Revolution: Philip Ludwell Lee of Stratford," http://www.stratfordhall.org/learn/lees/philip_ludwell_research.php.

15. The University of Chicago Press, *The Founders' Constitution*, vol. 1, chap. 13, document 6, http://press-pubs.uchicago.edu/founders/documents/v1ch13s6.html.

16. Jonathan Israel, *A Revolution of the Mind: Radical Enlightenment and the Intellectual Origins of Modern Democracy* (Princeton: Princeton University Press, 2010, Kindle edition), loc. 692–693.

17. Quoted in Louis B. Wright, *The Cultural Life of the American Colonies* (Minncola, NY: Dover Publications, Inc., 2002), 116.

18. MRCS: Member of the Royal College of Surgeons. See Irvine Loudon, "Why Are (Male) Surgeons Still Addressed as Mr.?," *British Medical Journal*, no. 321:1589 December 23, 2000, http://www.bmj.com/content/321/7276/1589.full.

19. Forbes, *Paul Revere*, 79.

20. Joan Patterson Kerr, "Benjamin Franklin's Years in London," http://www.americanheritage.com/articles/magazine/ah/1976/1/1976_1_14.shtml.

21. Flavell, *When London Was Capital of America*, 559.

22. See James M. Volo and Dorothy Denneen Volo, *Family Life in 17th-and 18th-Century America* (Westport: Greenwood Press, 2006), 153.

23. John J. McCusker and Russell R. Menard, *The Economy of British America, 1607–1789* (Chapel Hill: University of North Carolina Press, 1991), 315.

24. One-third of the city would burn in the great fire of 1776.

25. Bruce Blivens Jr., *Under the Guns: New York, 1775–1776* (New York: Harper & Row, 1972), 6–7.

26. McCusker and Menard, *The Economy of British America*, 80.

27. Stoll, *Samuel Adams*, 513.

28. Breen, *Marketplace*, 105–111.

29. Carroll Storrs Alden and Allan Westcott, *The United States Navy*, 5–6.

30. Arthur M. Schlesinger, "Colonial Merchants of the American Revolution, 1763–1776," Internet Archive, http://www.archive.org/stream/colonialmerchant00schlrich/colonialmerchant00schlrich_djvu.txt.

31. McCusker and Menard, *The Economy of British America*, 82.

32. Morison, *Sources and Documents*, 72.

33. Charles Fawcett, "The Stripped Flag of the East India Company, and Its Connection with the American Stars and Stripes," *The Mariners Mirror*, http://www.crwflags.com/fotw/flags/gb-eic2.html.

34. Marjorie Hubbell Gibson, *H.M.S. Somerset, 1746–1778: The Life and Times of an Eighteenth Century British Man-O-War and Her Impact on North America* (Cotuit, MA: Abbey Gate House, 1992), 2.

35. Fawcett, *The Mariners Mirror,* http://www.crwflags.com/fotw/flags/gb-eic2.html.

36. Labaree, *The Boston Tea Party,* 76.

37. Labaree, *The Boston Tea Party,* 77.

38. Claude Halstead Van Tyne, *The Loyalists in the American Revolution* (Ganesvoort, NY: Corner House Historical Publications, 1999), 11–12

39. William Peirce Randel, *The American Revolution: Mirror of a People* (Maplewood, NJ: Hamond Books, 1973), 157.

40. Randel, *The American Revolution,* 108–109.

41. McCusker and Menard, *The Economy of British America,* 179; 315.

42. Catherine E. McKinley, *Indigo: In Search of the Color that Seduced the World* (New York: Bloomsburg, 2011), 4.

43. McKinley, *Indigo,* 3.

44. McCusker and Menard, *The Economy of British America,* 61.

45. McCusker and Menard, *The Economy of British America,* 61.

46. Schlesinger, "Colonial Merchants," 113.

47. Between 1811 and1812, weavers and stocking knitters would lead the Luddite riots in Britain.

48. M. Dorothy George, *London Life in the Eighteenth Century* (Chicago: Academy Chicago Publishers, 1999), 167.

49. Simon Schama, *A History of Britain: The Wars of the British, 1603–1776* (New York: Hyperion, 2001), 186.

50. See Volo Volo, *Daily Life on the Old Colonial Frontier.* 51. M. Dorothy George, *England in Transition: Life and Work in the Eighteenth Century* (London: Penguin Ltd., 1964), 171.

52. George, *England in Transition,* 103.

53. Eric Robson, *The American Revolution in Its Political and Military Aspects, 1763–1783* (New York: W. W. Norton & Co., 1966), 7.

54. All of Massachusetts' paper was redeemed by 1773.

55. Miller, *Origins of the American Revolution,* 269.

56. The reader might want to compute the present day equivalent of a one night stay at a modest motel chain with free parking and a buffet breakfast, and compare it to an average person's wage in order to better visualize the value of a shilling.

57. McCusker and Menard, *The Economy of British America,* 339.

58. Labaree, 12.

59. See Volo Volo, *Daily Life in the Age of Sail,* 266–267.

60. Charles A. Beard and Mary R. Beard, *The Rise of American Civilization* (New York: Macmillan, 1927), 220–221.

61. Samuel W. Bryant, *The Sea and the States: A Maritime History of the American People* (New York: T. Y. Cromwell, 1967), 34.

62. See Oliver M. Dickerson, *The Navigation Acts and the American Revolution* (New York: A. S. Barnes, 1963), 63–102.

63. Dickerson, *The Navigation Acts,* 122–125.

64. Dickerson, *The Navigation Acts*, 208.

65. Dickerson, *The Navigation Acts*, 6–7.

66. Dickerson, *The Navigation Acts*, 296–297.

67. Dickerson, *The Navigation Acts*, 32.

68. Dickerson, *The Navigation Acts*, 48.

69. Dickerson, *The Navigation Acts*, 179.

70. Morison, *Sources and Documents*, 77.

71. Dickerson, *The Navigation Acts*, 172–183.

72. Dickerson, *The Navigation Acts*, 298.

73. Dickerson, *The Navigation Acts*, 299.

74. Stout, *The Royal Navy in America*, v.

75. Dickerson, *The Navigation Acts*, 4.

76. Dickerson, *The Navigation Acts*, 295.

77. Dickerson, *The Navigation Acts*, xiv.

78. Quoted in Peter Padfield, *Maritime Supremacy and the Opening of the Western Mind* (New York: The Overlook Press, 2002), 217.

CHAPTER 4

1. George F. Sheer and Hugh F. Rankin, *Rebels and Redcoats* (Cleveland, OH: World Publishing, 1957), 149.

2. Stoll, *Samuel Adams*, 40.

3. James Truslow Adams and Charles Garrett Vannest, *The Record of America* (New York: Charles Scribner's Sons, 1935), 83.

4. Adams and Vannest, *The Record of America*, 111.

5. Samuel Eliot Morison, *Sources and Documents Illustrating the American Revolution 1764–1788 and the Formation of the Federal Constitution* (New York: Oxford University Press, 1965), 17.

6. Adams and Vannest, *The Record of America*, 111.

7. Quoting British Secretary of State Conway in a letter to General Gage dated December 15, 1765 found in Stout, *The Royal Navy in America*, 99.

8. See Thomas Jefferson Wertenbaker, *Father Knickerbocker Rebels* (New York: Charles Scribner's Sons, 1948).

9. Roger Champagne, "The Military Association of the Sons of Liberty," *Narratives of the Revolution in New York* (New York: New York Historical Society, 1975), 1–11: 2.

10. Ibid.

11. Adams and Vannest, *The Record of America*, 82–83.

12. Richard N. Current and John A. Garraty, *Words that Made American History: Colonial Times to the 1870's* (Boston: Little, Brown and Company, 1965), 111.

13. Beard and Beard, *The Rise of American Civilization*, 216; also see Miller, *Origins of the American Revolution*, 244–246.

14. Adams and Vannest, *The Record of America*, 250.

15. Morison, *Sources and Documents*, 78.

16. Morison, *Sources and Documents*, 79.

17. Schlesinger, "Colonial Merchants," 211.

18. Adam Smith, *An Inquiry into the Nature and Causes of the Wealth of Nations*, Library of Economics and Liberty, http://www.econlib.org/library/Smith/smWN1.html#I.1.3.

19. Robert Carse, *The Seafarers: A History of Maritime America, 1620–1820* (New York: Harper & Row, 1964), 156.

20. Schlesinger, "Colonial Merchants," 109.

21. Adams and Vannest, *The Record of America*, 238.

22. Adams and Vannest, *The Record of America*, 238–239.

23. Michael Pearson, *Those Damned Rebels: The American Revolution as Seen Through British Eyes* (n.c.: DeCapo Press, 1972), 26.

24. Miller, *Origins of the American Revolution*, 266–267.

25. McCusker and Menard, *The Economy of British America*, 356.

26. Miller, *Origins of the American Revolution*, 261.

27. Russell Bourne, *Cradle of Violence: How Boston's Waterfront Mobs Ignited the American Revolution* (Hoboken, NJ: John Wiley and Sons, 2006), loc. 151–152.

28. Miller, *Origins of the American Revolution*, 266–267.

29. Stoll, *Samuel Adams*, 81–82.

30. Russell Bourne, *Cradle of Violence*, 151–152.

31. Miller, *Origins of the American Revolution*, 294–295.

32. Robert L. Heilbroner and Aaron Singer, *The Economic Transformation of America: 1600 to the Present* (New York: Harcourt Brace Jovanovich, 1984), 71.

33. McCusker and Menard, *The Economy of British America*, 356.

34. Labaree, *The Boston Tea Party*, 72.

CHAPTER 5

1. Claude Halstead Van Tyne, *The Loyalists in the American Revolution* (Ganesvoort, NY: Corner House Historical Publications, 1999), 7.

2. Letter of Lieutenant General Thomas Gage to Willian Legge, Earl of Dartmouth, on September 25, 1774, in Robert P. Richmond, *Powder Alarm, 1774* (New York: Auerbach, 1971), 35–36.

3. Breen, *Marketplace*, 53.

4. James R. Kennedy and Walter D. Kennedy, *The South Was Right* (Gretna, LA: Pelican, 1995), 164.

5. Breen, *Marketplace*, 59.

6. Breen, *Marketplace*, 169.

7. Quoted in North Callahan, *Royal Raiders: The Tories of the American Revolution* (New York: Bobbs-Merrill Company, Inc., 1963), 68.

8. William S. Sachs and Ari Hoogenboom, *The Enterprising Colonials: Society on the Eve of the Revolution* (Chicago: Argonaut Publishers, 1965), 68–69.

9. Jonathan Israel, *A Revolution of the Mind: Radical Enlightenment and the Intellectual Origins of Modern Democracy* (Princeton: Princeton University Press, 2010), loc. 192–195.

10. William H. Nelson, *The American Tory* (Boston: Beacon Press, 1961), 127.

11. Israel, *A Revolution of the Mind*, 192–195.

12. Israel, *A Revolution of the Mind*, 529–531.

13. Oliver Goldsmith, *The Vicar of Wakefield: A Tale* (n.p.: Public Domain Books, 2009, Kindle edition), loc. 1296.

14. Sterne, *The Life and Opinions of Tristram Shandy*, 1114.

15. John Locke, "A Letter Concerning Toleration," ed. William Popple, Project Gutenberg Consortia Center Collection, The World Public Library, http://WorldLibrary.net.

16. John Locke, "Second Treatise of Government," ed. C.B. McPherson, (Indianapolis and Cambridge: Hackett Publishing Company, 1980), 2.

17. Allen, , "An Oration," 25.

18. Miller, *Origins of the American Revolution*, 261.

19. Pauline Maier, *The Old Revolutionaries: Political Lives in the Age of Samuel Adams* (New York: W. W. Norton, 1990), 98.

20. This was a 450 percent increase from 1700 ($270, 000) to 1750 ($1,260,000). Sachs and Hoogenboom, *The Enterprising Colonials*, 26.

21. Paul A. Gilje, *Liberty on the Waterfront, American Maritime Culture in the Age of Revolution* (Philadelphia: University of Pennsylvania Press, 2004), 99.

22. Stoll, *Sam Adams*, 82.

23. Quoted in Barnet Schecter, *The Battle for New York, The City at the Heart of the American Revolution* (New York: Penguin Books, 2002), 166–167.

24. Israel, *A Revolution of the Mind*. Kindle Locations 212–213 and 1281–1282.

25. Sachs and Hoogenboom, *The Enterprising Colonials*, 68–69.

26. David Brion Davis, *Slavery in the Colonial Chesapeake* (Williamsburg: Colonial Williamsburg Foundation, 1994), 5.

27. Volo and Volo, *Daily Life on the Old Colonial Frontier*, 137.

28. Ibid, 134.

29. The word *pariah*, which can be used for anyone who is a social outcast independent of social position, reflects the rigid social system found in India, which designated only certain people Pariahs (proper noun) according to their birth. The caste system of India placed Pariahs, also known as Untouchables, on the very lowest level in society.

30. King James II (Stuart) was deposed in England in 1688 and the individual colonies returned to their previous form of local governance in 1691 by decree of William III and Mary II (Stuart), James' daughter.

31. William Peirce Randel, *The American Revolution: Mirror of a People* (New York: Routledge, 1973), 211.

32. North Callahan, *Royal Raiders: The Tories of the American Revolution* (New York: Bobhs-Merrill, 1963), 64.

33. Gordon S. Wood, *The Radicalism of the American Revolution* (New York: Vintage Books, 1993), 3.

34. Maier, *The Old Revolutionaries*, 274–275.

35. Schama, *A History of Britain*, 76.

36. Paraphrasing Moorehead Storey (1905) as quoted in George C. Herring, *From Colony to Superpower: U.S. Foreign Relations since 1776* (New York: Oxford University Press, 2008), 399.

37. Ralph Ketcham, ed., *The Anti-Federalist Papers and the Constitutional Convention Debates* (New York: New American Library, 1986), 4.

38. Jill Lepore, *The Whites of their Eyes: The Tea Party's Revolution and the Battle over American History* (Princeton: Princeton University Press, 2010), loc. 192.

39. James M. Volo, *A History of War Resistance in America* (Santa Barbara: ABC-CLIO, 2010), 42–43.

CHAPTER 6

1. T.H. Breen, *American Insurgents, American Patriots: The Revolution of the People* (New York: Hill and Wang, 2010, Kindle edition), loc. 77.

2. William Pitt, *The Speeches of the Right Honourable, the Earl of Chatham, in the Houses of Lords and Commons: With a Biographical Memoir and Introductions and Explanatory Notes to the Speeches* (London: Aylott & Jones, 1848), 74–76.

3. *Journal of the First Congress of the American Colonies, in Opposition to the Tyrannical Acts of the British Parliament,* held at New York on October 7, 1765 (New York, 1845), 27, http://www.ushistory.org/Declaration/related/bpb.htm.

4. Drake, *Tea Leaves*, 1073.

5. Stoll, *Samuel Adams*, 15.

6. Edmund Burke, *The Works of the Right Honourable Edmund Burke*, 6 volumes (London: Henry G. Bohn, 1854–1856), 1: 47.

7. Ibid.

8. See Roger Champagne, "The Military Association of the Sons of Liberty," *Narratives of the Revolution in New York* (New York: The New York Historical Society, 1975), 1–11: 2.

9. Stoll, *Samuel Adams*, 27–28.

10. Douglas E. Leach, *Roots of Conflict: British Armed Forces and Colonial Americans,1677–1775* (Chapel Hill: University of North Carolina Press, 1986), 25–30.

11. Drake, *Tea Leaves*, 166–203.

12. Nicholas B. Dirks, *The Scandal of Empire: India and the Creation of Imperial Britain* (London: Belknap Press, 2006), 38–39.

13. Philip Woodruff, *The Men Who Ruled India: The Founders* (New York: Schocken Books, 1964), 13.

14. Quoted in Dirks, *The Scandal of Empire*, 75–76

15. See Santhi Hejeebu, "Contract Enforcement in the English East India Company." *The Journal of Economic History* 65 (2005): 496–523.

16. Dirks, *The Scandal of Empire*, 118.

17. Dirks, *The Scandal of Empire*, 81.

18. Dirks, *The Scandal of Empire*, 30.

19. Gardner, *The East India Company*, 54.

20. Dirks, *The Scandal of Empire*, 65.

21. Quitrents had originated in Europe as a replacement for personal services or other obligations to the Crown.

22. Dirks, *The Scandal of Empire*, 12.

23. This was possibly a nephew or a cousin born in 1647 and who died in 1735 in New Haven. There are conflicting sources in the available genealogies.

24. Thom Hartmann, "Unequal Protection: The Boston Tea Party," Ukiah Blog, http://ukiahcommunityblog.wordpress.com/2011/04/07/unequal-protection-%e2%80%94-chapter-3-the-boston-tea-party-revealed/.

25. Franklin Bowditch Dexter, ed., "Documentary History of Yale University Under the Original Charter of the Collegiate School of Connecticut, 1701–1745," *Internet Achieve*, http://www.archive.org/stream/documentary histo00dextrich/documentaryhisto00dextrich_djvu.txt.

26. About Yale, "History," http://www.yale.edu/about/history.html.

27. See Edward S. Creasy, *The Fifteen Decisive Battles of the World* (New York: The Heritage Press, 1969), 3.

28. Warren Hastings was impeached in 1787 for corruption and not acquitted of charges for a decade. His main inquisitor was Edmund Burke.

29. See Roy Moxham, *The Great Hedge of India: The Search for the Living Barrier that Divided a People* (New York: Carroll & Graf Publishers, 2001).

30. Labarre, 44.

31. Labarre, 68–70.

32. Labarre, 63.

33. Labarre, 68–70.

34. Tyne, *The Loyalists in the American Revolution*, 23.

35. Tyne, *The Loyalists in the American Revolution*, 23.

36. William H. Sadler, *History of the United States* (New York: Smith and McDougal, 1879), 176.

37. Miller, *Origins of the American Revolution*, 385. Identical language had been used by the Puritans during the English Civil Wars of the mid-17th century.

38. Miller, *Origins of the American Revolution*, 379.

39. Miller, *Origins of the American Revolution*, 391.

CHAPTER 7

1. Simon Schama, *A History of Britain: The Wars of the British, 1603–1776* (New York: Hyperion, 2001) 108.

2. Stoll, *Samuel Adams*, 139.

3. Father Sabastien Rasles (sometimes spelled Rale') spent more of his life living among the Abenaki than he did in European society. He clearly incited the tribe to war on the English settlements.

4. John W. Thompson, "The Black Boys Rebellion—Racial Injustice or Patriotic Prelude to the American Revolution?" *William Smith House*, http://savesmithhouse.com/?p=530.

5. John Keegan, *Fields of Battle: The Wars for North America* (New York: Vintage Press, 1997), 135.

6. Samuel Eliot Morison, *Sources and Documents Illustrating the American Revolution 1764–1788 and the Formation of the Federal Constitution* (New York: Oxford University Press, 1965), xx.

7. Neil Harmon Swanson, *The First Rebel: Being a Lost Chapter of Our History and a True Narrative* (New York: Farrar & Rinehart, 1937), 54–55.

8. Morison, *Sources and Documents*, 11.

9. See Swanson, *The First Rebel*, 30–35.

10. See Thompson, "The Black Boys Rebellion."

11. Swanson, *The First Rebel*, 2194.

12. Marjoleine Kars, *Breaking Loose Together: The Regulator Rebellion in Pre-Revolutionary North Carolina* (Chappel Hill: University of North Carolina Press, 2002), 98–101.

13. Kars, *Breaking Loose Together*, 594.

14. James Webb, *Born Fighting, How the Scots-Irish Shaped America* (New York: Broadway Books, 2005, Kindle edition), loc. 335.

15. North Callahan, *Royal Raiders: The Tories of the American Revolution* (New York: Bobbs-Merrill, 1963), 77.

16. Sachs and Hoogenboom, *The Enterprising Colonials*, 127.

17. Sachs and Hoogenboom, *The Enterprising Colonials*, 128–129.

18. Schlesinger, "Colonial Merchants," 57, http://www.archive.org/stream/colonialmerchant00schlrich/colonialmerchant00schlrich_djvu.txt.

19. Schlesinger, "Colonial Merchants," 68.

20. Sachs and Hoogenboom, *The Enterprising Colonials*, 124–126.

21. Schlesinger, "Colonial Merchants," 25.

22. Paul A. Gilje, *Liberty on the Waterfront: American Maritime Culture in the Age of Revolution* (Philadelphia: University of Pennsylvania Press, 2004), 99.

23. Schlesinger, "Colonial Merchants," 45.

24. Gilje, *Liberty on the Waterfront*, 99.

25. Dr. Church later proved to have been a spy. See Schlesinger, "Colonial Merchants," 72.

26. See "The Sons of Liberty." USHistory.org, http://www.ushistory.org/Declaration/related/sons.htm.

27. Drake, *Tea Leaves*, 294.

28. Schlesinger, "Colonial Merchants," 72.

29. Schlesinger, "Colonial Merchants," 71.

30. Schlesinger, "Colonial Merchants," 72–73.

31. "Parker, James (1714–1770)," *American Eras*, 1997, *Encyclopedia.com*, http://www.encyclopedia.com/doc/1G2-2536600512.html.

32. Miller, *Origins of the American Revolution*, 304–305.

33. See Thomas Jefferson Wertenbaker, *Father Knickerbocker Rebels* (New York: Charles Scribner's Sons, 1948).

34. (Unidentified), *New York during the American Revolution* (New York: C. A. Alvord, 1861), 46–47.

35. Charles E. Green, *The Story of Delaware in the Revolution* (Wilmington, DE: William N. Cann, 1975), 16.

36. Schlesinger, "Colonial Merchants," 117.

37. Green, *The Story of Delaware*, 18.

38. Green, *The Story of Delaware*, 181.

39. Green, *The Story of Delaware*, 184.

40. Green, *The Story of Delaware*, 185.

41. Callahan, *Royal Raiders*, 100.

42. James M. Volo, *Blue Water Patriots: The American Revolution Afloat* (New York: Rowman & Littlefield, 2008), 26.

43. Quoted in Stout, *The Royal Navy in America*, 82–83.

44. Maier, *The Old Revolutionaries*, 107–108.

45. Stout, *The Royal Navy in America*, 49.

46. Morison, *Sources and Documents*, 17.

47. Quoted in Stout, *The Royal Navy in America*, 80.

48. Stout, *The Royal Navy in America*, 84.

CHAPTER 8

1. Roderick Nash, *Wilderness and the American Mind* (New Haven: Yale University Press, 1971), 6.

2. Frederick Jackson Turner, *The Significance of the Frontier in American History* (New York: Henry Holt & Co., 1920), 2.

3. Oscar Kuhns, *The German and Swiss Settlements of Colonial Pennsylvania: A Study of the So-Called Pennsylvania Dutch* (New York: Henry Holt and Company, 1901) 85–86.

4. Quoted in McCusker and Menard, *The Economy of British America*, 305–306.

5. McCusker and Menard, *The Economy of British America*, 301.

6. T. H. Breen, *The Marketplace*, 37.

7. From the inventory of Andrew Ferree of Lancaster County, PA in Kuhns, *The German and Swiss Settlements*, 87–88.

8. Richard A. Hofstadler, *America at 1750: A Social Portrait* (New York: Alfred A. Knopf, 1971), 11–12.

9. Quoted in Aaron Spencer Fogleman, *Hopeful Journeys: German Immigration, Settlement, and Political Culture in Colonial America, 1717–1775*, (Philadelphia: University of Pennsylvania Press, 1996) 33.

10. Margaret F. Hofmann, "The Land Grant Process in North Carolina," *The Colony of North Carolina, 1735–1764*, http://www.pipesfamily.com/land grant.htm.

11. By way of comparison, the author had 33 acres surveyed in 2001 at a cost of $1500, or almost $50 per acre.

12. David M. Friedenberg, "Life, Liberty, and the Pursuit of Land," the School of Cooperative Individualism, http://www.cooperativeindividualism. org/friedenberg_daniel_life_liberty_pursuit_of_land.html.

13. See Friedenberg, "Life, Liberty, and the Pursuit of Land."

14. See Friedenberg, "Life, Liberty, and the Pursuit of Land."

15. See Friedenberg, "Life, Liberty, and the Pursuit of Land."

16. Ronald Bailey, "A Surveyor for the King," *Colonial Williamsburg Journal*, Summer 2001, http://www.history.org/foundation/journal/summer01/surveyor.cfm.

17. See Bailey, "A Surveyor for the King."

18. Samuel Eliot Morison, *Sources and Documents Illustrating the American Revolution 1764–1788 and the Formation of the Federal Constitution* (New York: Oxford University Press, 1965), 8.

19. Edward Redmond, "George Washington: Surveyor and Mapmaker," *Annals of the Association of American Geographers* 23, no. 3 (September 1941): 147, http://memory.loc.gov/ammem/gmdhtml/gwmaps.html.

20. See Friedenberg, "Life, Liberty, and the Pursuit of Land."

21. See Redmond "George Washington: Surveyor and Mapmaker."

22. See Friedenberg, "Life, Liberty, and the Pursuit of Land."

23. Margaret F. Hofmann, "The Land Grant Process in North Carolina," *The Colony of North Carolina, 1735–1764*, http://www.pipesfamily.com/landgrant.htm.

24. Volo and Volo, *Daily Life during the American Revolution*, 84.

25. Fagan, *The Great Warming*, 30.

26. BBC Historic Figures, "Jethro Tull (1674–1741)," http://www.bbc.co.uk/history/historic_figures/tull_jethro.shtml.

27. "Jethro Tull," *Encyclopædia Britannica. Encyclopædia Britannica Online.* Encyclopædia Britannica, 2011, http://www.britannica.com/EBchecked/topic/608684/Jethro-Tull.

28. James M. Volo and Dorothy Denneen Volo, *Encyclopedia of the Ante-bellum South* (Westport, CT: Greenwood Press, 2000), 173.

29. "Ben Franklin, World of Influence," PBS Timeline, http://www.pbs.org/benfranklin/l3_world_agriculture.html.

30. McCusker and Menard, *The Economy of British America*, 301.

CHAPTER 9

1. David Hackett Fischer, *Albion's Seed: Four British Folkways in America* (New York: Oxford University Press, 1989), 6–11. The author is thankful to Fischer for his use of the term "folkways" to describe these characteristic categories.

2. Richard Hofstadler, *America at 1750: A Social Portrait* (New York: Alfred A. Knopf, 1971), 16

3. James Webb, *Born Fighting: How the Scots-Irish Shaped America* (New York: Broadway Books, 2005, Kindle edition), loc. 335.

4. Dirks, *The Scandal of Empire*, 7.

5. North Carolina was formed in 1712 under a council of proprietors, and Georgia, founded in 1732, was ruled by a council of trustees until 1755 when royal governors were appointed.

6. Drake, *Tea Leaves*, 1073.

7. Douglas E. Leach, *Roots of Conflict: British Armed Forces and Colonial Americans,1677–1775* (Chapel Hill: University of North Carolina Press, 1986), 25–30.

8. The *Patriot Whigs* was formed in Great Britain in 1725. See Roger Champagne, "The Military Association of the Sons of Liberty," *Narratives of the Revolution in New York* (New York: The New York Historical Society, 1975), 1–11: 2.

9. Harry Alonzo Cushing, ed., *The Writings of Samuel Adams*. 4 volumes (New York: G. P. Putnam's Sons, 1904–1908), 1:319.

10. Lieutenant Governor Thomas Oliver was no relation to Andrew Oliver who died in 1774.

11. Herbert H. Bankcroft, "Causes of the Revolutionary War," ed. Charles Leigh, *The Great Republic by the Master Historians*, volume II (1902), http://www.publicbookshelf.com/public_html/The_Great_Republic_By_the_Master_Historians_Vol_II/causesof_ca.html.

12. Oliver M. Dickerson, *The Navigation Acts and the American Revolution* (New York: A. S. Barnes, 1963), 157.

13. Dickerson, *The Navigation Acts*, 140.

14. Morison, *Sources and Documents*, 14.

15. Maine was then a province of Massachusetts. See Sachs and Hoogenboom, *The Enterprising Colonials*, 40–41.

16. Sachs and Hoogenboom, *The Enterprising Colonials*, 42.

17. Breen, *The Marketplace of Revolution*, 5000.

18. Dickerson, *The Navigation Acts*, 208.

19. John C. Miller, *Origins of the American Revolution*, 266–267.

20. Stout, *The Royal Navy in America, 1760–1775*, v.

21. See David Friedman, "Making Sense of English Law Enforcement in the 18th Century," http://www.daviddfriedman.com/Academic/England_18thc./England_18thc.html.

22. See Dickerson, *The Navigation Acts*, 299–300.

23. Morison, *Sources and Documents*, 78.

24. The Scots had been slaughtered mostly without trial after the battle of Culloden in 1746. The wounded were bayoneted on the field and the heads of the leaders placed on spikes over the gates of Scottish cities.

25. T. H. Breen, *The Marketplace*, 5025.

26. Pauline Maier, *The Old Revolutionaries: Political Lives in the Age of Samuel Adams* (New York: W. W. Norton, 1990), 98.

27. Sachs and Hoogenboom, *The Enterprising Colonials*, 26.

28. Practically all New England was composed of Congregationalists, and all North Carolina and Pennsylvania of Scotch-Irish Presbyterians or Quakers and Pietists,

29. Simon Schama, *A History of Britain: The Wars of the British, 1603–1776* (New York: Hyperion, 2001), 76.

30. William H. Sadler, *History of the United States* (New York: Smith and McDougal, 1879), 176.

31. The right to *happiness* was formerly the right to *property* or estate, but this was thought to isolate too many persons having no property who supported the idea of independence.

32. Gordon S. Wood, *The Radicalism of the American Revolution* (New York: Vintage Books, 1993), 3.

Selected Bibliography

Bernstein, Peter L. *The Power of Gold: The History of an Obsession.* New York: John Wiley & Son, 2000.

Breen, T. H. *The Marketplace of Revolution: How Consumer Politics Shaped American Independence.* New York: Oxford University Press, 2004.

Dickerson, Oliver M. *The Navigation Acts and the American Revolution.* New York: A. S. Barnes, 1963.

Drake, Francis S. *Tea Leaves.* Boston: A. O. Crane, 1884.

Fawcett, Charles. "The Stripped Flag of the East India Company, and Its Connection with the American Stars and Stripes." *Mariner's Mirror*, no. 4 (1937). http://www.crwflags.com/fotw/flags/gb-eic2.html.

Friedman, David. "Making Sense of English Law Enforcement in the 18th Century." http://www.daviddfriedman.com/Academic/England_18thc./England_18thc.html.

Gardner, Brian. *The East India Company.* New York: Dorset Press, 1971.

Hofstadler, Richard A. *America at 1750: A Social Portrait.* New York: Alfred A. Knopf, 1971.

Koebner, Richard. *Empire.* New York: Grosset and Dunlap, 1965.

Leach, Douglas E. *Roots of Conflict: British Armed Forces and Colonial Americans, 1677–1775.* Chapel Hill: University of North Carolina Press, 1986.

MacFarlane, Alan, and Iris MacFarlane. *The Empire of Tea: The Remarkable History of the Plant that Took Over the World.* Woodstock, NY: Overlook Press, 2004.

Maier, Pauline. *The Old Revolutionaries: Political Lives in the Age of Samuel Adams.* New York: W. W. Norton, 1990.

Marcus, Robert D., and David Burner, eds. *America Firsthand: From Settlement to Reconstruction.* New York: St. Martin's Press, 1995.

Millar, John C. *Origins of the American Revolution.* Boston: Little, Brown and Company, 1943.

Morison, Samuel Eliot. *Sources and Documents Illustrating the American Revolution 1764–1788 and the Formation of the Federal Constitution.* New York: Oxford University Press, 1965.

Morris, Richard B., and James Woodress, eds. *Voices from America's Past: The Times that Tried Men's Souls, 1770–1783.* New York: McGraw-Hill, 1961.

Moxham, Roy. *Tea, Addiction, Exploitation, and Empire.* New York: Carroll & Graf, 2003.

Sachs, William S., and Ari Hoogenboom. *The Enterprising Colonials: Society on the Eve of the Revolution.* Chicago: Argonaut, 1965.

Schama, Simon. *A History of Britain: The Wars of the British, 1603–1776.* New York: Hyperion, 2001.

Schlesinger, Arthur M. "Colonial Merchants of the American Revolution, 1763–1776." *Studies in History, Economics, and Law.* Vol. LXXVIII, No. 182. New York: Columbia University Press, 1918.

Stoll, Ira. *Samuel Adams: A Life.* New York: Free Press, 2008. Kindle edition.

Stout, Neil R. *The Royal Navy in America, 1760–1775.* Annapolis, MD: United States Navy Institute, 1973.

Volo, Dorothy Denneen, and James M. Volo. *Daily Life during the American Revolution.* Westport, CT: Greenwood Press, 2003.

Volo, James M. *Blue Water Patriots: The American Revolution Afloat.* New York: Rowman & Littlefield, 2008.

Volo, James M., and Dorothy Denneen Volo. *Daily Life on the Colonial Frontier.* Westport, CT: Greenwood Press, 2002.

Wood, Gordon S. *The Radicalism of the American Revolution.* New York: Vintage Books, 1993.

Index

About the Author

James M. Volo, Ph.D., has been teaching physics, physical science, and astronomy for the past 42 years. He received his bachelor's degree in American history from CCNY in 1969, his masters from American Military University in 1997, and his doctorate from Berne University in 2000. He is the author of several reference works regarding US military, social, and cultural history and has served as a consultant for TV and movie productions. Among his published works are *Blue Water Patriots: The American Revolution Afloat* (Greenwood, 2006), *Daily Life in Civil War America* (Greenwood, 1998), *Family Life in 19th-Century America* (Greenwood, 2007), *The Antebellum Period* (in the American Popular Culture through History series) (Greenwood, 2004), and *Encyclopedia of the Antebellum South* (Greenwood, 2000). Several of these are coauthored with his wife Dorothy Denneen Volo. Dr. Volo is presently teaching at Sacred Heart University in Fairfield, Connecticut.